NEW FOUNDATIONS THEOLOGICAL LIBRARY

General Editor
PETER TOON, MA, M.TH, D.PHIL

Consultant Editor
RALPH P. MARTIN, MA, PH.D

NEW FOUNDATIONS THEOLOGICAL LIBRARY

OLD TESTAMENT THEOLOGY:
A FRESH APPROACH
by R. E. Clements

EVANGELICAL THEOLOGY 1833–1856:
A RESPONSE TO TRACTARIANISM
by Peter Toon

NEW TESTAMENT PROPHECY
by David Hill

Other volumes in preparation

NEW TESTAMENT PROPHECY

DAVID HILL

Reader in Biblical Studies
University of Sheffield

JOHN KNOX PRESS

ATLANTA

Bible quotations in this publication are taken from the Revised Standard
Version of the Bible, copyright © 1946, 1952, 1957, and 1971 by the
Division of Christian Education of the National Council of the Churches
of Christ in the United States of America, and are used by permission.

Library of Congress Cataloging in Publication Data

Hill, David, Rev.
  New Testament prophecy.

  (New foundations theological library)
  Bibliography: p. 231
  Includes index.
  1. Bible. N.T.—Prophecies. I. Title. II. Series.
BS2827.H49 1979   225.1′5   79–16702
ISBN 0–8042–3702–6

Co-published by John Knox Press in the United States of America and
(in Marshalls Theological Library) by Marshall, Morgan & Scott in
Great Britain, 1979.

John Knox Press
Atlanta, Georgia

Printed in Great Britain

CONTENTS

ABBREVIATIONS

ALUOS	*Annual of Leeds University Oriental Society*
AV	Authorised (King James') Version
BJRL	*Bulletin of the John Rylands Library* (Manchester)
BZ	*Biblische Zeitschrift*
ET	English translation
ExpT	*The Expository Times*
EQ	*The Evangelical Quarterly*
HTR	*The Harvard Theological Review*
IDB	*The Interpreter's Dictionary of the Bible*, 4 vols, and Supplementary Volume (Abingdon Press, New York/Nashville, 1962, 1976)
JBL	*Journal of Biblical Literature*
JB	*The Jerusalem Bible*
JJS	*Journal of Jewish Studies*
JQR	*Jewish Quarterly Review*
JTS	*Journal of Theological Studies*
LXX	*Septuagint*
NEB	*The New English Bible*
NovT	*Novum Testamentum*
NTS	*New Testament Studies*
S–B	H. L. Strack and P. Billerbeck, Kommentar zum Neuen Testament aus Talmud und Midrasch (München, 1922–56)
SBL	*Society of Biblical Literature*
SDB	*Supplément au Dictionnaire de la Bible* (Paris, 1928–)
TDNT	*Theological Dictionary of the New Testament*, ET of *Theologisches Wörterbuch zum Neuen Testament* (ed. G. Kittel and G. Friedrich: Stuttgart, 1933–74)
ThZ	*Theologische Zeitschrift*
TLZ	*Theologische Literaturzeitung*
ZAW	*Zeitschrift für die alttestamentliche Wissenschaft*
ZNW	*Zeitschrift für die neutestamentliche Wissenschaft*

PREFACE

New Testament prophecy has never been at the centre of scholarly research. Normally it has merited little more than the amount of discussion that is appropriate and necessary in commentaries on certain New Testament books, especially 1 Corinthians and Revelation, and an entry, usually quite brief, in the various Bible dictionaries. In recent years, however, the subject has been commanding considerable attention, partly as a result of increasing interest in the investigation of the types and forms of New Testament material and partly as a consequence of the revival of prophecy in Pentecostal and 'charismatic' communities.

Since the last book to be published in Britain on New Testament Prophecy – that by H. A. Guy – appeared thirty years ago and is now out of print as well as out of date, the time is opportune for a fresh review of the evidence and recent discussion concerning New Testament prophets and their activity. One book which appeared recently in the United States may seem to duplicate much of the content of the present volume: I refer to *Early Christian Prophecy: A Study of its Origin and Function* by T. M. Crone, published by St Mary's University Press, Baltimore, in 1973, but, as the title shows, this book investigates the phenomenon of Christian prophecy beyond the New Testament and its value is reduced by reason of the fact that the author concerns himself only with those passages where the terms 'prophet', 'prophecy', and 'to prophesy' occur, without apparently being aware of the possibility that the phenomenon of prophecy cannot be adequately studied solely on the basis of the appearance of items from a single word-group. Anyone seeking information in English about Christian prophecy has had to rely mainly on G. Friedrich's work in Volume VI of the *Theological Dictionary of the New Testament*, and, if he has access to them, on articles which are included from time to time in the scholarly journals devoted to New Testament studies. Some of the best and most recent work on Prophecy in the New Testament comes from French and German authors, such as É. Cothenet, G. Dautzenberg, and Ulrich B. Müller, and I acknowledge indebtedness to their published essays and books.

An indication of the growing interest in Christian Prophecy may be seen in the fact that in 1973 the American Society of Biblical Literature established a continuing seminar (with wide terms of reference) on the subject. To the published discussion-papers contributed to that annual Seminar this book owes, in certain sections, a good deal. In September 1975 an international consultation on 'Prophetic Vocation in the New Testament and Today' was convened at the Ecumenical Institute, Bossey, Switzerland, and the papers (in English, French and German) read to that gathering of scholars (including my own contribution) have just been published by E. J. Brill, Leiden, under the title used for the consultation. It was indeed an invaluable privilege to meet and exchange views with a number of scholars currently working on this topic in New Testament research.

It would be pretentious to claim that this book – which appears as one in a series of volumes intended 'to provide theological students, ordained ministers and interested laity with a balanced selection of scholarly and readable books in the various departments of theology' – offers to the reader radically new views on the subject of Christian prophecy; if I had any such views, this would not be the appropriate place to make them known: rather, I have attempted to survey, in a comprehensive and balanced way, the relevant New Testament evidence and the views of scholars concerning the meaning of that evidence and, at the same time, to draw attention to what I consider to be most important for understanding the distinctive function of New Testament prophets. The core of the book is preceded by a concise study of background material which is of the utmost significance for an investigation of the phenomenon of New Testament prophecy and by a chapter on the prophetic characteristics of Jesus and his teaching. The final chapter (written at the publisher's request) is entitled 'Prophecy Today' and in it I attempt to assess – with a considerable degree of hesitation as to my ability and right to do so – the revival of prophecy in Pentecostal churches and in what are known as Neo-Pentecostal or 'charismatic' circles in relation to the New Testament evidence as I interpret it. It is my hope that my observations, presented with impartiality, caution and charity, will be of assistance not only to those who are anxious about the presence of the remarkable 'gifts of the Spirit' in the life of the Church but also to those who may be exposed to the danger of over-emphasising their importance.

I wish to thank the Syndics of the Cambridge University Press for permission to use, in the relevant chapters of this book, material from the articles I contributed to Volumes xviii and xx of *New Testament Studies* under the titles 'Prophecy and Prophets in the Revelation of St John' and 'On the Creative Role of Christian Prophets': and I am grateful to the publishing house of E. J. Brill, Leiden, for permission to reproduce portions of the paper I read to the Bossey Consultation and which appears in the book *Prophetic Vocation in the New Testament and Today* under the title 'Christian Prophets as Teachers or Instructors in the Church'.

The biblical quotations are taken from the Revised Standard Version (RSV) unless otherwise indicated. The Notes are provided and the Bibliography annotated in order to enable students of the subject to follow up points raised in the discussion and to know which books and articles are most worthy of attention. I would stress, however, that the Notes are not absolutely necessary to an understanding of the argument. The book could be, and I suppose will be, read by many without reference to them: but their inclusion will, I hope, help those who want to know where the source material is to be found and take their own study of the subject to a more advanced level.

My thanks are due, and gladly given, to Marshall, Morgan and Scott for the invitation to write this book, and to the editorial staff of the series and of the publishing house for advice and co-operation. I must also express my deep sense of gratitude to many friends in Coleraine and Sheffield who have supported me as I have been writing this book, during a year which has been exceedingly troubled and stressful: some of them are included in the dedication of the completed work to the minister and members of the church in which I was baptised and ordained to the Christian ministry.

The University
Sheffield   DAVID HILL

November 1977

CHAPTER ONE

MATTERS OF DEFINITION AND BACKGROUND

Before we embark upon the examination of the New Testament materials for evidence of the existence and activity of Christian prophets two preliminary tasks must engage our attention.

The first is a matter of definition: what do we mean by the term 'Christian prophet'? Although no definition offered will be entirely satisfactory or universally acceptable, it is necessary to have some kind of reference point, some fairly precise understanding of what we are looking for, if our attempt to identify and characterise Christian prophets and their utterances is to be viable and productive. Terms like 'prophet', 'prophecy', 'oracle of the risen Lord' and 'prophetic' have been and still are used, with reference to phenomena in the New Testament, in a confusing variety of ways, but the initial discussions of the American Society of Biblical Literature (SBL) Seminar on 'Early Christian Prophecy' are extremely valuable in providing guide-lines towards a useful working-definition of the subject of its wide-ranging investigation. Although the scope and depth of our examination of Christian prophecy is necessarily more limited than those proposed for the deliberations of this on-going Seminar, we shall derive assistance from its suggested definition, as well as from consideration of the methods by which it has been reached.

The second preliminary task is to survey the phenomenon of prophecy in the periods before and contemporaneous with the New Testament era in order to open the way for subsequent discussion of areas of continuity, comparison and contrast. In order to be adequate, such a survey would demand at least a monograph to itself; but, since no book on New Testament prophecy can responsibly omit some consideration of materials outside the primary sources, the reader's indulgence is sought for the brevity with which the body of material will be presented and discussed in the second part of this chapter.

A. ON DEFINING THE TERM 'CHRISTIAN PROPHET'[1]

Obviously it is not the adjective 'Christian' which requires explanation, but the noun 'prophet' (*prophētēs* or, in the feminine, *prophētis*), whose characteristic action is 'to prophesy' (*propheteuein*) and whose product is 'prophecy' (*prophēteia*), the latter term being also used to describe the phenomenon as a whole. For the formulation of a usable and explanatory (i.e. nominal) definition of 'prophet' several methods, not altogether mutually exclusive, are available. One approach is to regard the linguistic antecedents of the word as decisive, or at least of very great importance, in determining its meaning – witness the age-old and continuing debate concerning the derivation of *nābî'* among Old Testament scholars, and the introductory sections of many of the *TDNT* articles, including the one on 'Prophet'. But while the usefulness of etymological information is not here contested we must recognise that the semantic value of a word is not determined by its derivation, but by its usage in contexts. Attempts to relate *prophētēs* to the verb *prophēmi* and to prove that the prefix *pro-* is in each case to be understood 'originally' in something like a spatial ('forth-tell') rather than a temporal ('fore-tell') sense may arrive at a correct conclusion, but on insufficient grounds. Etymological considerations may be helpful in discovering the reason why a particular word was used in preference to another; they may also assist in illustrating the meaning of a word arrived at on other grounds, but they cannot be normative in deciding what that meaning is. A word *means* what it comes to mean in a particular literary and historical context.[2] Therefore a working-definition of *prophētēs* must be related to the way in which this word (and the word-group of which it is part) was used in the contexts where it appears.

Why not then simply concentrate attention on the occurrences of the word and word-group? This approach assumes that the phenomenon to be defined will *always* be so labelled in the materials being investigated, and, if we were to follow it, we would scan the New Testament for the use of the word *prophētēs* (and in the case of sources in Hebrew the word *nābî'*) and base our understanding of prophecy on an analysis of those texts in which it appears. This procedure – which is employed in the making of a dictionary – may be used on the one hand to provide a 'lowest common denominator' meaning, which will embrace all the discovered occurrences of the word, with the result that the definition frequently becomes too general to be of much use: on the other hand, this approach may lead to a virtual refusal to define at all, by saying, in effect, 'the word *prophētēs* denotes in a given period those persons who are so labelled'. Although this statement, being tautologous, cannot be falsified, the procedure on which it is based is useful only for determining how a particular *word* was used in a given time and place, but is of little assistance in understanding a particular phenomenon which may occur in connection with a given word *as well as apart from it*. Is the phenomenon of 'prophecy/ prophet' always and necessarily absent when the word *prophētēs* is not found? What then of Josephus's work, certain Johannine material, and Paul himself? The exclusiveness of this method of definition (by 'label') is a serious drawback to its usefulness, as is the great variety of figures designated by the word *prophētēs*. Of course, the strength of this approach is obvious: it will not call anyone a prophet who is not so designated in the sources. Great though this strength is, our disinclination to assume that the phenomenon of prophecy was *always* bound in a one-to-one correlation to the word or word-group causes this approach to the material to have limited value in our investigation.[3]

Another possible approach to definition might be to adopt a particular instance of the literary deposit of early Christian prophecy (e.g. the Revelation of St John) or a description of an early Christian prophet (e.g. Agabus in Acts, or from inferences drawn from 1 Cor. 14) as definitive and to measure the prophetic character of all else by this. But even if it were agreed that the book of Revelation is definitive of what we mean by Christian prophecy, it could not be 'definitive' in any absolute sense without amplification by other definitions, for the question could not be suppressed: '*What* is it about the book of Revelation which *constitutes* it as prophecy?' An answer to that question requires consideration of other approaches to definition. One such might be to claim that a certain kind of message is 'prophetic' and that whoever delivers such a message must and will be regarded as a prophet. But what kind of content is to be definitive? The demand for social justice, integrity and righteousness, in the tradition of Amos? This view seems to underlie the commonly-expressed desire that ecclesiastical leaders should speak a 'prophetic' word to our contemporary situation. Or will the definitive content be the apocalyptic speculation (in the tradition of Daniel) and the disclosures of events to come, as some Fundamentalist and millenarian groups seem to assume? Unless we are prepared to decide in advance that a certain product in the New Testament is 'prophecy' – and what or whose criteria shall we employ? – this approach has very limited usefulness in our search for a definition.

A functional approach is the most appropriate for the study of the phenomenon of Christian prophecy. A prophet is defined then in terms of his essential function, the function which constitutes him a prophet. Admittedly this approach is not entirely free from objections: how do we determine what is 'essential' and how is it to be abstracted from the non-essential? and what is the 'constitutive' function which makes someone a prophet? Questions like these, however, can be dealt with satisfactorily and a sound beginning made possible, if we make the following procedure the (implicit) foundation of our work. Since it is Christian prophets, and especially those of the New Testament era, who are the subjects of our primary interest, our definition should be formulated by commencing with those who are specifically called 'prophets' in the earliest Christian literature: to that extent the label-type of definition, despite its limitations and exclusive character, forms a convenient and useful starting-point. Then the group so labelled as 'prophets' should be used as a kind of sample-group for the purpose of formulating a working-definition. This core-group will include the prophets mentioned in Acts and in the Pauline letters, the book of Revelation, perhaps Mark 13 and parallels and Matthew 7, the

Didache, and the Shepherd of Hermas (depending on the dating of these last-mentioned documents): this group has sufficient variety to keep the definition from being too narrow, yet has sufficient in common (in terms of function) to keep the definition from becoming so broad and vague as to be meaningless. This core-group should be analysed in order to determine what function(s) they have in common and which differentiate them from other functionaries, i.e. which function(s) constitute them as prophets. Finally, this prophetic function should then be described and used as the working-definition, and whoever performs it should be considered a 'prophet', whether or not he bears the label in the sources, especially if some valid explanation can be offered for the absence of the specific term, as can be done in the case of the rabbis, the Qumran community, and, perhaps, the Fourth Gospel.

To be a convenient tool any definition should be brief, giving only the essential, the *sine qua non* functions of the prophet, and, because it therefore is a functional definition, it should avoid, as far as possible, the debate that revolves around 'office and charisma in the early Church'.[4] Whether the Christian prophet is to be identified in terms of a special 'office' is a question best left open in formulating a working-definition. So too is the question of the uniqueness of the phenomenon, for, although the definition must be constructed on the basis of Christian sources, it is very unlikely that Christian prophecy was *completely* discontinuous (or indeed completely continuous[5]) with what preceded it or existed alongside it. Even if Christian prophecy should prove to be unique in some features or many, the definition should not be composed around these features, unless it is they which constitute Christian prophecy as *prophecy*: unique features of Christian prophets are, in fact, likely to be what makes them *Christian*, not what makes them prophets.

Working along these lines, M. E. Boring offered and defended the following definition for use by the SBL Seminar: *A prophet is an immediately inspired spokesman for the (or a) deity of a particular community, who receives revelations which he is impelled to deliver to the community.*[6] In this definition the claim to inspiration is the *sine qua non* of a prophet, whose essential role is that of messenger: he is therefore different from the mystic who seeks the deity and whose communion with the deity is an edifying end in itself in that he is sought or called by God into a communion in which he receives the message for the community. Boring insists that, while prophetic immediate-inspiration (in whatever manner or degree, but always declaring the present immediate voice of the deity) excludes such devices as the casting of lots and the examination of the entrails of dead animals in order to deduce the message, it does not exclude the use of sources, traditional materials, or the reflections of the prophet himself which are inseparably involved in the delivery of what he has received to the community.

> The prophet presents all that he utters as a prophet as the immediately-inspired present address of the deity to his community. This message may well include material taken from tradition and the prophet's own reflection, consciously or unconsciously, with or without re-interpretation, but it is not presented as material which a past authority once said, but as what the deity now says. The same material may be presented by the non-inspired teacher or preacher, but with the formal and functional difference that this claim to immediate inspiration is not made.[7]

This is a significant qualification of his definition ('receives revelations') in view of the frequently repeated claim that a prophet does *not* declare what he has taken from tradition (that being the task of the preacher) but only divine revelations.[8]

This definition is intended by its author to mark itself off from three related phenomena in early Christianity which are sometimes regarded as prophetic: (i) the general 'prophetic' character which the early Spirit-filled Christian community possessed whereby all members may have been considered as potentially prophets: only prophets in the strict sense of the word (i.e. those who function according to the terms of the definition) are included in the definition; (ii) the general phenomenon of the risen Lord's voice being heard in the early Church through the rehearsal of the whole, diverse tradition of Jesus' words; and (iii) the understanding of the living Christ (or the Holy Spirit) as active in the general preaching ministry of the Church in all generations, as expressed in several major streams of Christian theology (most notably, in the Barthian): in this 'prophetic' interpretation of preaching it is a matter of the sovereignty of the Word itself, or of the exalted Christ himself, rather than of the essentially and specific claim to immediate inspiration.

Boring's definition of 'prophet' is made specific to the Christian prophet in the following way: *A Christian prophet is a Christian who functions within the Church as an immediately-inspired spokesman for the exalted Jesus, who receives intelligible revelations which he is impelled to deliver to the Christian community.*[9] A revised definition was proposed by David E. Aune,[10] which is responsible for the addition of the word 'intelligible' to the original, but Boring asserts that there is nothing in it which conflicts with his own definition, when fully understood. Aune's definition is as follows: *The Christian who functions in the prophetic role (whether regularly, occasionally or temporarily) believes that he receives divine revelations in propositional form which he customarily delivers in oral or written form to Christian individuals and/or groups.* Boring would exclude 'to individuals' here, if this is intended in some non-community sense, since he thinks that relationship to the community (i.e. the whole Christian community as manifested in a particular congregation) is of the *esse* of Christian prophets. Delivering purported messages from the deity to an individual which have no bearing on the life of the community is a function beyond the bounds of 'prophecy' as Boring thinks it should be defined. However, since very few, if any, Christian prophetic messages to individuals are likely to have had no bearing whatever on the life of the Christian community in any of its particular manifestations, we would be prepared to accept Aune's inclusion of the words 'Christian individuals'.

Before offering our own definition – a functional definition – of 'Christian prophet', we must in fairness comment on the two definitions already given and provide some justification for not accepting either as it stands. Both definitions lack any specific reference to 'call': it is implied by both scholars in their definitions, but, in our view, it requires explicit statement. The prophet knows that he has never chosen his role: he has been chosen, called and commissioned by the deity. This attribute is strongly emphasised by J. Lindblom in his general characterisation of the prophetic class among *homines religiosi*, a passage which evokes comparison with the definitions suggested by Boring and Aune:

> They are entirely devoted, soul and body, to the divinity. They are inspired personalities who have the power to receive divine revelations. They act as speakers and preachers who publicly announce what they have to say. They are compelled by higher powers and kept under divine constraint. The inspiration which they experience has a tendency to pass over into real ecstasy. One further attribute may be added: the special call. A prophet knows that he has never chosen his way himself: he has been chosen by the deity. He points to a particular experience in his life through which it has become clear to him that the deity has a special purpose with him and has designated him to perform a special mission.[11]

In Aune's definition we miss the reference to divine constraint or compulsion that is present in Boring's phrase 'impelled to deliver': neither definition includes a precise reference to the authority of a prophet's message, and, although it is probably implied by both scholars, it ought to be stated clearly: Boring's claim that the Christian prophet functions as the 'spokesman for the exalted Jesus' seems unnecessarily restrictive and may carry hidden presuppositions about the relation of prophetic words to 'oracles of the risen Lord', and therefore, in a definition, we prefer the more open terminology employed by Aune in this respect, though, in general, Boring's language is more attractive.

So, while acknowledging indebtedness to both Boring and Aune (and to Lindblom as well), we propose the following definition of 'Christian prophet' as the reference-point for the subsequent discussions in this book: *A Christian prophet is a Christian who functions within the Church, occasionally or regularly, as a divinely called and divinely inspired speaker who receives intelligible and authoritative revelations or messages which he is impelled to deliver publicly, in oral or written form, to Christian individuals and/or the Christian community.*

B. PROPHECY IN THE HEBREW – JEWISH TRADITION (PALESTINIAN AND HELLENISTIC)

In this section it is our intention to survey briefly the pheno-menon of prophecy in the periods before and (roughly) con-temporaneous with the New Testament. The title under which the survey will be conducted may seem, to some, much too nar-row: was not prophetism one of the ways in which the *Zeitgeist* expressed itself in Greek and Roman religion? It was: but, even at a time when New Testament scholarship has belatedly learned that what is termed 'Hellenistic' cannot be distin-guished, neatly and conclusively, from what is 'Jewish' because of the cultural cross-fertilisation which took place over several centuries, there will be few scholars, if any, who will wish to claim that prophetic phenomena in Greek and Roman religion provide *primary* evidence for the understanding of Christian prophecy. Similarities may be culled from sources (widely diverse in time, location, character and intention) and listed under the broad headings of call, inspiration, ecstasy, com-munion with deity, the reception of revelations, and even the obligation to deliver a divinely given message.[12] But in only one source do we find *all* these aspects of the prophetic experience attributed to a single individual, and that is in the First Tractate (*Poimandres*) of the *Corpus Hermeticum* – which C. H. Dodd called 'a first-hand document of the prophetic consciousness'[13] – which has to be dated in the second, if not the third, Christian century.

The so-called 'prophetic' activity in Greek religion was carried on mainly by 'soothsayers' (*manteis*) who employed in-cantations and practised divination by material signs (e.g. the interpretation of omens, stars, etc.), or, in later tradition, by men like Apollonius of Tyana and Peregrinus who were called by their biographers 'seers' (*goeis*), probably because, as E. Fascher suggests,[14] *prophētēs* was an honorific title and *goēs* a term of abuse. From a papyrus from Upper Egypt (dating probably from the beginning of the second century B C) which lists as last in a procession in honour of the oracle of Apollo Coropaeus 'the scribe (*grammatea*) of the god and the prophet' we learn that the word *prophētēs* designated either the interpreter of the oracle or the proclaimer of the interpretation – and 'proclaimer' or 'announcer' is the general definition which Fascher thinks fits best the various occurrences of this skeletal word (*prophētēs*) which had no specific content of its own, but drew its precise meaning from its diverse contexts (poetical, philosophical and religious). Helmut Krämer draws attention to several broader uses of the term: it may refer to members of an Egyptian priestly class, the advocates of some particular philosophy, to the 'specialist' in botany and to the 'quack' in medicine; even the heralds who declared the victor at games could be called 'prophets'.[15]

The famous Pythia or priestess of the Delphic oracle gave forth inspired utterances in a condition of ecstasy, partly accounted for by the intoxicating vapour which arose from the earth at Delphi but officially explained as the sign of the temporary presence of the god in the medium, a condition which Plato describes as *entheos*. The Pythia herself could be called a *promantis* (with respect to her disclosures of the future) or, more frequently, a *prophētis* (with respect to her role as a mouthpiece of the god): but the *prophētēs*, the prophet, was one who heard her words and then interpreted and proclaimed them to the inquirers who were seated in another room; he was presumably not divinely inspired, but simply one who translated the priestess's semi-coherent babblings into an intelligible reply. The Hellenistic mystery-cults, with their longing for salvation, enlightenment and the release of the soul from the body in order to enjoy an immortal communion with the divine, were once thought to be closely connected with Christianity (both in its character as 'mystery' and in its sacramental practice)[16] but, for the purposes of our inquiry, it is sufficient to note that the 'prophetic' condition in the mysteries seems always to have been associated with ecstasy: the initiate showed by his behaviour that he was *entheos*, no longer controlled by the mind but possessed by the deity, and therefore able to speak in his name, sometimes in intelligible language, sometimes in rapt utterances and ejaculations resembling glossolalia: but – and this is important in view of our definition of a (Christian) prophet – the initiate was not required, as a rule, to proclaim a message publicly; his experiences were, by their very nature, a secret not to be divulged.

Whereas prophetism seems to have been natural to the Greek temperament, it never blossomed among the Romans. Virgil alone bears witness to a sympathetic awareness of the Greek conception of ecstasy which produced messages in the case of the Sibyl in Apollo's temple at Cumae (*Aen.* vi. 44–51, 77–82). Sufficient has been said to justify the contention that 'prophetic' phenomena in Greek and Roman religion do not form *primary* sources – either in language used or experience described – from which we may seek illumination, by comparison, on Christian prophecy: more striking in fact are the suggested contrasts. Therefore we turn to the Hebrew–Jewish sources (both Palestinian and Hellenistic, though these are often intertwined) in the expectation that they will provide evidences of continuity and similarity.

I. OLD TESTAMENT PROPHECY

So numerous are the books and articles written on prophecy and prophets in ancient Israel and dealing with various stages of the prophetic phenomenon (from the early ecstatic seers – and an element of the supranormal never completely disappeared from the phenomenon, even though the enduring significance of prophecy was not dependent upon it – to the postexilic prophets and the later writers of apocalypses), as well as with specific aspects of the phenomenon (the call, the forms of speech employed, the relation of prophets to the cult and to the priestly and wisdom traditions), that any attempt to provide a short sketch of Old Testament prophecy, such as is required here, is to undertake a difficult task and one likely to invite criticism of its inadequacy. Nevertheless, we must try to set out the chief features and characteristics of the Old Testament prophetic experience if for no other reason than that (i) the prophets of the Christian community share the same title of dignity as the prophets of the old Covenant, *prophētēs* – a term not very frequently found in the vast range of non-Biblical Greek literature – being universally employed by the Septuagint (LXX) translators to render the Hebrew word *nābî'*; and (ii) early Christian prophecy, according to Acts 2 : 17f. represents the revival in the end-time of prophecy promised in the Old Testament (Joel 2.28–29).

Those whom we normally have in mind when we speak of 'the prophets of Israel' based their credentials neither on any hereditary right nor on any political appointment to an official position, but on their direct call by God himself: in other words, their status was not hierarchical but charismatic. They were inspired men who had a personal and extraordinarily direct encounter with God, and from this experience came their conviction that they spoke, with authority – indeed, absolute authority, if they were 'true' prophets – the word of the Lord. The great Jewish scholar, A. J. Heschel, states this admirably: 'the first and main feature of a prophet is his own claim to be a prophet: his own testimony to an experience of the Supreme Being addressing himself to him for the purpose of conveying a message to others; his own consciousness of an event in which both decision and direction come upon him as a transcendent act'.[17] Whether the unsought revelatory encounter with the divine is described in terms of a dream, a vision, an audition, or of an invasion or possession by the Spirit, the prophet transcends normal self-assertive consciousness and participates in a highly receptive state. The vocation and, more frequently, the commission (narrated in order to legitimise the message and sometimes give it dramatic form) were often accepted quite reluctantly both because inadequacy was felt and expressed and because testing hardship was entailed in being directly exposed to the will of God as well as in being the channel for its communication to others.

The most common form of prophetic communication was the oracle, a message from God, spoken by the prophet (on behalf of God) in the first person, usually with the explicit introductory formula 'Thus says the Lord', or 'This is the word of the Lord'. In his essay 'The Prophet as Yahweh's Messenger'[18] J. F. Ross interestingly and provocatively expands on this aspect of the prophetic task:

> The prophets, although they seldom call themselves 'messengers', used the form of the *Botenspruch* [messenger-speech] and claimed that their authority was of one sent by Yahweh or from his council (*sôd Yhwh*). They did not identify themselves with the one who sent them: there is no 'mystic union' with the divine. Nevertheless they did not 'prophesy the deceit of their own heart' (Jer. 23.26) for they had 'stood in the council' of Yahweh. The line is not easy to draw: does a messenger speak only the words of his Lord, or are they in some sense his own? Perhaps we may say more than we know when we refer to 'the message of the prophets'.

This quotation helps forward our discussion in several ways.

(1) The question whether the prophet's words were in some sense his own does not (and, in our view, is not intended to) open up the possibility of regarding prophetic messages as spontaneous or intuitive inventions, expressions of ideas which God approves, or simply true thoughts about God; but it does open up the question concerning the prophet's relatedness to tradition and his awareness of indebtedness to tradition. When a prophet asserted the divine origin of his message and affirmed that he had been specially chosen and called by God to proclaim it, he was undoubtedly testifying to a particularly immediate consciousness of God; yet, at the same time, in its speech-forms, motifs, ideas and themes, that message – and this is true not least of classical prophecy – shared a connection (not always of an affirmatory kind) with earlier prophetic messages (cf. Amos's influence on Isaiah and Hosea's on Jeremiah) and also with other areas of Israel's religious life. The former relation might be developed in the direction of bringing out the fresh significance of a prophecy for a later age: the latter, while including individual religious experience and its recollection, focuses attention on the cult. The extent to which cultic features are reflected in the description of prophetic calls, etc., is a debated issue; but, on the more general question of the prophets' participation in regular cultic ceremonies, we may be

certain that as private persons and especially as representatives of God they did participate, though not necessarily as specific cult functionaries or members of cultic associations. Ancient ritual was loose enough in organisation to give opportunity for various kinds of person to speak to any audience that was willing to listen: indeed, there was expectation and hope for special divine relevations. And some prophecies, such as those of Amos, were delivered at festivals and very probably transmitted later within some cultic/prophetic organisation. The Psalms – in addition to quoting a number of divine declarations (e.g. in Pss. 2, 60, 68, 87 and 89) – contain oracular expressions which are general in application, addressed to the 'wicked' (Pss. 50.16, 75.4) or to those who trusted in God. These general oracles – belonging to the sphere of the liturgist or cultic singer – are similar to, but not identical with, prophetic words which deal with *specific* situations. To sum up: the prophet's consciousness of being called to deliver a message directly given by God does not imply a total abandonment of tradition: the prophet drew upon, modified and added to the religious traditions of Israel, sometimes rejecting them, sometimes affirming them.

(2) That the prophets did not 'prophesy the deceit of their own heart' (Jer. 23.26), i.e. their own imaginings or inventions, leads to the question of true and false prophecy and prophets. Divergences in the messages of prophets were usually explained in terms of a charge that opponents had not received a genuine and therefore unquestionably authoritative divine word because they were morally or spiritually corrupt (Isa. 28.7; Jer. 23.16f.; Ezek. 13.10; Mic. 3.5) or even apostate (Deut. 13.1–3; Jer. 2.8). An oracle could, of course, be verified in hindsight, if it was fulfilled (1 Kgs. 22.28; Jer. 28.9), but this was only one criterion of genuineness: equally valid were conformity to accepted tradition and – a theological or dogmatic criterion – conformity with known revelation, 'the covenant faith' (Deut. 8.11 ff. and 13:2–4). In distinguishing between the true prophet and the false the criterion was ultimately the validity of his call. In Jeremiah, where false prophets so often are presented as opposing the divinely appointed messenger of God, it is stated several times that they were not commissioned by God, and

that their words were not from him (Jer. 14.14, 23.21–2, 28.15): the message of the divinely commissioned prophet was self-authenticating and unchallengeable.

(3) Although, as we have indicated, the messenger-formula 'Thus says the Lord' – whereby the prophet speaks the words of the one who sends and wherein the sender later speaks (usually, if not exclusively) in the 'I'-form, thus making the prophet himself a kind of letter from God – is the main form of prophetic speech, it may itself have more than one form of expression, and there are other patterns of prophetic speech. Specially worthy of note in connection with the 'Thus says the Lord' formula is its appearance in the covenant lawsuit (*rîḇ*), whether explicit (as in Isa. 1 and Mic. 6) or implicit: this is a court scene in which it is not a case of God being presented in the role of judge and Israel in that of the accused, but rather of God bringing the accusation or complaint that the covenant-bond has been broken and Israel attempting to defend her innocence by suggesting that God has not been active or faithful. In this kind of scene, God's case is put on the prophet's lips (in the 'I'-form, cf. Mic. 6.3) and at the same time the prophet, as the partner in God's cause and reading in an inspired, theological way the events of his time, calls Israel to acknowledge that God is right and that she is in the wrong, thus opening the way towards restoration of the covenant-relationship and salvation. The prophetic oracle thus becomes a vehicle of exhortation or, if necessary, in the judgment scene, a word of reprimand (*Scheltwort*) or an oracle of woe (*Drohrede*).

A distinctive view of the function of prophets which may be considered at this point finds expression in 2 Kgs. 17. 13–14:

> Yet the Lord warned Israel and Judah by every prophet and every seer, saying, 'Turn from your evil ways and keep my commandments and my statutes, in accordance with all the law which I commanded your fathers, and which I sent to you by my servants, the prophets.' But they would not listen, but were stubborn, as their fathers had been, who did not believe in the Lord their God.

Two observations on this passage are pertinent: in the first place, the prophets are presented as preachers of repentance, whose message was a call to return to the law (*tôrâh*) which had itself been given to the people by prophets: this is a strongly Deuteronomic (or Levitical) interpretation of prophets and their function inspired by its assessment of Moses as the prophet *par excellence*, who enjoyed the unique privilege of being addressed by God 'face to face' (Num. 12.6–8; Deut. 34.10) but who, incidentally, does not employ the usual prophetic messenger-formula 'I' when speaking for God, but always 'he' – the mark of the preacher; as the mediator and proclaimer of the law (cf. Deut. 18.15 ff.); and also as servant ('*ebed*) of the Lord. Secondly, the interpretation of the role of the prophets – and the Deuteronomic writer probably had in mind the succession from Moses, through Nathan and Elijah, up to Amos and possibly even beyond – continues with a statement about Israel's stubborn rejection of this call to repentance and obedience from her own prophets – a view which, as O. H. Steck has demonstrated,[19] was later developed into the presentation of the prophet as a martyr figure. This consciousness of rejection is certainly a marked feature of the understanding of the prophetic task in the call-narratives of Isaiah, Jeremiah and Ezekiel, and is probably reflected in Amos. 2. 10–12 (cf. Deut. 29.4). 'The prophets were sent to the people of Israel, but they expected to be heard only by the Israel of faith.'[20] The prospective destiny of the prophet was misunderstanding and distrust, at least, but not infrequently rejection (2 Chr. 36.16), imprisonment, and even death (2. Chr. 24.21, Jer. 26.20–23).

To return to the prophetic forms of communication: in addition to funereal complaint (cf. Amos 5.2), parable (Isa. 5), enigmatic statements, predictive utterances and diagnostic commentary on God's word, we may draw attention to three further forms: (*a*) salvation-speeches (*Heilsreden*) of an oracular or proclamatory kind; (*b*) the prophetic action – like the purchase of the field (Jer. 32), the naked and barefoot walk (Isa. 20), and possibly Hosea's marriage – which is not so much a symbolic act, but words in action, spoken and speaking actions, or, as von Rad describes them, 'intensified forms of prophetic speech';[21] and (*c*) prophetic intercession with God on behalf

of his people (Amos 7, and later witnessed to in 2 Macc. 15.17):
whether this is best understood in relation to a cultic setting
or otherwise is secondary to the fact that this intercessory role
indicates the solidarity of the prophet with the people, or a remnant of the people, whom he seeks to create into a prophetic
community with a prophetic mission – most clearly mirrored,
in the view of some, in the Isaianic Servant of the Lord, interpreted as the true prophetic Israel.

(4) The fact that the prophet-messenger claims to have stood
in the council of the Lord, or to have come from it, implies
that he witnesses to the topicality of the divinely given word.
Although the early prophet-seers in ancient Israel might be
consulted by individuals (1 Sam. 9.6–9) and by kings and military leaders (1 Sam. 23.2–4; 2 Kgs. 3.11), such consultation
was apparently not routine (cf. 1 Kgs. 22.5), because reliance
regarding political decisions was often placed upon the advice
of the 'wise' man (2 Sam. 16.23; cf. Isa. 19.11), a fact which
could lead to rivalry between the two 'professions' (Isa. 29.14 f.).
The classical prophets, however, did not want consultations:
they *declared* a message from the Lord's council. Consequently,
in addition to lamenting over immorality, sacred prostitution
(Hos. 4.14), sabbath violation, disrespect towards parents
(Mic. 7.6), murder, adultery, theft, selfish aggrandisement
(Mic. 2.2), drunkenness, charging interest on loans (Ezek.
22.12), and all other forms of evil and iniquitous practice, the
prophets attacked merchants for cheating and rapacity (Amos
8.4–6; Hos. 12.7 f.) and condemned the leaders of the country,
individually or collectively. Priests were criticised for failing to
mediate and follow divine instruction and for being eager to
receive expiatory sacrifices and other remunerations (Hos. 4.6–
8; Mic. 3.11; Zeph. 3.4): prophets were accused of violating
the norms of their profession (see above pp. 14–15): the 'heads',
'princes' or members of government were condemned for ignor-
ing basic morality, accepting bribes, for lack of concern for the
weak and for exploitation (Hos. 5.10, 7.3; Isa. 1.23, 3.14; Amos
6.1–6; Mic. 3. 1–3, 9–11). Of special concern to prophets was
the placing of national confidence in military or other human
operations (e.g. Isa. 30. 15–17, 31.1; Jer. 17.5; Hos. 10.13), and

both idolatry and oppression are seen as evidences of mis-
directed trust (Isa. 30.12, 42.17; Hab. 2.18). The downfall of
foreign nations was sometimes attributed to their arrogant self-
confidence (Isa. 10.12–16; Jer. 50.31; Obad. 3): but more often
the nation was held guilty of insolent 'oppression' (Isa. 14.4),
i.e. of destructive activity towards Israel and others (Amos 1.3–
2.3; Jer. 51.25–49; Obad. 10–14; Nahum 3.1). For the Israelite
audience (within which the prophet stood) the thrust of oracles
against foreign nations was to create or support trust in the
Lord: in fact, the difference between words of condemnation
and of promise lies, to a large extent, in the situation of the
hearers, in terms of whether they inflict, or need rescue from,
oppression or other forms of violence and wickedness.

Unsurpassed, perhaps unequalled, as a reforming political
force the prophets may have been, but it would be a mistake
to think that they dealt only with immediate problems and
situations. In the 'council of the Lord' they saw deeply into the
realities of existence and their expressions of what they learned
not only offered guidance to their immediate audience but possessed such personal and religious authority and ethical value
as to make them resound over many centuries. They affirmed
that the clashes and tensions which afflict national life would
be overcome only in an ultimate intervention of God, in his
way and in his time ('the day of the Lord'): they hoped, in
God's name, that men and nations would realise their peril and
trouble and be led to a self-transcending acknowledgment of
guilt, to a turning or repentance which could give rise to the
expectation of divine graciousness (Zeph. 3.8–18). On the other
hand, some major prophetic voices were raised to assert that
only after downfall would reconstitution be possible, a reconstitution or eschatological resolution whose various names bear
witness to the diverse kinds of tradition prophets drew upon
– a new exodus, a new covenant, a new Zion, a new creation.
When Israelites lost control over political power, classical prophecy ended. (It is a striking fact that prophecy effectively
begins and ends with the 'kingdom': during the Exile it
remained linked to the 'kingdom' and the state of Israel; but
after the Exile prophecy is but an echo or reminiscence of the

past, not a fresh, independent epoch.) The emphasis therefore shifted from concern about national or social evils towards expressions of confident perseverance, in the midst of suffering, inculcated by apocalyptic, with its announcement of a totally new world-order.

Since the relationship of prophecy to apocalyptic will be briefly dealt with later in this book (in the discussion of the book of Revelation), we may end our survey of prophecy in the Old Testament with a short statement on its relation to the two other major aspects of Israelite religion and culture: the priestly tradition and Wisdom. These aspects were by no means always isolated and could be combined in a single person's life, and even in a single utterance. A prophetic message could and often did contain elements more characteristic of priesthood or Wisdom. Perhaps the combination of functions is older than their separation since societal development generally runs in the direction of increasing specialisation. Prophecy is distinctive within but not separate from the rest of Israelite life, culture and religion.

Prophecy shares with priestly tradition a strong emphasis on divine revelation, expressed stylistically by God's speaking in the first person. It differs from priestly tradition in that the priest presents above all the traditions of the sacred past which were believed to have general and continuing significance for Israelite life, whereas the prophet responds, in the main (as we have stressed), to particular and immediate situations. It could be argued, however, that the priestly tradition, being institutional and conservative, is foundational, and therefore forms the context within which the prophet operates, sometimes approvingly, often critically. The general applicability of priestly speech implies that it did not require for itself constantly fresh revelation: it relied on and elaborated (as in Deuteronomy) a message received earlier by a mediator of revelation, who may be called a 'prophet', or, in the case of Moses, 'more than a prophet'. The desired domination of the priesthood in Israelite religion was finally achieved when it ranked the law (_tôrâh_) above the prophetic corpus. Although this may have happened as a result of the demands of practical life, rather than as a matter of theological theory, it effectively gave to Israel's religion the conservative and legalistic character that eventually stifled prophecy and stopped the springs of inspiration.

Wisdom found an early home in Israel, and its intellectual vitality and moral persuasiveness made it an important aspect of Israelite culture. Some see Wisdom as primarily a court activity (like state-craft) and others as a more domestic pursuit rooted in the folk ethos of early Israel's clan and tribal structured society. In fact it could be and was both, with result that we cannot accept any specially direct connection of Wisdom with any one class or group – politicians, scribes, educators or *élite* court-circles. Since the whole setting of Wisdom and the identity of 'the wise' thereby become much looser, we cannot set neat boundaries around 'wisdom' and 'prophecy' and expect to trace, easily, the influence of one on the other. Moreover, so-called 'wisdom' forms of speech and methods of argumentation may be more of the nature of stylistic, didactic devices and types of artistic speech, rather than fixed oral forms which prophets, such as Amos and Isaiah, are supposed to have employed. No more can themes, units of vocabulary, and idiom that appear in Proverbs and other wisdom-writings prove Wisdom influence on prophets who employed them. Wisdom themes, forms (like riddle and proverb) and vocabulary are part of the common oral and literary heritage belonging to a nation's whole culture. Their presence in a prophetic book may suggest, but cannot be decisive for 'wisdom' influence, any more than the presence in Wisdom books of prophetic-like themes and forms (e.g. Prov. 1–9) signifies direct prophetic influence.

The most decisive material for studying the part played by Wisdom-traditions in the preaching of the prophets remains those passages, especially in Isaiah and Jeremiah, where explicit reference is made to those who are or claim to be 'wise' and who make use of a special wisdom. And here the note struck is consistently one of conflict, indicating a sharp collision between policies advocated by rulers and governments and those urged on the people by prophets 'in the name of the Lord'.

Yet even here it is not simply a matter of an inherent and inevitable conflict between secular, political, anthropocentric
empiricism and divinely revealed message. It is the immediate
situation – not a fixed dependence on clearly identifiable and
opposed traditions or 'world-views' – that creates the conflict,
when certain prophets came face to face with men who supported their policies and advice with an appeal to their own
wisdom and insight. There was a religious element and motiva-
tion in early Wisdom, and there was a degree of common interest between prophecy and wisdom in their concern for morality
and for order and harmony in society. A measure of tension
between them is understandable, but it was not 'institutionally'
inevitable: and the book of Daniel is a late witness in the Old
Testament to a combination of both (together with apocalyptic), even if his book was not placed in the canon of Prophets.
Finally, we should note that when 'prophecy' in its distinctive
form died out, Wisdom lived on, as the book of Ecclesiastes, for
instance, shows, as well as the literature of the intertestamental
period.

2. THE INTERTESTAMENTAL LITERATURE

Before engaging with this body of literature two points must
be made concerning the end of Old Testament prophecy. The
prophetic movement which had flourished in various forms
from the beginning of the Israelite monarchy eventually came
to an end in the period following the Babylonian exile: its last
representatives were Haggai, Zechariah, and the shadowy
figure of Malachi, and after them the canon of the latter Prophets received no further addition. There can be no doubt that,
long before the turn of the eras, the Jews believed that prophecy
as such had ceased in Israel and that the prophetic Spirit had
withdrawn. Biblical passages of post-exilic origin substantiate
this fact (Zech. 13.4–6; Mal. 4.5–6 and perhaps Ps. 74.9). But
it is likewise clear from certain specific passages that there was
a definite belief, even in the biblical period, that in the future
prophecy would be revived. The passages in Malachi and Joel
which promise the return of the prophet Elijah (Mal. 4.5–6)
and of the prophetic spirit (Joel 2.28–29) bear witness to this

expectation and should not be overlooked in any study of the history of the phenomenon of prophecy.

In connection with the intertestamental literature two general observations may be made at the outset. In the first place, with few exceptions, the writings are pseudonymous. This must surely imply that the authors realised that their books could not gain general acceptance as prophetic utterances (where appropriate) on the basis of their own authority. The authority derived from the action of the prophetic Spirit had been withdrawn along with that Spirit. Secondly, with one possible exception (which we shall deal with later) the name 'prophet' is attributed to no person after Malachi in the entire literature of the intertestamental period. What these two points suggest is confirmed by explicit statements that prophecy had ceased and that there were no more prophets in Israel. No other book contains more references than 1 Maccabees. The distress that afflicted Israel after the death of Judas Maccabaeus is described as 'worse than any since the day when prophets ceased to appear among them' (1 Macc. 9.27). Earlier in the narrative, when the friends of Judas were uncertain about what to do with the defiled stones of the altar in the Temple, they agreed to leave them in an appropriate place 'until a prophet should arise who could be consulted about them' (1 Macc. 4.45–46). Again in 14.41 we read that 'the Jews and their priests confirmed Simon as their leader and high priest in perpetuity until a trustworthy (*piston*) prophet should appear'. Both these passages – if 4.46 is not just an expression of a tactical compromise between disputing parties – seem to confirm the expectation of a revival of prophetic activity (cf. Sib. Orac. III, 781): but it is worth noting that the prophet envisaged is a person with decision-making power, a man of insight, rather than of inspired authority, and, although his coming is placed in the future, the context does not appear positively eschatological.

Because 1 Maccabees was written at a time of lively eschatological thinking in Palestinian Judaism, and because the reappearance of prophecy was expected to coincide with the arrival or near approach of the messianic era, some scholars[22] think that the prophet was eschatological and the expectation derived from Deut. 18.15 ff. where the Moses-like prophet is described as invested with legal functions. This view is at least more probable than that of J. Klausner[23] who maintains that the prophet mentioned in the two passages from 1 Maccabees is Elijah, because, in rabbinic teaching, it is said that when Elijah returns, with the coming of the messianic age, he will interpret the law and settle legal disputes (cf. the expression 'it must be left undecided until Elijah comes'), a tradition that can be dated as early as the middle of the second century (M. Eduyoth 8.7). But in view of the probable date of 1 Maccabees (c. 125–100 BC) it would seem more likely that the task assigned to Elijah in rabbinic literature does not explain the tradition in 1 Maccabees, but rather the reverse: the existence of difficult religio-legal problems suggested that a trustworthy prophet would come to decide them and later this task was attributed by some rabbis to Elijah when he returned to function as reconciler, restorer of Israel and peace-maker (Mal. 4.6; Ecclus. 48.10) as well as forerunner of Messiah (Mal. 4.5; 1 Enoch 90.31, 37).

R. Meyer[24] has argued that long-range expectation is absent from the passages under consideration in 1 Maccabees, on the grounds that the guiding theme of the book is the fluctuating rise of the Hasmonean dynasty up to Simon and its continuation by John Hyrcanus (135–104 BC), the new priest-king (1 Macc. 16.11–22). John has passed into history as the bearer of the threefold gift – prophecy, priesthood and kingship – and the references to a coming prophet in 1 Maccabees would have a satisfactory sense when referred to this figure, a high priest and ruler who was endowed with the ability to make valid decisions on religio-legal matters, despite the fact that he is nowhere called *prophētēs* in the book.

In connection with this identification of the expected prophet of 1 Maccabees – if it is a genuine expectation at all and not (as we suspect) simply a formulaic expression of pious reserve in making decisions (cf. our 'God willing ...') – we may now refer to the possible exception mentioned earlier to the intertestamental literature's consistency in not attributing the term 'prophet' to anyone after Malachi. The Testament of Levi

– which, though it received Christian interpolation, came into being, substantially, not later than the first century B C[25] – contains the following passage: 'And the third shall be called by a new name, because a king shall arise in Judah and shall establish a new priesthood, after the fashion of the Gentiles. And his presence is unutterable (?), as a prophet of the Most High, of the seed of Abraham our father' (8.14). Both R. H. Charles[26] and Otto Eissfeldt[27] have interpreted this passage as referring to John Hyrcanus. Charles contended that it was written at the height of his success when some Jews apparently regarded John as the Messiah, a view he finds confirmed by the Testament of Benjamin 9.2: 'Nevertheless the temple of God shall be in your portion, and the last (temple) shall be more glorious than the first. And the twelve tribes shall be gathered together there, and all the Gentiles, until the Most High shall send forth his salvation in the visitation of an only-begotten (?) prophet'. For Charles, this passage is pre-Christian (though it seems to contain clear Christian interpolation) and refers to Hyrcanus for, in his time, the twelve tribes did again meet in the temple for worship, and in his triumphs the hope was raised that there would be a widespread conversion of the Gentiles.

These two passages from the Testaments of the Twelve Patriarchs substantiate the claim that the gift of prophecy was expected to return to Israel, the second suggesting that it was looked for in a messianic-type figure. It is of more than incidental interest in this connection that, according to Josephus (*Antiq.* XIII.299), John Hyrcanus was accounted worthy of the three greatest privileges, the rule of the nation, the dignity of high priest and the gift of prophecy (*prophēteia*), for the deity was with him and enabled him to foresee and foretell the future (cf. *Bell.* 1.68): in neither place is John called *prophētēs*). Since Josephus attributes to John alone the gift of prophecy (even though it denotes 'prediction'), this may provide support for Charles's view that Testament of Levi 8.14 refers to the same figure, since it (and Testament of Benjamin 9.2, if pre-Christian) is the only place in the intertestamental literature where prophecy is attributed to a specific individual.

It has to be admitted that the intertestamental literature,

even if we were to include discussion of the Sibylline Oracles
– a literary form adopted and adapted from the Greek Sibylline
literature for propagandising purposes, and related to apocalyptic both in form (e.g. pseudonymity) and content much
more clearly than to Hebrew prophecy – does not yield a rich
harvest of material for understanding prophecy in the post-
biblical period. What it does suggest is that, with the cessation
of divinely inspired prophecy, a hope remained, in at least some
quarters, for divine guidance through an individual or individuals who would be endowed with the gift of insight, or even
of revelation, but would not function with the divinely given
authority of the Old Testament prophetic messengers. Even if
we were to consult the large body of Jewish apocalyptic literature, the result would be similar. Although these works are
pseudepigraphal, the revelatory experiences related by the
alleged authors presumably reflect genuine revelations given
to the actual authors. Whether these authors regarded their
works as equal in authority to the Old Testament prophets but
hid that (pretentious) claim in a pseudepigraphal guise to avoid
the displeasure of the Jewish religious officials, or whether they
thought of their work as revelation of an important, but nevertheless inferior, sort, is a matter difficult to determine with certainty.
Although, on the one hand, there is a deep consciousness of the
privileged reception of divine revelations (Ass. Mos. 1.13–18;
2 Enoch 33.5–6. 36.1; 3 Bar. 1.3–8; 4 Ezra 14.7–8, etc.), there
is, on the other hand, such a notable absence of claims to inspiration by the Holy Spirit and, in much of the literature (with
the exception of the Similitudes of Enoch, 1 Enoch 37–71), of
the 'Thus says the Lord' form of introduction, that the second explanation seems, on balance, to be preferable and more probable.

3. JOSEPHUS

For the understanding of prophecy in Judaism during the first
century A D, including prophecy in early Christianity, the writings of Josephus, unlike the intertestamental literature, are
of great importance. But it would be simplistic and unprofit-
able for our purpose merely to catalogue his references to
prophet-like figures as evidence of the lively and multi-faceted

continuance of the prophetic phenomenon in the Judaism of, or roughly contemporaneous with, New Testament times.

Whatever we may think of the justification offered for his change of allegiance to Rome, a passage in the *Bellum* (III.351–4) is of considerable significance in connection with Josephus's claim to prophetic powers and his own self-understanding as a prophet, and it will conveniently form the reference-point for this brief discussion. The passage relates to the time, during his command in Galilee, when in acute danger from Nicanor, Josephus recalled

> those nightly dreams in which God had foretold to him the impending fate of the Jews and the destinies of the Roman sovereigns. He was an interpreter of dreams and skilled in the divining of the meaning of ambiguous utterances of the Deity: a priest himself and of priestly descent, he was not ignorant of the prophecies of the sacred books. At that hour he was inspired (*enthous genomenos*) to read their meaning and, recalling the dreadful images of his recent dreams, he offered up a solemn prayer to God. 'Since it pleases thee', so it ran, 'to break thy work, since fortune has wholly passed to the Romans, and since thou hast made choice of my spirit to announce the things that are to come, I willingly surrender to the Romans and consent to live, but I take thee to witness that I go not as a traitor, but as thy minister (*diakonos*)' (Thackeray's translation).

Although neither here nor anywhere else in his writings does Josephus refer to himself as *prophētēs* (that title being reserved for biblical prophets alone) because for him, as for the rabbis who were his contemporaries, the era of genuine prophecy was past (*Apion* 1.41), this passage offers valuable insights into Josephus's own prophetic experience and activity from which we may understand better what he says of other prophet-like figures.

(1) Boastful Josephus's claim may be here (and again in *Bell.* III.399–408, where he claims to have predicted correctly the overthrow of his Galilean headquarters, his own capture by the Romans, and the accession of Vespasian and Titus to the

emperorship), but the very fact that he could write in such a way – in a situation and with a message not dissimilar to Jeremiah's (cf. Jer. 1.4–19, 15.10–21, 20.7–18) – shows that, although prophecy as such was believed to have ended, it was still possible to conceive that a favoured individual might be endowed with the gift of insight into the future. And for Josephus prophecy consists principally in prediction. The rationale for this view lies in the fact that (a) he understood the biblical prophets as historians (which explains the attribution of the historical books to prophetic authors: they were in fact the historians *par excellence* because they obtained information about the past in the best and surest fashion, i.e. under divine inspiration (*kata tēn epipnoian tēn apo tou theou: Apion* 1.37): (b) he himself, by commencing his writing roughly where the prophets left off and by claiming an inspiration comparable to though less than that of the canonical prophets, is competent to take up and complete this prophetic task. Precedent or justification for Josephus's interpretation of his life's work as historian as being a prophetic task could be found, as J. Blenkinsopp suggests,[28] in the work of the author of Chronicles–Ezra–Nehemiah who refers to prophetic sources – one of which is 'the midrash of the prophet Iddo' (2 Chr. 13.22) – to such an extent and in such a way as to leave little doubt that he regards the writing of history, admittedly in a midrashic form, as a prophetic task; Josephus owes much to this biblically based tradition of history and midrash as being prophetic genres: (c) biblical prophets – both the very early ones like Balaam, Moses and Samuel and the canonical prophets – were involved in predicting the future course of events, and in his own re-telling of the biblical story Josephus is eager to take note of their predictions and their fulfilment (cf. *Antiq.* IV.125, 303, 313 f.; V.350; IX.276; X.79; XIII.62 ff.).[29] So much then the passage quoted tells us: prophetic revelation which comes through inspiration (*enthous genomenos*) has to do with future events in the political sphere.

(2) This kind of prophetic revelation is mediated through the dream (as in the case of Daniel, whom Josephus holds in particularly high regard by reason of the accuracy of his prophecies), but even more importantly through the ability to

explain 'ambiguous utterances of the Deity' and to know the meaning of the sacred prophecies: prophetic prediction rests on the inspired interpretation of biblical texts. This view of prophecy is not essentially different from that of the Essenes, concerning whom Josephus says that 'there are some among them who profess to foretell the future, being versed from their early years in sacred books, holy writings and the sayings of the prophets' (*Bell.* II.159): in short, Essene prophesying is based on midrash or scriptural exegesis, and references elsewhere in Josephus to particular Essene prophets and their prophecies (*Antiq.* XIII.311–13; XVII.346–8; XV.373 ff.) confirm this conclusion. The same holds true for the little Josephus has to say about prophecy among the Pharisees (*Antiq.* XVII.43 ff.). Predictive prophecy implies exegetical skill combined with divine inspiration.

While Josephus does not refer to those who, like himself, were genuine predictors as *prophētai*, he does not hesitate to use the term *pseudoprophētēs* both of individuals who falsely claimed prophetic status and of individuals who announced things that were not, or did not, come true. This Greek word made its entry into the language in the Septuagintal translation of Jeremiah, where it is used nine times to refer to persons who were no better than pagan divinators (*manteis*).[30] This particular implication, however, is absent from Josephus's use of the word: the *pseudoprophētēs* in the biblical period and on the contemporary scene is an individual who either falsely lays claim to or has ascribed to him prophetic status or predicts falsehoods. Among such are Theudas who promised the repetition of Joshua's miracle in the cleaving of Jordan (*Antiq.* XX.97 f.), the prophet from Egypt who held out the prospect of a repeat performance of the Jericho miracle at Jerusalem (*Antiq.* XX.169 ff., *Bell.* II.261–4), and the unnamed false prophet who tried to rally the defenders of the Temple with promises of miraculous, divine intervention towards the end of the siege of Jerusalem (*Bell.* VI.283 ff.). Josephus speaks of these men as magicians or imposters (*goētēs*), acting under the pretence of divine inspiration (*Bell.* II.258; *Antiq.* XX.168), as pretended messengers (*angeloi*) of the Deity (*Bell.* VI.288), and thus as claiming prophetic status within the context of events interpreted as heralding messianic times when, it was believed, the spirit of prophecy would again be operative. They are generally distinguished from the bandits of the time (*lēstai*) and the difference is not unimportant, for Josephus's criticism of these prophet-like figures is that they were, implicitly, pretenders to a nationalistic messiahship, being convinced that the age of salvation was imminent and that they were called, as a second Moses or Joshua, to bring matters to a head. And for Josephus (who desired to conceal Jewish messianism as much as possible, for apologetic reasons) such political messianism was pseudo-prophecy (in claim and content) for two reasons: first, the predictions of divine assistance did not come true, as anyone writing after AD 70 knew very well; and secondly, these persons perverted the sense of the biblical prophecies (*Bell.* 1.342). Jesus ben-Chananiah, who prophesied the destruction of the Temple as early as AD 62, falls into a different category: though Josephus calls him neither *prophētēs* nor *pseudo-prophētēs*, he stands close to the Old Testament prophets of doom in the content, form and manner of delivery of his woe-oracle (*Bell.* VI.300 ff.).

(3) Reverting to the passage from *Bell.* III.351–4: the description of Josephus's own inspiration as *enthous genomenos* might easily give the impression that the vocabulary used with reference to predictive prophecy implies a thoroughly Hellenistic understanding of the prophetic experience. But what we have said thus far should have given a contrary impression, and it is confirmed by a closer look at the terminology used by Josephus for this general phenomenon. Language associated with mantic and oracular prophecy is far from frequent in his writings. Admittedly, the Essene seers, Judas and Simon (*Bell.* 1.78–80; II.112) are called by the title *mantis*, the words *manteia* and *manteuma* are occasionally used of politically oriented oracles and the verb *manteuomai* is employed in the account of Saul's visit to the witch of Endor: but otherwise these terms are used, mainly if not exclusively, of non-Jewish individuals and phenomena. Nor does the word-group *mania*, *mainesthai* and *mainomenos* occur with anything like the frequency it does in Philo. It would seem clear that Josephus is well aware of the difference between Jewish and non-Jewish prophecy: even if his own

emphasis on prophecy as political prediction fits in well with popular and current Hellenistic religious ideas, that too, as we have suggested, has biblical justification.

(4) At the end of the passage quoted from *Bell.* III Josephus refers to himself as God's 'minister' (*diakonos*). The restriction of the term *prophētēs* to the canonical prophets is accompanied by the use of various synonyms for later figures to whom genuinely prophetic characteristics could not be denied. One such would be *diakonos* (which is the LXX rendering of *'ebed* in Hag. 1.12 f.) and another would be *angelos* (cf. *Bell.* VI.288), a noun which renders *mal'ak* in the LXX of Mal. 3.1. The *angeloi* sent by God to teach the Jews doctrines and laws (*Antiq.* XV.136) are also probably intended to be prophets.

(5) Finally, we may draw attention to the fact that in *Bell.* III.351 Josephus affirms that he was not ignorant of the prophecies of the sacred books because he was a priest himself and of priestly descent (cf. *Vita* 2–6). It is clear from the way he speaks about his priesthood that it is closely associated in his mind with the prophetic gift. Now we know independently of Josephus that from the time of the Hasmoneans the prophetic endowment was believed to inhere *de iure*, if not always *de facto*, in the high priest, and we have already drawn attention (pp. 23–24) to the fact that, according to Josephus, John Hyrcanus was the only one to unite in his person the three most noble privileges, supreme command of the nation, the high priesthood and the gift of prophecy (viewed in terms of prognostic ability), *Antiq.* XIII.299 ff. This combination of high priesthood and prophecy is attested independently in Testament of Levi 8.11–15 (discussed earlier) and in the Talmud. In this connection, the prophecy of the high priest recorded in John 11.51 should be borne in mind, for it has to be understood within the same frame of reference.[31] All this reflects the sacral and cultic associations of prophecy in Israel, and at several points in his narrative Josephus speaks of the Temple as the locus of prophetic activity: it owed its existence in the first place to a prophetic oracle (*Antiq.* VII.90 ff.), and, at its dedication, received a portion of the divine Spirit (*Antiq.* VIII.114), which, for Josephus as for the rabbis, was pre-eminently the spirit of prophecy.

To sum up: Josephus knew that the age of immediately inspired and unquestionably authoritative prophecy was past and gone, yet he believed that God still made use of certain individuals for the purpose of revealing the course of future events and guiding the destinies of his people. These could not be called by the honoured title 'prophet', although those who wrongly claimed to be such could be called 'false prophets'. Since Josephus himself believed that he had been entrusted with this kind of task, he was under obligation to provide a context in which the claim could be made credible and intelligible. His political predictions and his activity as an historian provided an available connection with earlier and current understandings of the role of the prophet. A less obvious, but perhaps no less important, aspect of the process of legitimisation arose directly out of his priestly and Hasmonean (therefore high priestly) descent. With this he associated not only his divinely inspired, and therefore legitimate, interpretation of prophetic texts, but also his prophetic (or, as some will wish to say, quasi-prophetic) role in the actual unfolding of events.

4. PHILO JUDAEUS

In Pharisaic Judaism Torah – which contains all revealed truth – is the raison d'être of prophets and prophetic activity in that prophets are regarded as the bearers or transmitters of the tradition ultimately derived from that single and supreme revelation. In Alexandrian theology it is Wisdom (*Sophia*) – 'the cause of all things, a breath of the power of God' (Wisd. 7.25) – that brings prophets into the world: 'in each generation she passes into holy souls and makes them friends of God and prophets' (Wisd. 7.27). Among such 'holy souls' were Abraham, Jacob, Joseph and, especially, Moses, so that the early history of God's people (narrated in Wisd. 10–19) was almost entirely guided by prophets in whom Wisdom made her home. For Philo too Torah – in the sense of the Pentateuchal tradition – is the prototype and starting-point of the whole history of salvation: consequently, the patriarchs and Moses in particular are presented as prophets in a special sense, together with men of Israel's later history.

For instance, Abraham steadfastly apprehended the wisdom of God (*Heres* 313–15) and because of this upward direction of his thoughts he experienced the highest form of *ekstasis*, the experience of divine seizure and inspiration (*entheos katokōchē te kai mania*) which is designated 'prophecy' (the other three forms being delusion or folly, excessive stimulation or consternation, and quietude or passivity): Abraham was inspired and God-possessed; the divine reason passed into him and he became the mouthpiece of God (*Heres* 263–66), having nothing of his own to say since it is really another who speaks in him. As the clinching proof-text for Abraham's prophetic status, Philo quotes Genesis 20.7, but his interpretation of the passage contains some very significant words: 'the holy word (*hieros logos*) assures prophecy to every worthy man (*panti asteiō*)' (*Heres* 259), which implies that, contrary to the common Jewish view that authoritatively inspired prophecy had ceased at the time of Ezra, it is a continuing phenomenon – in the sense of knowing things beyond sense-perception and reason – available to Philo's contemporaries and successors through their own religious experience. In this assumption Philo was certainly modifying, if not ranging far from, his Jewish base. What follows the sentence quoted is of importance for Philo's understanding of prophecy: 'for a prophet, being a spokesman, has no utterance of his own, but all his utterance comes from elsewhere, echoes of another's voice (*hypēchountos heterou*). The wicked may never be an interpreter of God, so that no worthless person is God-inspired (*enthousiā*) in the proper sense. The name only befits the wise since he alone is the vocal instrument of God, smitten and played by his invisible hand. Thus all whom Moses describes as just are pictured as possessed and prophesying (*katechomenous kai prophēteuontas*)' (*Heres* 259–60).

From this passage, and from others which testify to his own pneumatic experiences – such as his occasional seizure by the divine (*katochē entheos*) which left him unconscious of everything else (*Mig. Abr.* 35) and his likening of himself to persons possessed and corybants filled with inspired frenzy 'even as the prophets are inspired' (*Heres* 69 f.) – we may learn something about Philo's understanding of the prophetic experience.

(1) It is the highest form of ecstasy, a state of divine possession in which the mind is no longer in its own keeping, a state in which the divine Spirit plays on the vocal organism and makes sounds (*krouei*) which express its message.

(2) The language employed by Philo in describing the experience(s) is almost entirely derived from non-biblical Greek: *thespizō* ('foretell'), *katokōchē* ('possession'), *enthousia(z)ō* ('be inspired'), *mania*, *theophorētos* ('possessed or inspired by God'), *hypēcheō* ('echo' or 'prompt'), etc.

(3) In affirming that the gift of prophecy is available 'to every worthy man' and therefore to his contemporaries, Philo is at odds with known Jewish (rabbinic and non-rabbinic) views.

(4) His claim that a prophetic utterance is not the individual speaking, but the echo of another's voice reminds one of the rabbinic doctrine of the *baṭ qôl*, the organ of inspiration during the absence of the Holy Spirit of prophecy; but Philo localises the experience within the individual, whereas rabbinic usage (as we shall see) thinks of the 'voice' coming to the recipient from the heavenly sphere.

In Philo's writings we find either an acute hellenisation of the Jewish concept of prophecy,[32] or a hellenistic view of prophecy justified on a biblical basis:[33] whichever view of the matter we take, it must be admitted that it certainly represents a significant departure from what is reflected in other extant Jewish literature of the general period.

5. RABBINIC TEACHING

Although rabbinic testimonies on prophecy (as on other subjects) are for the most part late and although it is theoretically possible that some of them are due to reaction against Christianity, nevertheless we must pass in review the major points of interest.[34]

Again and again we find the dogmatic assertion that Haggai, Zechariah and Malachi were the last of the prophets and that with their departure the Spirit of God or the Holy Spirit, who is equated with the Spirit of prophecy, ceased to be active in Israel (Tos. Sot. 13.2): in this situation the divine will is made known by means of the *baṭ qôl* (lit. 'daughter of a voice'), not by human means, for no person was thought worthy to receive the Holy Spirit (and so become a prophet): even if such an individual existed, the iniquity of the present age made it impossible for him to receive the prophetic spirit. It is said, for example, of Hillel, one of the pillars of Pharisaism in the early first century A D:

> When the elders came to the house of Gadia in Jericho, a *bat qôl* proclaimed to them: 'There is a man among you worthy of the Holy Spirit, but this generation is unworthy of it.' They fixed their eyes on Hillel the Elder.
>
> (Tos. Sot. 13.3; bSot. 48b; jSot. 24b)

The *bat qôl* is a remarkable idea or phenomenon: the term is normally translated 'heavenly voice', but one cannot help wondering if that is not to overdo its significance for the scribes: for them 'heavenly voices' merited at least some respect by reason of their warnings, but the *bat qôl* (certainly after A D 90) was merely a poor substitute for prophetic revelation,[35] an echo of God's voice, deserving even less attention than the scriptural exegesis of the scribes who, in their own way, laid claim to inspiration. In any case, the 'voice' or 'echo' had no authority, in normal circumstances, in matters relating to *halakah* (i.e. instruction on conduct), a discipline which was to be constructed not on the basis of fresh and immediate revelation but on written, scriptural tradition and reason, or even group-decisions (bBab. Met. 59b; jBer. 3b; bBer. 52a). The activity of the *bat qôl* was confined to bearing testimony to a person's holiness, as in the case of Hanina ben-Dosa and Samuel the Little, to reciting Scripture for men's guidance, and, occasionally, to conveying a divine command (for example, Jonathan ben-Uzziel was forbidden by a *bat qôl* to publish the Targum of the Writings, bMeg. 3a).

We have mentioned the fact that Josephus speaks, on a few occasions, of Pharisees who had the gift of prophecy (*prognōsis*), and we have just referred to one Pharisaic teacher who was judged worthy of the spirit of prophecy and therefore inspired, viz. Hillel, and others could be Simon the Just, Onias the Circle-maker, and Hanina, who actually rejected the title 'seer' or 'prophet' by referring to Amos 7.14: cf. bBer. 34b; bYeb. 121b: in keeping with this attestation of charismatic or inspired activity attributed to individual Pharisees is the fact that the Pharisees, as a group, saw *themselves* as heirs of the great prophetic tradition. They took over, in pairs (Aboth 1.1), the transmission of the tradition – the Mosaic 'oral' law – from the men of the Great Synagogue who received it from the last in the line of the prophets. As expert interpreters of the sacred Scripture, it is probable that the Pharisees, and in particular their scribes, saw themselves as engaged in a process which was the closest approximation possible *at the time* to the revelation mediated through the prophets in an earlier era. It was, of course, an activity brought to bear principally on Torah and issued in $h^a la$-kôth: and in consequence the Pharisees tended to view the prophets as exponents and traditioners of Torah, themselves saying nothing, and their successors (the 'wise men') saying nothing that was not already contained in the Sinai revelation – hence, perhaps, the saying attributed to Hillel (jShab 19.1 [Schwab III, 178]; bPes. 6) concerning the Pharisees and their successors, 'If they are not prophets, yet are they sons of the prophets:' It is on the basis of this kind of outlook (where Torah expounds itself in the prophets) that we can understand why, in the rabbinic view, the prophets did not have anything like the same canonical validity and status as the Law.

Did rabbinic Judaism expect a revival of prophecy? To answer that question with precision would require knowledge of the importance accorded by Judaism to the chief Old Testament testimony to a renewal of the era of prophecy (Joel 2:28–29). The texts provided as evidence by Strack-Billerbeck are few and relatively late (Num. Rab. 15, 25 and one passage from Deut. Rab.). Since we find no allusion to the Joel passage in the Testaments of the Twelve Patriarchs, nor in the Qumran texts, we cannot easily argue that the rabbis expunged references to it from their texts as a reaction against its use in Christianity – a use which surely comes out of its own early experience and not one based on preconceived ideas. We may therefore affirm, with M. A. Chevallier,[36] that the expectation of a new era of prophecy constituted only a peripheral element in the hopes of Judaism: the outpouring of the prophetic spirit was a phenomenon which did not really touch men's hearts, but acted as a sign of a return to a golden age of bliss when Israel was full of prophets rather than as the cause of or a factor in general spiritual renewal.

More significant, perhaps, is the expectation of an eschatological prophet who would appear in the messianic era, either as a prophet-Messiah, in fact if not in name, or as a precursor of the Messiah or as the partner of Messiah.[37] The idea of an eschatological prophet *like* Moses (as distinct from the conception of a returning Moses, i.e. Moses *redivivus*) was based on one of several possible interpretations of Deut. 18.15 ff., but evidence for the messianic interpretation of that passage is lacking in early rabbinic literature: it is the Fourth Gospel which provides us with surer evidence that Deut. 18.15 ff. was interpreted messianically in certain circles within Judaism (perhaps at Qumran, though the relevant passages are difficult to interpret) and amongst the Samaritans whose expected messiah, named *Taheb* (=restorer), had, in addition to royal and priestly features, the gift of prophecy and was undoubtedly like Moses, if not in fact identified with him as Moses *redivivus*: he was expected to have the characteristic features of the prophet in that he would perform miracles, restore the law and true worship and also bring knowledge to other nations, and, like Moses, he was to die at the age of 120 years. That Moses would accompany Messiah at his coming may be deduced from a passage in *Codex Neofiti*,[38] but the translation and interpretation of the reference is by no means certain. Better attested is the tradition concerning the coming of Elijah, based on Mal. 3.23 and Ecclus. 48.10, whose future functions varied from being the agent of reconciliation and of the restoration of Israel (Mal. 3.24; Eduy. 8.7) to that of being, in the view of some, a quasimessianic figure in his own right before the coming of the Lord (Targ. Mal. 3.1, 23-4), or, in the opinion of others, the forerunner or companion of the Messiah.[39]

These varied and interesting expectations in Judaism of a future prophet-like figure should not be allowed to overshadow the significance of the rabbinic (that is, the official Pharisaic-scribal) view that the era of prophets had ceased: contemporary 'prophets', in the sense of foretellers of future events, they might accept, but they could not tolerate prophets in the strict sense, prophets who, without reference to Scripture, could proclaim 'Thus says the Lord'.[40] In theory the era without prophets was for the rabbis only a temporary tragedy: in fact it was an unavoidable consequence of the conviction that revelation in its totality had been given at Sinai. There is no place for genuine prophecy in the sense of immediately inspired and authoritative utterances in a religious milieu dominated by scribes, whose task is solely the interpretation of that which has already been given. 'It is no accident that the power, originality and driving force of the Rabbis ... did not lead to immediate deliverances of their own personal certainties, but were canalised within the framework of tradition.'[41] But the Spirit of God, the prophetic Spirit, could not be imprisoned in a dogmatic and scribal schema: the belief in men of God as bearers of the divine Spirit must have continued among simple and ordinary people, and powerful eschatologically oriented charismatic phenomena (in the time of Vespasian and Hadrian) were to reveal the insufficiency of early Pharisaic-scribal dogmatic rigidity.

6. THE QUMRAN SCROLLS

For the members and teachers of the Qumran community the law of Moses was the only rule of life and the revelatory words of the Old Testament prophets their only guide to the events of the last days. The programmatic statement of its functions may be seen in 1QS 8.15 f.: the community separates itself from ungodly men and enters the wilderness to make straight in the desert a path for God (Isa. 40.3) – 'this (path) is the study of the Law which he commanded by the hand of Moses, that they may do according to all that has been revealed from age to age, and as the Prophets have revealed by His Holy Spirit'.

In the Law of Moses, says the Damascus Rule (16.2) 'all things are strictly defined': consequently the sole aim of the members of the community was 'to seek God with a whole heart and soul, and do what is good and right before Him as he commanded by the hand of Moses and all His servants the Prophets'

(1QS 1.2–3). Any member who deliberately transgressed even one of the precepts promulgated was expelled from the sect's *élite* stratum, the Council of the Community (1QS 8.21–23); and any member who sinned inadvertently was excluded, for up to two years, in order to do penance (1QS 8.24–9.2). The Law was indeed the charter or foundation of the community, but the interpretation of the Law in the community was the final rule. 'Whoever approaches the Council of the Community ... shall undertake by a binding oath to return with all his heart and soul to every commandment of the Law of Moses in accordance with all that has been revealed of it to the sons of Zadok, the Keepers of the Covenant and Seekers of his will' (1QS 5.8–9; cf. CD 15.13), i.e. the priestly leaders and teachers of the sect. In other words, the only valid observance of the Law was that which followed the official interpretation taught by the community, an interpretation which was marked by a rigidity and exclusiveness more strict that the *halakah* ('instruction for conduct') of the great legal codes of Mishnah and Talmud:[42] any interpretation other than that of the sons of Zadok was, in their eyes, an obstacle to true righteousness, a 'snare of Satan' (CD 4.15–17). 'The perfect way' or 'perfection of way', so frequently spoken of as the ideal for the members of the community, was attainable only through absolute and total obedience to the revealed interpretation of the Law handed down and developed by the sect (1QS 9.17 ff.).

The disclosure of the revealed will of God from the Law is the function of priestly teachers in the first place: in every group of ten men of the Council of the Community there had to be a seeker or interpreter of the Law (probably a priest) who spent night and day in continuous study and who shared with his brethren the truth he discovered (1QS 6.6–7). (Is this the *Sitz im Leben* of the numerous interpretations, or *pesharim*, found in the Qumran texts?) But the tradition of an esoteric revelation goes back to the Teacher of Righteousness (the 'right' or 'rightful' Teacher). The Damascus Rule (3.13 ff.) mentions the 'hidden things' revealed to the earliest remnant and emphasises the validity of the legal enactments of the founders of the sect (who dug a well [CD 6.3], i.e. the Law). It is therefore legiti-

mate to suppose that the sect regarded the Teacher of Righteousness as one of those who discovered or had revealed to him
the true interpretation of Torah. Support for this view would
be strong if some of the references to the 'Interpreter of the Law'
– not all of them, of course, since the task of interpreting Torah
had to continue after the original (or first) Teacher's death –
are references to the function of the Teacher of Righteousness:
and this view is consonant with the suggestion that the Teacher
of Righteousness was an aspirant to the office of high priest as
described in 2 Chronicles 15.3 f., i.e. a chief priest as a teaching
priest whose prerogative it was to teach or expound the Law.[43]

If the Teacher's claim to possess and deliver revealed interpretations of Torah is plausible, in the matter of the interpretation of the prophets it is certain. The books of the prophets form
authorities that demand obedience (CD 7.15–18) and their importance for the community was enormous, for God 'through
the words of his servants, the Prophets, foretold all that would
happen to his people and his land' (1 QpHab 2.9 f.). But what
the prophets said, like the words of the Law, remained a mystery until explained or interpreted. One notable passage from
the Habakkuk Commentary illustrates their exegesis (known
as *pesher*-interpretation) of a prophetic text. In Habakkuk 2.2
God tells the prophet, 'Write down the vision and make it plain
upon the tablets, that he who reads may read it speedily': this
is interpreted as follows: 'God told Habakkuk to write down
that which would happen to the final generation, but He did
not make known to him when time would end. And as for that
which he said, "that he who reads may read it speedily", interpreted, this concerns the Teacher of Righteousness to whom
God made known all the mysteries of the words of his servants
the Prophets' (1 QpHab 7.1–5).

Several of the sect's basic beliefs about prophecy are
expressed in this text. In the first place, the words of the prophets are mysteries which have a hidden significance that must
be discovered by further revelation. Secondly, this hidden
meaning has to do with what is to take place in the last days.
Thirdly, the end is near and therefore the prophecy applies to
the writer's own generation and movement. Fourthly, and most

important of all, the person to whom all these mysteries are revealed is the Teacher of Righteousness himself.[44] In short, biblical prophecy – whose meaning was *not* known to the prophets themselves – was made comprehensible to the community alone, and much of it was already or about to be fulfilled in the community's own history. For instance, the words of Hab. 1.5, 'For I accomplish a deed in your days but you will not believe it when told', were interpreted as concerning 'those who were unfaithful, together with the Liar, because they did not listen to the word received by the Teacher of Righteousness from the mouth of God' (1 QpHab 2.1–2).

The men of Qumran never employ the term 'prophet' with reference to the Teacher; but then Josephus did not use the term either of himself and his historical writing or of the Essenes who could foretell the future on the basis of scriptural study (see above, pp. 26–28) : yet they share the conviction that the real meaning of texts, in both the Law and the Prophets, is revealed to the inspired exegete as a result of direct divine illumination. Is not such an inspired interpreter of biblical texts, with reference to their present and future fulfilment, in many respects a 'prophet' according to our definition? The Teacher's words are received 'from the mouth of the Lord' (1QpHab 2.2, according to a reasonable reconstruction of the text) and he is instructed by God himself (1 QpHab 7.4).

If, as many scholars are convinced, the Teacher was the author, in whole or in part, of the Qumran hymns (*Hodayoth*), then we see further prophetic features in his self-understanding. Speaking to God, he describes himself as one 'into whose mouth Thou hast put doctrine and into whose heart Thou hast put wisdom that he might open a fount of knowledge to all men of insight' (1 QH 2.17–18): again, 'through me Thou has illumined the face of many and hast shown thine infinite power, for Thou has instructed me in thy marvellous mysteries' (4.27–28). For his mission he claims the presence of the Spirit: 'I thank Thee Lord for ... Thou hast shed Thy Holy Spirit upon me that I may not stumble' (7.6–7): 'I, the master (of wisdom), know Thee, O my God, by the spirit which Thou hast given me, and by Thy Holy Spirit I have faithfully hearkened to Thy marvellous counsel' (12.12). Moreover, in a kind of visionary experience (4.2–3) in which God appears to him, he is able to declare that his enemies – teachers of lies and false prophets – will not or do not listen: 'they hearken not to Thy voice nor give heed to Thy word; of the vision of knowledge they say "It is unsure", and of the way of Thy heart "It is not (the way)"'. In view of these features of his claim, endowment and character, as well as in view of the fact that just as the prophets are called 'God's servants' (1 QS 1.3; 1 QpHab 2.9) so does he refer to himself frequently in the Hymns as 'God's servant', can we deny a genuine prophetic experience and mission to the Teacher, even if the name 'prophet' is not used of him? We cannot: yet, at the same time, we must recognise at least one very significant distinction between the Teacher and the Old Testament prophets. Although the Teacher is inspired by God to unravel the secrets of the words of the prophets which would remain hidden mysteries to the community apart from his exposition, he does not create new prophecies of equal authority; he does not add, through his teaching, to what is written, but bases that teaching solely upon the written word. He has been given by God a right understanding in order that he may bring his community into the Covenant by which they may live according to the Law, that is, according to the will of God.[45] Inspired interpretation, however authoritative, is not the same as the direct and immediate address from the 'council of the Lord' in the messenger form 'Thus says the Lord'.

Two further points of relevance require discussion. The first concerns the use and meaning of the term maśkîl (pl. maśkîlim) in the texts from Qumran.[46] In the book of Daniel the maśkîlim) are pious men who are endowed with the gift of insight into the divine wisdom and teachers of that wisdom: 'the maśkîlim of the people shall give understanding to many' (Dan. 11.33). The word maśkîl (and its plural form) plays an important part in the Scrolls: many of the documents are addressed to him, and some scholars (rightly, in our opinion) suggest that he is to be identified with the Interpreter of the Law, who is, in turn, the Teacher of Righteousness. But when the community as a whole, or a group within the community, calls itself (among

other titles) the *maśkîlîm*, it seems obvious that they are laying
claim to be teachers of wisdom, the wisdom imparted to them
by the Teacher of Righteousness on the basis of his inspired
interpretation of both Torah and prophets.

Secondly: while we have no wish – and fortunately for our
purposes it is not necessary – to enter into the debate about
Qumran Messianism, it cannot be left unsaid that the belief
in a/the eschatological prophet forms part of their expectations.
The men of holiness, according to 1QS 9.11, 'shall be ruled by
the primitive precepts ... until there shall come the Prophet
and the Messiahs of Aaron and Israel'. On the basis of certain
passages in the Damascus Document some have thought that
only one anointed figure, not two, is intended: the evidence
of the so-called 'Messianic Testimonia' from Cave 4 (4 QTest)
has been employed to confirm the eschatological trinity of 1QS
9, but the identification of the texts cited in this anthology so
as to make them refer to the prophet and the two Messiahs is
regarded by other scholars as dubious.[47] In any case, the
reference to the prophet of the end-time in both places seems
assured. He could be Elijah, but the quotation of Deut. 18.18–
19 in 4 QTest 5, 8 makes it far more likely that he is the promised
prophet like Moses. Attempts have been made to identify the
prophet of 1QS 9.11 with the Teacher of Righteousness, mainly
on the basis of the similarities of language with CD 6.11 ('until
he comes who shall teach righteousness at the end of days'):
but we are inclined to agree with G. Jeremias[48] that there is
no *text* – and plausible interpretations and amalgamations of
texts are a different matter – which conclusively identifies the
Teacher of Righteousness with the prophet promised in Deut.
18.

Never called a prophet – perhaps because the Qumran community flourished during that period when prophecy was
regarded as having ceased, and perhaps because of his own consciousness of his particular task of bringing men back to the practice of the Mosaic Torah – the Teacher of Righteousness nevertheless has prophetic features, such as Josephus would have
recognised, and which are in considerable accord with our
working-definition. This makes his significance for our on-going

inquiry very real. But it is probable that John the Baptist – despite all the parallels (and contrasts as well) that may be drawn between his teaching and practice and those of Qumran – was more truly a successor of the Old Testament prophets than was the Teacher of Righteousness or any of his disciples.

7. JOHN THE BAPTIST

No survey of the prophetic phenomenon in the periods before and roughly contemporaneous with the New Testament could responsibly omit discussion of John the Baptist. To place him in this context, however, does not imply agreement with Conzelmann's view that John was the last and greatest prophet of the old era, described in the categories of the old epoch, and therefore separated from the central epoch in the history of salvation, the ministry of Jesus.[49] Conzelmann's view is based on Luke 16.16, but his interpretation of the significance of that verse contradicts its literal translation which dates the beginning of the era of salvation from the time of John's manifestation. This interpretation is confirmed by the synchronism of dates in Luke 3.1–2 (which makes John the inaugurator of the decisive period) and by Luke 3.2–7, 10–14, 18; 7.26.[50] John belongs to the period of fulfilment, but he is excluded from the actual period of Jesus' ministry because his work was of a preparatory kind, but nevertheless was necessary to the fulfilment which he inaugurated.

Further justification for treating John in this chapter rather than in a special section lies in the fact that Josephus (*Antiq.* XVIII. 116–19) makes explicit reference to John *ho baptistēs*, thus implying that his memory was honoured by at least some Jews long after his death. Josephus's testimony to John is that he was a pious man, a preacher of morality who invited Jews to a baptismal rite of consecration or purification; that his appeal won him a large following which Herod feared might be the beginnings of an insurrection; and that his imprisonment and death were due to Herod's suspicion of his influence among the people.

While it is possible that Josephus's version of the nature of John's baptism reflects adaptation to Graeco-Roman taste, it

is not at all improbable that he is right in asserting that the
Baptist's imprisonment and death were due to Herod's fear that
his movement was another in the succession of Galilean upris-
ings against Roman or Roman-backed authority. The supplementary and more lurid details concerning John's death,
recorded in the Gospels, are not inconsistent with this view:
for any charges that John might have brought – in the style
of ancient seers condemning royal transgressions of God's commandments – against immorality or riotous living in court-
circles were subject to being regarded as incitement to insurrection because they would have tended to undermine confidence
in Herod's right and ability to rule. But Josephus's résumé of
John's activity differs from what we find in the Gospels in two
important respects: there is no hint at the eschatological
character of the Baptist's message, and his baptism is a con-
secratory or purificatory rite (like the Qumran baptisms) and
not a single and unrepeatable baptism of repentance for the
remission of sins. In one respect, however, and that the most
important for our purposes, Josephus and the Q tradition
agree: John's preaching included moral exhortation. According to Matthew 3.7–10 and Luke 3.9 the Baptist was pre-
eminently a preacher of repentance and a prophet of judgment.

In the wilderness of Judaea (the location of the Qumran sect)
– a place of refuge and a focus of religious hope (Matt. 24.23–
26) – John steps forth as a prophet proclaiming the eschatological day of the Lord: 'Prepare the way of the Lord; make his
paths straight'. Of priestly origin, according to the birth-narra-
tives of Luke 1 (which many think emanate from a non-Chris-
tian Baptist community[51]), endowed with the Holy Spirit from
his mother's womb, he stands in the prophetic tradition of Elijah (though only Matt. 17.12–13 openly identifies him with Elijah, Mark's introduction presupposes it: but cf. Mark 9.11)
who, as we have seen, was expected by the Jews to return and
play an important role in the ushering in of the messianic era.
John's simple dress and ritually pure diet (Mark 1.6; Matt. 3.4)
– even more strict than Qumran asceticism – bespeak his rejection of the corrupt society of his time and his strict adherence
to the laws of Moses, if not to a Nazirite vow. He proclaims

that the judgment of God was imminent and the need for repentance urgent since the wrath of God was about to be poured out on all the unrighteous (Matt. 3.7–10, 11b–12; Luke 3.7–9, 16b–17), and his metaphors – the axe laid to the root of the tree, and the sifting of the winnowing fan – are in the genuine prophetic tradition (Ezek. 17.24, Jer. 1.10; 15.7, Isa. 41.16, Mal. 4.1). According to Luke's account John's baptism was accompanied by ethical instructions of a general kind (on sharing food and clothing) and by specific injunctions to meet the exigencies of the moment: tax-collectors were to take no more than was their due; soldiers were to be content with their rations and refrain from improving their lot at the expense of helpless civilians (Luke 3.10–14).

In their present form these injunctions may reflect the problems which confronted an early Baptist-community which faced the issues that were presented to the early Christian church, viz. the delayed consummation of the *eschaton* and the consequent necessity of giving advice to those who, while waiting the consummation, still had to deal with the stern realities of finding daily food and other necessities of life in a situation of oppression by the Romans. It is certainly not possible to say to what extent these teachings are directly from John, but they do underline his *known* concern for righteousness (Matt. 21.32; Mark 6.20; Jos., *Antiq.* xviii.116 ff.) Do the ethical instructions reflect perhaps John's picture of a corrupt society which would soon be swept away, a society dominated by inequality, abuse of power and oppressive taxation – the very issues which a prophet like Amos attacked with vigour and authority? It is noteworthy that the Synoptic gospels describe the call (cf. Luke 3.1 with Jer. 1.1; Hos. 1.1; Joel 1.1; Zech. 1.1, etc), the appearance (cf. Zech. 13.4 and especially 2 Kgs. 1.8, with reference to Elijah) and the preaching of John wholly after the manner of Old Testament prophets, and his baptism is open to interpretation as a prophetic sign or action for all those who penitently received the eschatological message of salvation.

The narrative in Luke 7.24–35 (Matt. 11.7–19) treats of the relationship between Jesus and John. In this passage John is designated as a prophet, indeed as more than a prophet – and this is almost certainly an authentic saying of Jesus since it is opposed to a later tendency to depreciate John – the 'moreness' being explained as his role as the preparer of the way of the Lord, that is, in this context, the Messiah Jesus. The endorsement of John in this narrative seems to be modified by the apparent depreciation of John in Matthew 11.11b (Luke 7.28b), although it may be argued that the latter *logion* depreciates all men in general (of whom John still represents the best) in relation to those men in particular who enter the Kingdom. Some regard the passage as a mosaic of authentic *logia* and later additions, but it is possible that the pericope was found as a unity (within Q) which, on the one hand, affirms the greatness of John ('more than a prophet') and, on the other, draws attention to his position as least (even as representative of Judaism at its best) in the Kingdom of God. The narrative witnesses to a relationship between John and Jesus of this kind: the preacher of repentance and prophet of judgment becomes the preparer of the way of Jesus Messiah; the Baptist receives his greatness only from the greatness of Jesus.

If the short and probably misplaced controversy-narrative (Mark 11.30–32) about the source of John's baptism is authentic, as it appears to be, then it is interesting to observe that all the people regarded John as a prophet: if the Jews took that seriously, then they must have been forced, according to their own presuppositions, to face the question whether the Jesus proclaimed by John was in fact the Messiah: if a true prophet had arisen, then Messiah must be very near or indeed must have come. It was impossible to acknowledge John as a prophet without arousing messianic expectations.

Two final points: first, in connection with John's death: he meets the virtually inevitable end of a prophet, that of persecution and death. The idea of the prophet as a martyr-figure is one which has a long tradition, reaching back into the Old Testament, and Mark 1.14, 6.17–29 and 9.11–13 (where in 12b Elijah is identified with the Baptist) form a sequence, possibly as a result of Marcan redaction, which sets out the inevitable fate of Jesus in parallelism with the already accomplished and violent end of John.

Secondly: recent research on the Baptist has been focused more on the origins of traditions about John and their use by the various evangelists than on attempting to describe his own life and work. The book by Walter Wink, *John the Baptist in the Gospel Tradition*, is evidence of this trend, as is his contribution to the Supplementary Volume of *IDB*, from which we derive the following quotation:

> Behind this striking diversity in the evangelists' treatments of John lies a surprising unity: each continues to make him the 'beginning of the gospel'. Jesus himself appears to have been the source of this estimate of John's role in God's saving activity. The conviction that John is 'the beginning of the gospel', and all of the Christian elaborations thereof, are but the theological expression of a historical fact, that through John's mediation Jesus perceived the nearness of the Kingdom of God and his own relation to its coming. Each evangelist has developed this tradition in the light of urgent contemporary needs, but also in faithfulness to Jesus' basic conception of John as the one through whom the eschatological event is proclaimed to be 'at hand' even though it may seem to be indefinitely remote (p. 488).

But the proclamation that the eschatological event of judgment is at hand is one thing; the proclamation of the *presence* of God's eschatological grace and the 'not just yet' of his final judgment is another; and it is this latter which lies at the heart of Jesus' preaching in word and in deed. He believed that the shift in the aeons had already taken place, that the Kingdom was present in his own ministry, that the Spirit was upon him (a conviction mediated through, or as a result of reflection upon, his baptism by John) and powerfully at work through him. These assertions lead us directly into our next chapter.

CHAPTER TWO

JESUS: 'A PROPHET MIGHTY IN DEED AND WORD'

From the statement in Revelation 19.10b, 'the testimony of Jesus is the spirit of prophecy' (*hē martyria Iēsou estin to pneuma tēs prophēteias*), we may infer that the phenomenon of prophecy in the New Testament church, at least in some quarters, was regarded as having its inspiration, perhaps even its norm, in the 'witness' or 'testimony' of Jesus, or (on the interpretation of *martyria Iēsou* as 'witness to Jesus') that the central concern of Spirit-inspired prophecy was bearing witness to Jesus. It is therefore imperative that we give consideration to the prophetic status of Jesus and the prophetic features of his ministry.

At the end of the preceding chapter we drew attention to the distinctiveness of Jesus over against John the Baptist: we return briefly to that theme as our way into the examination of Jesus' prophetic role. John proclaimed, 'Judgment is at hand: repent!' Jesus proclaimed, 'The kingly rule of God is now dawning.' John the Baptist, however much he is the beginning of the Gospel, remains within the framework of expectation: Jesus brings the fulfilment. His conviction that the Kingdom had become a present factor in history came to Jesus through his baptism by John, and probably through his subsequent reflection on that event. How then did Jesus understand his baptism? Since it was after his baptism that Jesus commenced his ministry of preaching, teaching and healing, of calling men to follow him and of consorting with outcasts, the evident effect of his baptism upon Jesus was to cause him to embark upon this ministry: it was in fact his 'call' to this particular ministry. Moreover, at Jesus' baptism the Spirit of God descended upon him. The descriptive and explanatory details found in the various narratives concerning the event may be later christological elaborations of what was implicit in it, but all the accounts agree on the endowment with the Spirit for his ministry. In the Judaism of the time, as we have seen, the imparting of the Spirit almost always meant prophetic inspiration: a man was grasped by God and authorised to be his messenger and preacher. So when it is said that the Spirit descended on Jesus – and we are not here concerned with the specific passages 'quoted' by the *bat qôl* – the meaning is that Jesus is both called and charismatically endowed to be God's messenger, and that the ending of the era of the quenched Spirit (already initiated by John) is further confirmed: the prophetic Spirit has again been given.

Among Jesus' authentic sayings about the Baptist there are a few which shed light on his understanding of his baptism. In the puzzling – and by that token, probably primitive – pericope Mark 11.27–33 Jesus is asked about the basis of his authority. His counter-question, 'Was the baptism of John from heaven or from men?' (which can hardly be construed as mere evasiveness), implies that his (Jesus') authority (*exousia*) rested upon and was indissolubly bound up with that of John. In other words, it was from what happened in his baptism by John that Jesus derived the authority 'from heaven' (i.e. from God) for his ministry. Secondly, Matthew 11.12 – a verse whose very difficulty argues strongly for its genuineness – says, 'From the days of John the Baptist until now the kingdom of heaven has suffered violence (*biazetai*) and men of violence (*biastai*) take it by force'. However the problematic terms are translated and interpreted, the saying makes it clear that, for Jesus, John stood at the 'turning-point of the aeons', and therefore the baptism by John is the moment when Jesus passes from the era of expectation and hope into the era of inauguration and fulfilment. This does not mean that Jesus merely carried John's ministry one stage further. The similitude of the children playing at weddings and funerals (Matt. 11.16–19) makes it clear that, whereas John's ministry was a stern and preparatory ministry of repentance, Jesus' ministry was the joyful ministry of grace and salvation. Again, it may be said, John's baptism marks the time when Jesus' awareness of the dawning, indeed the presence, of the eschatological salvation breaks through.

Jesus, then, understands his baptism by John as his call to ministry and his endowment with authority and the (prophetic) Spirit to carry out that ministry in which the Kingdom becomes a present reality in history. This is summed up in the programmatic statement in Luke 4, where Jesus applies the words of Isaiah 61.1 f. to himself: 'The Spirit of the Lord is upon me, because he has anointed me to preach good news to the poor ...'. Lucan this may be, and Luke's interest in the Spirit is well known; but in view of the remarkable statements made by the Teacher of Righteousness at Qumran about himself (since he is in all probability the author of at least some of the Hymns) and his reception of an effusion of divine Spirit, its authenticity is not nearly so inconceivable as it was a short time ago. As one on whom the Spirit rests, Jesus is, according to the Jewish thought of the time, a prophet and engaged on a ministry marked by numerous prophetic features.

I. JESUS ACKNOWLEDGED AS PROPHET

In certain respects Jesus' activity had similarities with that of the scribal teachers of his day. He gave much of his teaching to a group of disciples: he debated the interpretation of the Law: he was approached for legal decisions (Mark 12.13–17; Luke 12.13 ff.): he preached at synagogue services, though it is very doubtful if the privilege of expository preaching was reserved to scribes in the first century AD; and he was frequently addressed as 'Teacher' (*didaskalos*) and 'Rabbi', though the latter was commonly used as a mark of respect in the first century. But there are many differences. In addition to the fact that Jesus associated with women and with outcasts (tax-collectors, prostitutes and sinners) whom the scribes despised, that he did not have recourse in his teaching to the sayings of past authorities, that he was not training his disciples to succeed him in the office of rabbi, for they were always to remain disciples (Matt. 23.8), Jesus was, so far as we know, lacking in the basic requirement for the profession of a scribe: he had not undergone the disciplined and structured theological education of the scribal school. His teaching was direct and authoritative because it was charismatic rather than professionally learned, as Mark 1.22

demonstrates to the satisfaction of most, but not all interpreters of the verse.[1]

The conclusion to be drawn from Jesus' manifest inspiration and authority was that he was a prophet, and some of his contemporaries certainly regarded him as such. In Mark 6.15 and 8.27 f. it is reported that some people (not disciples) considered him to be '(like) one of the prophets', i.e., according to a Semitic idiom, a man belonging to the prophetic type, not one particular prophet.[2] This popular estimate of Jesus appears again in Matthew 21.11 and 46, but many scholars tend to regard these verses as editorial additions to the Marcan narrative:[3] the former assertion, 'This is the prophet Jesus from Nazareth of Galilee', may be a reference to *the* prophet of the End-time by reason of the fact that Jesus has just been acknowledged as 'Son of David'. Even the Pharisees are recorded as having known or shared this contemporary assessment of Jesus: Simon the Pharisee observes that if Jesus were a prophet (as presumably some considered him to be) he would have known about the murky past of the woman who anointed him (Luke 7.39), and the demand for a sign made by the Pharisees (Mark 8.11 and par.) in all probability carries with it the assumption that Jesus is a prophet who ought to authenticate his claim. Even the Emmaus disciples, according to Luke 24.19, considered Jesus during his lifetime to be 'a prophet mighty in deed and word before God and all the people': but since this is Lucan and Luke makes Peter see in Jesus the promised prophet of Deut. 18.15 ff. (cf. also Stephen's speech, Acts 7.37) it is possible that the words of Luke 24.19 reflect an interpretation of Jesus as the prophet like Moses, who was indeed powerful in speech and action before God and men.[4]

There is no passage in the Q stratum of Gospel material that supports the popular view that Jesus was an ordinary prophet: this is probably due to the absence of narrative material from that source as it is generally reconstructed. Nevertheless, despite the absence of evidence from Q, there is sufficient attestation of the popular estimate of Jesus as a prophet, and to what we have set out there might be added the testimony of the Samaritan woman (John 4.19) and of the man born blind (John 9.17).

One little episode from the trial scene – the insignificance of which may give it considerable historical value – may be mentioned at this point. In a kind of 'blind-man's-buff' game that the Sanhedrin guards played with Jesus at some interval in the proceedings Jesus is called upon to 'Prophesy!' (Mark 14.65) by telling who smote him (cf. Matt. 26.68 and Luke 22.64). Since the mockery of the condemned man travestied the charge brought against him – the white robe of Luke 23.11 was the characteristic garb of the national Jewish king, and the red cloak and crown of thorns (Mark 15.16–20 and par.) mimic the purple robe and garland of Hellenistic princes – the covering of Jesus' eyes and the demand to prophesy (to prove his ability to reveal hidden information) strongly suggests that Jesus was accused before the supreme council of being a false prophet: and as a false prophet he had to die (Deut. 18.20) and the sentence had to be carried out at the feast, 'when all the people shall hear it', in order that others might be deterred from the crime (Deut. 16.16 and 17.10–13). This ugly little scene, which Mark and Luke hand down independently and without christological elaboration (cf. Matt. 26.68), offers an incidental piece of information about the charge, or at least one charge, levelled against Jesus by the supreme Jewish authority,[5] and thereby indicates that even his enemies thought of Jesus in terms of 'prophet', albeit a false one.

There are in the Gospels a number of passages in which it is reported that Jesus was regarded by some of his contemporaries, not as a person conforming to the general prophetic type but as one of or a specifically named (or implied) one of the Old Testament prophets *redivivus*. To make that kind of comparison or identification may have seemed natural, but most of the passages which attest it are secondary. For instance, in Luke 9.8 and 9.19 the evangelist has changed Mark's 'a prophet like one of the prophets' (i.e. an ordinary prophet of the times) to 'one of the old prophets', that is, one of the Old Testament prophets, without further specification, raised from the dead. But the report that some thought Jesus was John the Baptist or Elijah *redivivus* occurs in a primary source (Mark 6.14f. and 8.28) and is reaffirmed in the Matthean and Lucan parallels. Now there is no unambiguous evidence that the post-Easter church ever regarded Jesus as John the Baptist *redivivus* or even Elijah *redivivus*,[6] though, as we shall see, certain traits from the Elijah tradition were taken up into the later conception of Jesus as an eschatological prophet. Rather, in Christian tradition, John the Baptist himself became Elijah *redivivus* (Mark 9.13). Consequently it would appear that on traditio-historical grounds, Mark 6.14 and 8.28 should be regarded as preserving genuine historical reminiscence. Evidently some among Jesus' contemporaries considered him to be an eschatological prophet, not in the sense that he himself was the inaugurator of the End (the role which, in our view, Jesus understood himself to be called and equipped to play in God's purpose) but in the sense that he was the herald of the End.

Further evidence of this is found by some scholars in the crowd's response to the miraculous raising of the widow's son at Nain: 'a great prophet has arisen among us and God has visited his people' (Luke 7.16). A careful comparison of this Lucan story with the LXX of 1 Kgs. 17.7–24 reveals a number of striking similarities in the characters involved, the location of the incident and in the language employed.[7] Does this suggest that Luke's reference to 'a great prophet' means that for him Jesus is a new Elijah or that Elijah has returned to earth? This is very doubtful: what Luke is affirming through the story – a kind of Elijah midrash – is that Jesus is a prophet like, or as great as, Elijah *in his power to raise the dead*, for, in the following paragraph, the testimony that Jesus gives to John's disciples to relate to their master includes a reference to the raising of the dead (Luke 7.22). Despite the presence of the adjective 'great' in relation to Jesus as prophet, it seems improbable that we should regard this as implying a reference to Jesus as Elijah *redivivus* or any eschatological prophet.[8]

That Jesus was considered to be the eschatological prophet 'like unto Moses' – an expectation based on Deut. 18.15 ff. – seems clear in Matthew and John, as well as in the primitive christology (as witnessed to in Acts 3.21 f., 7.38) and in the Jewish Christianity following the apostolic period (e.g. *Kerygmata*

Petrou, and the *Pseudo-Clementine Homilies and Recognitions*). It is probable that we should understand the words 'listen to him' (Mark 9.7 and par.) as an intended allusion to the 'him shall you heed' of Deut. 18.15, and it is in the Transfiguration narrative of Matthew (17.1–9), together with the Sermon on the Mount (chaps. 5–7) that the Mosaic-prophet theme comes to the fore with clarity, though not to the exclusion of other imagery and not just as 'a second edition of Moses, as it were, on a grand scale, but one who supersedes him'.[9] In John's Gospel we find, as one aspect of the portrayal of Jesus, clear indications that he is the fulfilment of the Deuteronomic passage. The sayings in 7.40 and 6.14 are based on the expectation of the prophet like Moses. In the former verse the people affirm 'This is really the prophet', because it was expected that the prophet like Moses would repeat the miracle of the dispensing of water at Horeb: and if we adopt the reading of P[66] in John 7.52 (as, in our view, we should) then what is contested is that the eschatological prophet (like Moses) will come from Galilee. After the miracle of the loaves it is said, 'This is indeed the prophet who is to come into the world' (6.14), for what has been experienced is reminiscent of the miracle of the manna. In connection with this verse it should be noted that *ho erchomenos* is exactly the same expression as used in the Baptist's question to Jesus: 'Are you he who is to come (*ho erchomenos*)?' (Matt. 11.3, Luke 7.19) – surely an authentic episode and question – and this suggests that *ho erchomenos* had titular significance, possibly designating Messiah (cf. the LXX and Targumic interpretations of Gen. 49.10, and the Jewish interpretation of Hab. 2.3),[10] but more probably a designation of the expected eschatological prophet.[11]

The pericope John 10.34–36 has long been a *crux interpretum*. In answer to the charge of blasphemy Jesus says to his Jewish opponents: 'Is it not written in your law, "I said, you are gods"? If he called them gods to whom the word of God came (and scripture cannot be broken), do you say of him whom the Father consecrated and sent into the world, "You are blaspheming" because I said, "I am the Son of God"?' Exegetes frequently have recourse to a rabbinic interpretation (from the

middle of the second century AD) of the words quoted from Ps.
82.6–7 in which the phrase 'You are gods' is made to refer to
the entire people of Israel to whom God gave the privilege of
avoiding death through obedience to the Torah revealed on
Sinai. This attractive explanation is embarrassed by the fact
that the expression 'the word of God' (in the singular) does not
appear to have been a designation of the Law in contemporary
Judaism, nor by the evangelist John himself.

Recently M. E. Boismard has offered a fresh approach to the
passage.[12] He draws attention (i) to the fact that the expressions
'to whom the word of God (the Lord) came' and 'he whom
the Father consecrated and sent' clearly recall Jer. 1.4–7 and
that John wishes to establish a parallelism between the vocation
of Jesus and that of Jeremiah, a fact which suggests that the
theme of 'prophet' plays a significant role in the argument that
the evangelist attributes to Jesus; (ii) to the fact that the call
narrative of Jeremiah offers so many literary contacts with the
passages where Moses's call is dealt with that a literary dependence is likely between the groups of texts;[13] (iii) to the evidence
that within as well as outside John 10.24–39 (cf. John 8.28 f.
and Exod. 4.12, and John 12.48 f. and Deut. 18.18 f.) there
are allusions to the different accounts of Moses's call: e.g.
Exodus 4.1, 9 are recalled in John 10.25–27, 37–38; and (iv)
to the datum that Moses exercises the function of judge – and
it is to judges that Psalm 82.6 is addressed – which is indirectly
implied in Deuteronomy 1.9–18 and Exodus 18.13–26, passages
which show that at first Moses alone functioned as judge (judge
par excellence) but was forced to delegate some of the judicial
powers to the leaders of the people. Boismard therefore concludes that in the person of Moses the roles of prophet and judge
tend to coalesce (cf. also Num. 11.16 f., 24–30): even as prophet
Moses transmits to the people the commandments, the divine
injunctions, as well as their interpretation. Therefore if the
expression in John 10.35 '(those) to whom the word of God
came', alludes primarily to the judges referred to in Psalm 82,
there is nothing to prevent us from relating to these words the
expressions 'consecrated' and 'sent' (from v. 36) in order to see
in them an allusion to the prophetic call of Jeremiah, which

in turn equally easily evokes the call of Moses (cf. Ecclus. 45.4 which uses 'sanctified' or 'consecrated' of Moses). In short the Johannine passage means this: since Scripture, whose witness cannot be contested, calls 'gods' and 'sons of the Most High' (Ps. 82.6) those who were instituted judges or prophets ('to whom the word of God came'), at the head of whom stands Moses with whom God spoke face to face (Num. 12.6–8), how can the Jews dare to accuse Jesus of blasphemy when he calls himself 'son of God', in view of the fact that he is the prophet *par excellence*, the new Moses announced by Deuteronomy 18, as the works which he does in the name of the Father prove? If this argument by Boismard is convincing (and it certainly has much of value in it) then it is one more section in John's Gospel where Jesus is presented by the evangelist as the Moses-like prophet, although this is not all that John wants to say about Jesus: for him Jesus infinitely surpasses the person of Moses, as 1.17 clearly demonstrates.

The review of Boismard's essay introduced a mention of Jeremiah. It is of more than a little interest that Matthew 16.14 alone suggests that some of Jesus' contemporaries thought he was Jeremiah. Why should Matthew include his name in particular? He was not the most celebrated or popularly quoted prophet (that honour would belong to Isaiah): nor was he regarded as a precursor of Messiah (for 2 Macc. 2. 1.12 and 15.13–16 offer insufficient proof of that): and surely not because he was the first of the *writing* prophets according to canonical order (bB.Bat. 14b). Can the name of Jeremiah have been introduced simply because some of Jesus' contemporaries saw in him certain traits of the figure of Jeremiah, the link being based on the similarities between their persons and missions? Both Jeremiah and Jesus proclaimed a salvation that was not an easy option, each forecasting (even desiring) for his adversaries the judgment of God, and for his supporters the persecution of men. Is it just accidental that Matthew includes this estimate of Jesus? More likely is it that either Matthew himself saw the pertinence of it and included it or that he is the sole preserver of a piece of tradition that is genuine, simply because it is so unusual, accurate, and unexpected.[14]

But we have been straying, at too early a stage, from the historical into the redactional and explicitly christological understanding of Jesus. What our investigation so far permits us to say is that (i) some of his contemporaries certainly regarded Jesus as a prophet (i.e. one of the prophetic type), or as an eschatological prophet (either John the Baptist or Elijah *redivivus*), or as the prophet like unto Moses; and (ii) that Matthew, Luke, and certainly John considered the category of 'the eschatological prophet' (and especially the 'prophet like Moses') an appropriate though by no means sufficient vehicle of christological statement. It is the first of these assertions that is most significant for our purposes. The recognition of Jesus as a prophet is not the same as the attribution of the honorific title 'rabbi': the acclamation was fraught with eschatological significance: the 'drought of the Spirit' was over and the beginning of the End had arrived; the gift of prophecy had reappeared and been acknowledged to be present in Jesus of Nazareth.

But did Jesus understand himself as a prophet? There are only two *logia*, explicitly containing the word *prophētēs*, to be considered. The first is the proverbial saying 'A prophet is not without honour, except in his own country' (Mark 6.4 f. and par.), and the second an expression of a generally accepted truth, 'It cannot be that a prophet should perish away from Jerusalem' (Luke 13.33). In neither case is 'prophet' a self-designation, but Friedrich's remark is both penetrating and pertinent: 'Jesus is not describing himself as a prophet but quoting a common view. Nevertheless, by not merely adopting the view but also preparing to exemplify it, Jesus numbers himself among the prophets.'[15] In other words, without using 'prophet' as a direct self-designation, Jesus clearly indicates that he understands his role in prophetic terms in so far as it involved rejection, persecution and martyrdom – the fate of prophets according to certain strands of Old Testament thought (1 Kgs. 19.10; Neh. 9.26), popularised in apocryphal works (like the Ascension of Isaiah 5.1–14) and testified to in many passages in the New Testament (Matt. 23.31 and 37, with their Lucan parallels; Acts 7.52). We observe that in the reported speech of the Q tradition Jesus' work appears in the frame of the prophetic: in his lament over Jerusalem his appeal parallels the tragic appeal of the ancient prophets.

However, we are not confined to the appearance of the term *prophētēs* as a self-designation in order to affirm the prophetic character of Jesus' teaching and actions. Our definition of prophecy allows us to look at other features which may imply prophetic status and the genuine prophetic claim. It is to these, in relation to Jesus, that we now turn.

2. PROPHETIC CHARACTERISTICS IN JESUS' MINISTRY

We have already mentioned the fact that Jesus understood his baptism by John as a call to embark upon his ministry, and as the occasion of his anointing and empowering by God's Spirit to carry out that ministry. Within the Judaism of the time, the possession of the holy Spirit, the Spirit of God, was regarded as *the* mark of prophecy: therefore Jesus' inspiration and equipping for ministry by the Spirit of God signifies that he was (and probably regarded himself as) a prophet. His claim to possess the Spirit is quite explicit if 'the blasphemy against the Holy Spirit' (Mark 3.29) is rightly interpreted as the denial of the *divine* source of the spiritual power with which Jesus casts out demons, an activity which indicates that the Kingdom of God, or God's sovereign rule – itself another characteristic theme of Old Testament prophetic proclamation – is breaking through and becoming a present reality in history (Luke 11.20).

Some of the more obvious indications of continuity between Jesus and the prophets of the Old Testament may be briefly mentioned. Much of Jesus' teaching has been shown by the specialists in Aramaic studies to have been delivered in poetical form(s), using parallelism, rhythm, paronomasia, etc., as was the teaching of the Old Testament prophets: the parable form – so very characteristic of Jesus' method of teaching – has precedent also in prophetic speech (2 Sam. 12.1–7; Isa. 5.1–7) and beatitudes, especially in the second person – as in Luke, who is usually regarded as having preserved the more original form – whose tone is that of consolation and assurance rather than of paraenetic exhortation, are not without a few parallels in prophetic or prophetic-apocalyptic speech (Deut. 28.3 – words of Moses; and Isa. 32.20), and woe-sayings (like those found in Luke in association with the Beatitudes) are frequent in the speech of Old Testament prophets, even in a series (cf. Isa. 5.8–23).[16] To understand the Beatitudes in the dynamic, prophetic context of proclamation and response (rather than in a Wisdom setting which makes them universally valid conditions for obtaining blessedness) is to maintain their distinctive character and intention in Jesus' preaching: the future blessing of salvation is so announced in Jesus' word of authority that the hearer becomes a new person through his summons, a person called by God and therefore blessed, for whom the Kingdom is realised, even now, if he responds.

From time to time the Gospels suggest that Jesus had visions, auditions and ecstatic-prophetic experiences. At his baptism he sees the heaven rent open and the Spirit descending like a dove and also hears a voice from heaven (*bat qôl*): although these features in the narrative (as in the Transfiguration story, and note also John 12.28) possibly owe more to the evangelists' employment of traditional motifs and ideas belonging to what we would call 'disclosure situations' than to Jesus' own testimony to his actual, historical experience, they nevertheless confirm the view that the writers saw Jesus as sharing pneumatic traits associated with prophecy and apocalyptic. The unparalleled statement in Luke 10.21 that Jesus 'rejoiced in the Holy Spirit' must mean that the evangelist regarded the sayings which follow as an inspired or even ecstatic prophecy of peculiar significance. It is of interest that this Lucan statement follows upon the return of Jesus' disciples who have found that demonic powers were subject to their commands: news of this elicits from Jesus the exclamation 'I saw Satan fall like lightning from heaven' (Luke 10.18), which is most naturally interpreted in terms of a visionary experience. The genuineness of this *logion* should not be dismissed too lightly: Jesus claimed that his ability to cast out demons derived from the power or Spirit of God (Luke 11.20; cf. Matt. 12.28) and that these victories over evil were manifestations of the dawn of the era of salvation:

he confers this authority (*exousia*) upon his disciples for their mission, and news of its effectiveness confirms his own assurance that Satan's realm is not only under attack but actually being vanquished. Jeremias' observation on this passage is very illuminating:

> The casting of Satan out of the heavenly world presupposes an earlier battle in heaven, like that described in Rev. 12.7–9. Jesus' visionary cry of joy leaps over the interval of time before the final crisis and sees in the exorcisms performed by the disciples the dawn of the annihilation of Satan. This stage has already been reached: the evil spirits are powerless, Satan is being destroyed (Lk. 10.18), paradise is opening up (v. 19), the names of the redeemed stand in the book of life (v. 20). There is no analogy to these statements in contemporary Judaism: neither the synagogue nor Qumran knows anything of a vanquishing of Satan that is already beginning in the present.[17]

The Spirit-inspired interpretation of his Spirit-endowed authority is surely no insignificant witness to Jesus' authentic prophetic consciousness.

Equally if not even more indicative of the charismatic nature of Jesus' prophetic role is his possession of the gift of insight into the innermost thoughts and motives of people in his company. The ability to reveal the secrets of a man's heart was regarded by Paul as a distinctive mark of the effectiveness of prophesying (1 Cor. 14.24–25: see below pp. 123 f.) and it seems to have been considered a mark of the prophetic phenomenon by Jesus' contemporaries, if Luke 7.39 ff. is any guide. This manifestation of inspired knowledge is attributed quite frequently to Jesus: so well established is the tradition in the Gospel materials (Mark 2.5, 8 and pars.; Mark 9.33 ff., 10.21 and pars.; 12.15 and pars.; Luke 6.8, 9.47, 11.17, 19.5; Matt. 12.25 and par.; John 2.24 f., 4.17 ff.) that it would be difficult if not presumptuous to deny its presence in the historical ministry of Jesus. Undoubtedly he possessed the prophetic power to scan the thoughts and impulses of men.[18]

But Jesus possessed not only prophetic insight: he possessed prophetic foresight. Some of the instances of foreknowledge have the character of momentary disclosures of the future: cf. Mark 10.39, 14.8 and pars.; 14.30 and pars. 'In these cases', says Dunn,[19] 'we see not logical corollaries drawn from wider expectations but the partly detailed partly obscure premonitions ... which are the mark of the charismatic and inspired prophet.'

Two points about Jesus' prophetic foresight demand further comment. There can be no doubt that Jesus foresaw and announced his suffering and death. Constantly under threat from his opponents, he had to reckon with the possibility, indeed the likelihood, that he would meet the fate of the prophet – persecution and martyrdom. The three passion predictions (Mark 8.31, 9.31 and 10.33, with their parallels) bear the signs, in their present form, of having been given greater precision in the light of subsequent events, but underlying them is an early Aramaic sentence, 'God will (soon) deliver up the man to men' (Mark 9.31a) whose authenticity is guaranteed by the presence in it of three stylistic characteristics preferred by Jesus – the puzzle or riddle form, the passive voice denoting divine action, and paronomasia.[20]

Of particular interest in this connection is Luke 13.32–33: 'I cast out demons and perform cures today and tomorrow, and the third day I finish my course (*teleioumai*). Nevertheless I must go on my way today and tomorrow and the day following; for it cannot be that a prophet should perish away from Jerusalem.' Whether we regard this *logion* as one which has undergone later interpolation or as a unity, comprising two parallel sets of Aramaic couplets, is secondary to the fact that its substance is free from any suspicion of later church theologising. Here, in an indubitably authentic saying, Jesus affirms that his mission is not exhausted in the exorcisms and healings, the signs of God's eschatological action in him: there is a 'must' (*dei*) which extends beyond healing and exorcism, namely his death at Jerusalem where the eschatological challenge of his ministry is issued at the very heart and centre of Judaism. And he reaches his goal, finishes his course, and 'passes on' as a prophet, experiencing the martyrdom which was, at that time, considered to be inherent in the prophetic vocation and exemplified in John the Baptist's fate. But this inevitable *dénouement*, like the healings and exorcisms, is accepted as part of the dawning of God's Kingdom – a view which Mark 14.25 clearly confirms, by showing that between Jesus' last meal on earth and the consummation of the Kingdom lies the decisive event of his own death. In both Luke 13.32–33 and Mark 14.25 the inevitability and the fact of Jesus' death are related to the consummation in a very short time – for the Semitic idiom 'after three days' or 'on the third day' means, as in the case of the passion predictions, 'soon' – of his life's work in the coming of God's salvation: this is *vindication*, and it may well be that it is on the basis of this kind of expectation that the prediction of *resurrection* 'after three days' (=God's 'soon') was formed, with the aid of the Aramaic interpretation of Hos. 6.2 in which the national revival spoken of by the prophet was interpreted with reference to the awakening of the dead.[21] Be that as it may, what we can say on the basis of authentic sayings of Jesus is this: as a prophet he foresaw his violent death in terms of prophetic martyrdom and probably foresaw his vindication as well in relation to his wider expectation that the consummation of the Kingdom was at hand.

The second point concerning Jesus' prophetic foresight brings us to the much-debated thirteenth chapter of Mark's Gospel. This is not the place, nor have we the space, to enter upon detailed discussion of this so-called apocalyptic discourse.[22] We must content ourselves with four observations. (i) However much of this chapter we may think belongs to the formulation of the Christian community (either before or after Mark, or even on the part of Mark himself), we cannot easily deny the prophetic foresight of Jesus in predicting the fall of the Temple (v. 2, though some think that this verse does not form part of the discourse proper): this prophecy of the doom of the Holy Place, which is consonant with Old Testament prophecies of disaster, is definitely older than the event; that Jesus himself could have made the prediction is no more improbable than that Jesus ben-Chananiah should have done so in AD 62

(Jos. *Bell.* VI. 300 ff.) : indeed, the destruction of the Temple was one of the most important elements in post-Herodian messianism, and not every reference to it requires a date after AD 70. (ii) The amount of genuinely apocalyptic material – in the third person – in the discourse is much less than many have imagined. (iii) The nucleus of the chapter (probably formed by the four temporal clauses followed by imperatives, i.e. vv. 7, 9, 11, 14, 15, 16, 18, 21 and 23) is instruction for the community in the face of an actual danger which was threatening and advising non-involvement: if this state of affairs is taken to refer to the events just before AD 70, is it inconceivable that the Jesus who predicted the fall of the Temple should have guided his followers on how to behave in the situation immediately preceding that catastrophe? (iv) As is well known, there are many links between Mark 13 and various Old Testament passages, particularly Dan. 7–9 and 11–12: although this feature may not offer a solution to all the problems raised by the chapter, the fact that parts of it and much of the nucleus mentioned above look like a midrash or exposition of Danielic texts[23] may bear the weight of the suggestion that Jesus himself was the source of this reinterpretation of prophecy with reference to events, not of the present but relating to the 'end' which he believed to be imminent (Mark 13.30, treated as an authentic logion). In short, a case can be made out for suggesting that within Mark 13 we find traces of Jesus' activity as prophet, in terms of foresight or prediction, in terms of exhortation and instruction, and in terms of the inspired application of scriptural prophecy to the events of the End-time which would soon engulf his people. For the last-mentioned type of prophetic activity there is precedent in the prophet-like Teacher of Righteousness's *pesher*-exposition at Qumran, and for the others throughout the Old Testament prophetic material.

A further indication that Jesus may have set himself within the prophetic tradition is provided by his performance of symbolic acts. In this connection the entry into Jerusalem, the cleansing of the Temple and, above all, the eschatological meal, the Last Supper, spring to mind. It may be in terms of prophetic symbolic action that we should also approach the narrative of that more obscure meal in the desert, 'the feeding of the five thousand', and the puzzling story of the 'cursing of the fig tree' (Mark 11.12–14, 20–24).

If Jeremias's interpretation of Matthew 11.27 ff. (cf. Luke 10.22 ff.) in terms of a concealed Aramaic parable-form is correct,[24] then the affirmation amounts to a central statement about Jesus' mission. His Father has granted him the revelation of himself as completely as only a father can disclose himself to his son: and therefore only Jesus can pass on to others the real knowledge of God. This consciousness of being, in a quite singular way, the recipient and mediator of knowledge of God is implied elsewhere: for example in Mark 4.11 where 'the mystery of the Kingdom' is disclosed to the disciples, and in Luke 15, where Jesus' actions and words reflect and vindicate the divine attitude to sinners. There is a certain, though limited, parallel here to the prophet who comes from 'the council of the Lord' and declares the divine message with authority and immediacy. We have commented already on the authority (*exousia*) of Jesus (derived from his being in possession of the Spirit and therefore a prophet) in relation to his works of exorcism and healing by which the presence of the Kingdom breaks through into history: now we must turn our attention to the authority with which he declared his message.

The form of words which most clearly enunciates this authority is 'Truly, I say to you ... (*amēn legō hymin*)'. The Hebrew word '*amēn*, taken over into Aramaic, means 'certainly' and is found in the Old Testament as a solemn formula used in answers assenting to the words of another, in oaths, blessings, curses, doxologies and suchlike contexts. Occasionally in the New Testament, in liturgical formulae (cf. 1 Cor. 14.16; 2 Cor. 1.20; Rev. 5.14, 7.12, 19.4, 22.20), it is found with this connotation of assent or response. In the Gospels, however, and in every strand of Gospel tradition, *amēn* is used, without exception, to strengthen a person's own words, and in this unprecedented sense it is strictly confined to the words of Jesus, a sign that the tradition strongly felt that his way of speaking was new and unusual. So impressed is he by the significance of this feature of Jesus' speech that H. Schlier claims that christology as a whole is contained *in nuce* in this *amēn*-usage.[25] Jeremias claims that an explanation of its meaning must commence from observing that in the words of Jesus *amēn* is always followed by *legō hymin (soi)*. 'The only substantial analogy to *amēn legō hymin* that can be produced is the messenger-formula "Thus says the Lord", which is used by the prophets to show that their words are not their own wisdom but a divine message. In a similar way, the *amēn legō hymin* that introduces the sayings of Jesus expresses his authority.'[26]

Since Jeremias first put forward the thesis outlined above about *amēn* and the *amēn legō hymin* formula, at least two scholars have given intensive consideration to his case. From the standpoint of redaction-criticism V. Hasler[27] claims that the formula arose in the liturgy of Jewish-Hellenistic communities and was only secondarily placed on the lips of Jesus, a view which he justifies by asserting that even in Judaism *'amēn* had lost the character of a response and was used to strengthen a man's subsequent statement: hence it would not be peculiar to Jesus with this sense. Klaus Berger[28] undertakes a semantic and form-critical investigation of the formula: he puts Jesus' use of *amēn* within a wider context of similar expressions in Hellenistic-Jewish apocalyptic literature, and identifies *amēn* as an oath formula characteristic of apocalyptic speech (hence its link with, if not entry into, the New Testament), especially the LXX formula for introducing prophetic messages in Ezekiel. Of the many uses of the formula in Jewish apocryphal and early Christian literature some introduce paraenetic and eschatological sayings; Jub. 35.6 uses it to introduce a saying about the speaker's fate; and especially frequent are sayings in which the form legitimises the speaker's witness to knowledge obtained by revelation.

Berger has been rightly criticised for trying to make all *amēn*-sayings (including the New Testament examples) fit the procrustean bed of an apocalyptic framework: Hasler for his lack of responsibility in the use of evidence to support his case. Nevertheless, their work, when taken together, has diminished the strength of Jeremias's claim that the *amēn legō hymin* formula is completely new on the lips of Jesus and that his use of *amēn* to strengthen an affirmation is entirely unprecedented. J. Strugnell[29] has recently drawn attention to the use of '*mn* in a seventh century BC Hebrew ostracon – which of course calls into question both Hasler's and Berger's view that the usage is not Hebraic but Judaeo-Greek word-play – where the meaning is '*Truly*, I am innocent': this is hardly responsorial (as Jeremias would have us think) but a strongly affirmatory legal statement.

To sum up: Jeremias's dogmatic claim about the quite unprecedented use of *amēn* to strengthen an affirmation cannot be upheld: and his claim that Jesus' use of the formula *amēn legō hymin* is new and unusual requires modification. Nevertheless, its persistence in the Gospel tradition, together with its relatively infrequent appearance earlier, makes a cogent case for regarding it as authentic. Its similarity to the LXX formula for the introduction of Ezekiel's prophetic message(s) confirms, not that it is a mark of solely apocalyptic speech but that its equivalent lies in the substance of the prophet's 'Thus says the Lord', the divinely authorised messenger's formula. In the sayings with *amēn legō hymin* – and it is not necessary to regard every one as authentic – we have clear affirmation of Jesus' authority as a teacher and preacher who stands in the prophetic tradition. This authority manifests itself with special strength in the antitheses contained in the Sermon on the Mount (in the form 'But I say unto you ...'), where Jesus presents himself as the true interpreter of the Law in its radical intensity, the unique and definitive teacher of men.[30]

The claim by Jesus to authority, even to finality, for his mission finds expression in sayings which take the form 'I came (*ēlthon*)' (Mark 1.38 and pars.; 2.17 and pars.; 10.45; Matt. 5.17, 10.34–36; Luke 12.49 (Q?), Matt. 11.19 f. and par.) or 'I was sent (*apestalēn*)' (Mark 9.37; cf. Matt. 10.40; Luke 10.16 (Q?); Matt. 15.24). In his form-critical analysis of these sayings Bultmann admits that 'There is no *a priori* objection against the possibility that Jesus should have spoken of himself and his coming in the first person. After all, that would accord with his prophetic self-consciousness.'[31] Nevertheless Bultmann proceeds to eliminate most of them as church formulations on grounds of content, leaving only Luke 12.49, Mark 2.17 and Matthew

15.24. These he then eliminates also, because they all look back on Jesus' ministry as a completed fact of the past. It would appear that Bultmann wants to get rid of these sayings at all costs. But in Luke 12.49 Jesus is clearly speaking of his ministry as still in progress and of his tension until it is completed. The saying does not look back upon a ministry already finished. Mark 2.17 also speaks of Jesus' Galilean ministry to the outcasts, not necessarily of his entire saving work up to and including the cross. Matthew 15.24 is rather more dubious in its attestation and may represent the evangelist's own redaction, and Bultmann suspects that this saying originated in the debates of the Palestinian church about the Gentile mission.

But quite apart from the problem as to whether or not this represents the precise attitude of the Palestinian church towards the Gentile mission (and the language of the verse does offer evidence for its Palestinian provenance), the question has to be faced as to whether this was the *original* application of the saying. It could very well have referred originally to Jesus' ministry to the outcasts, in which case it is similar in significance to Mark 2.17. Furthermore, if, as is often suggested, the Q form of Matthew 11.18 f. (and par.) has changed an original 'I' saying to a 'Son of man' saying, a strong case can be put forward for the authenticity of that *logion*; and again it has to do with Jesus' eating with outcasts. It seems certain that we must reckon with an original nucleus of genuine 'I came' and 'I was sent' sayings which formed the model for the later church formulations, especially frequent in the Fourth Gospel.[32] And these sayings do bear witness to Jesus' prophetic self-consciousness, to use Bultmann's phrase.

It is of interest to note that the authentic core of sayings of the 'I came' or 'I was sent' kind around which later tradition built concerns Jesus' ministry to the outcasts from religion and society. It was in this connection that his consciousness of mission appears to have been most strongly expressed. Yet it is precisely here that his activity passed beyond that of a prophet, even of an eschatological prophet, whose task was to proclaim a salvation that was yet to come. In Jesus the salvation is breaking through and its consequences breaking out in his own mission of grace and acceptance. Just as there is a difference between 'Thus says the Lord' and 'I say unto you', there is a corresponding difference between the prophet who, like John the Baptist, looked forward to a greater than himself, and the more-than-prophetic Jesus who affirmed that God's decisive action and revelation was taking place in himself. That is why the interpretation of Jesus as a prophetic reformer is an insufficient assessment of his self-understanding, and that is why Vermes's impressive portrayal of Jesus as a charismatic prophet in the tradition of the Jewish *ḥāsîd*[33] – a view which incidentally goes back to R. Otto's *The Kingdom of God and the Son of Man*, published in 1938 – must be criticised for the selectivity on which it bases its conclusion.

It is true that from the historian's point of view the working concept which guided Jesus in the task of his ministry was that of 'prophet': true also that as far as speech-forms, authority, action and attitude are concerned, we can point to many similarities between Jesus and Old Testament prophets, as well as the charismatics of his day, which are sufficient to justify his being called 'a prophet' or 'the prophet' by some of his contemporaries. But this 'prophet' was unique in the sense that his proclamation and activity were confronting men and women with the present saving action of God in the midst of history, and that his commitment and obedience to God made him the channel of that gracious and saving action. When those claims came to receive explicit exposition in christology the term 'prophet' was deemed to be insufficient – save in a few circles in Jewish Christianity which produced the *Gospel of the Hebrews* and the *Kerygmata Petrou* – to do justice to Jesus' identity, claim and achievement.[34] Despite this fact, however, the investigation of the prophetic characteristics of Jesus' ministry in word and deed remains, in our view, a necessary part of the prelude to the examination of Christian prophecy. Jesus can be accommodated within our working definition of 'prophet': but far more important is the likelihood that many of the characteristics of the Old Testament prophets may have been mediated to the earliest Christian prophets through Jesus' exemplification of them in speech and action,[35] and the fact that, to return to our starting-point, the inspiration and chief concern of Christian prophecy was 'the testimony of Jesus', the witness he bore – as prophet and more-than-prophet – to the word and the purpose of God. But that is to move into the subject-matter of the next chapter.

CHAPTER THREE

THE BOOK OF REVELATION AS CHRISTIAN PROPHECY

In approaching the primary documents which directly yield information concerning New Testament prophecy we must decide where to commence the investigation. The choice in fact has to be made from Paul and his letters, the Acts of the Apostles and the book of Revelation. All are valuable sources, as we shall see, but none is without its distinctive and different problems, as this and later chapters will show: nevertheless Revelation commends itself as the best starting-point for our inquiry, for it is the earliest extant Christian book, and the only New Testament document, which is written with the explicit claim to be, in its entirety, prophecy (cf. Rev. 1.3; 22.7, 10, 18 f.). On the basis of this claim we might feel inclined to proceed, without further discussion, to ask what Revelation can tell us about Christian prophetic activity in its time[1] and place (Asia Minor),[2] were it not for the fact that the claim is not universally, indeed not widely, accepted as indicative of the genre of the book. In the opinion of many, the title of the book and its opening words ('The revelation – *apokalypsis* – of Jesus Christ, which God gave him to show to his servant . . .'), as well as its contents, decisively locate it in the category of apocalyptic literature, not prophetic. To this matter we must give some attention.

I. REVELATION: APOCALYPTIC OR PROPHETIC?

Before attempting to answer this question we ought to remind ourselves that it is not always easy to draw clear lines of demarcation between prophecy and apocalyptic, and biblical scholars differ considerably in the identification of the characteristics which belong to each genre, as well as in the interpretation of the relationship between them. The commonly held view that apocalyptic represents a continuation or development of prophecy[3] is contested by P. Vielhauer who argues that, while it was the intention of apocalyptic writers to continue prophecy, this did not in fact take place, and the dualism, determinism and pessimism of apocalyptic form the gulf which separates it from prophecy.[4] With his customary vigour G. von Rad declares that the view that apocalyptic literature is the child of prophecy is 'out of the question', and claims that the decisive factor is 'the incompatibility between the apocalyptic literature's view of history and that of the prophets'.[5] Some of these conflicting issues will be taken up in what follows, but in an area where opinions conflict so clearly we must tread with great care and responsibility.

And responsibility requires us to acknowledge the fact that some of the features of Revelation are widely regarded as evidence of its sharing in the tradition of what is termed, rather loosely, 'Jewish apocalyptic'. The language of the book and its imagery, occasionally weird and grotesque, betray the influence of the apocalyptic genre. There is a certain determinism in that the plan of God is unalterably laid down in the book with seven seals, and, once this has been opened by the Lamb, the divine plan is unfolded without obstruction: this looks like a Christianised form of an old apocalyptic motif. The same may be said of the dualism in the book: heaven and earth, space and time pass away to make room for the new heaven and the new earth; the Church is locked in antagonism with the pagan world power, and this is but the foreground of the struggle between Christ and Satan. Again, in its insistence on the imminence of the End and in its interest in the End-events, especially those that concern the Church, Revelation shows its indebtedness to the apocalyptic world of ideas. But do these features make the book as a whole apocalyptic? Or do they form part of the apparatus of apocalyptic taken over and made to serve a purpose or intention other than that normally served by apocalyptic writing? The answers to these questions will become clearer in the ensuing discussion, but we must now look at features of the book which mark it as distinct from the writings of apocalyptic.

It has been suggested that in its denunciations of evil and exhortations to pure and noble living, and in its possession of the quality of real inspiration over against the gloomy pedestrianism of much Jewish apocalyptic writing, Revelation stands close in tone to the work of the Old Testament prophets.[6] If the charge of subjectiveness may be brought against that view, a rather more objective criterion by which to assess the character of the book has been introduced by James Kallas.[7] He argues that the real touchstone of apocalyptic thought was its attitude towards the nature, purpose and source of suffering: suffering was brought on the elect by forces opposed to God which were active in the universe; in the end, they and the suffering caused by their activity would be destroyed by God. This – the apocalyptic view – is not shared by the writer of Revelation: he is closer to the prophetic view, in which suffering was regarded as being of God and therefore, ultimately, a good thing to submit to and accept. However, the fact that the attitude towards suffering in Revelation (and in the apocalyptic literature as well) is not so consistent as Kallas implies raises a question about the reliability and the validity of this criterion.[8]

One of the most commonly adduced and significant features which distinguishes Revelation from apocalyptic writings is the absence of pseudonymity and, with it, of the fictitious claim to antiquity for the book. The apocalyptist did not write under his own name but under that of some ancient worthy (Elijah, Enoch, Ezra, Baruch) and from the disguise he borrowed an authority he did not possess, in contrast to the writing prophets. The likelihood that the book of Revelation is pseudonymous is exceedingly small: 'John' (whoever he may be) writes under his own name and he is known to the church(es) he addresses, and he writes in his own authority *as one called and addressed by Christ* and who even dares to claim 'canonical' authority for his book (22.18).[9] The book nowhere lays claim to fictitious antiquity, nor does it regard itself as having been sealed up and secretly preserved from olden times till the end of days (cf. Dan. 12.9; 4 Ezra 12.35–38, 14.7, etc.).

What is written here is not esoteric knowledge or secret wisdom, but an unsealed, open, clear, eschatological message and exhortation which is related to the present and immediate future. Indeed, the sealing up of the revelation for disclosure in a distant future is strictly opposed (22.10): the author insists that his writing should be understood as an 'ecumenical letter', not as a secret document (1.4, 11, 19, 22.16, 21). In this respect the writing stands closer to the prophetic tradition than to the apocalyptic. This should not surprise us, for the author's own description of his book, as he opens and concludes it, is 'prophecy' (1.3, 22.7, 10, 18 f.). The opening sentences of the book recall at a number of points the first words of the prophetic books (cf. Isa. 1.1; Amos 1.1. and especially Amos 3.7), and the writer, in his address to the churches, casts himself in the role of a prophet through whom the Spirit speaks. Again, in chapter 10, John is the recipient of a clear prophetic call, the symbolic account of which recalls the vocation of Ezekiel (cf. Ezek. 2.8–3.3) and the content or charge – to proclaim the oracles of God on the nations – resembles that of Jeremiah (cf. Jer. 1.10). The intention here may be to suggest, as J. Comblin argues,[10] that with John there is a renewal or recommencement of prophecy (if *palin* is capable of bearing this significance in v. 8): prophecy which relates to all nations and which includes words of promise as well as of judgment (10.7, 14.6 ff.) begins again with him, and it is committed by him to the Church for transmission (chapter 11).

In connection with John's understanding of his role, one wonders if the phrase 'I was in the Spirit' (1.10, 4.2) and even the words 'he carried me away in the Spirit' (17.3, 21.10: cf. Ezek. 3.12, 14 and 37.1) are intended to denote, not the ecstatic trance-like rapture characteristic of advanced apocalypticism but action in the sphere of and under the inspiration of the Spirit (of God) which, in the Jewish-Christian circles in Asia Minor from which the book emerged, would probably still have been understood, at least partly, in terms of the spirit of prophecy. W. C. van Unnik has drawn attention to the parallel to 1.19, 'Write what you see, what is and what is to take place hereafter' – which may contain a rough outline of the book – found in the Apocryphon of John ('Now I am come to reveal to thee what is, what was and what shall be, that thou mayest know the invisible things like the visible . . .') and in the Epistle of Barnabas 1.7 where it is connected with (Christian) revelation through the prophets: he claims that the verse in Revelation and in the Apocryphon of John (despite their variation in order and wording) use the same formula to describe the office and privilege of a prophet as one who has insight into the totality of history, past, present and future.[11] One further point from the opening verses: it cannot be without significance that John declares that he is bearing witness to the *logos tou theou*, the *d^ebar Yahweh* which came to the prophets and revealed the divine purpose, and then calls his witness *logoi tēs prophēteias*.

According to von Rad, apocalyptic (which he thinks has much in common with Wisdom literature[12]) and prophecy are to be sharply differentiated by their distinctive views of history, the prophetic message being firmly rooted in the saving history,[13] whereas apocalyptic had little serious concern with those acts of God on which salvation was based and which gave to the nation its birth, a history and an identity. For the apocalyptists the events of their own time were not a locus of divine action and revelation: the present age was meaningless and evil, and would be swallowed up and destroyed in the End-time. The prophetic *Heilsgeschichte*, on the other hand, speaks, not of the termination of history but of its fulfilment through God's disclosure of himself in history. It is this view of history, and not Jewish apocalyptic eschatology, which underlies the Church's proclamation of the decisive, divine action in Christ and of the efficacy of his word within history:[14] and it is in terms of its attitude to history that the character of the Revelation as a whole may be discerned.

The task undertaken by John in his prophetic vocation consists essentially in the interpretation of history, more particularly, perhaps, the interpretation of present and future history (1.19). But the method of interpretation is not that of the Jewish apocalyptists: from a fictitious standpoint in the past, they present surveys of world-history, in the form of predictions, which depend on the absolute predetermination of successive epochs, and their real interest lies only in the last generation and the events immediately preceding the End. John's starting point, on the other hand, is the saving action of God in Christ:[15] this event is the pivot of his confidence in the power and victory of God in the present and throughout the short space of time till the establishment of God's sovereignty. Like the prophets, John takes his standpoint in his own day and age and emphasises his contemporaneity with his readers: he offers no review of past history: the period which he interprets is bounded by the death and resurrection of the Lamb and his parousia, when those God-opposing forces which stand behind the actual historical conflict of the Church with a pagan political power will be destroyed. The idea of *Heilsgeschichte* is the foundation of the view of history which underlies Revelation, and it is from this perspective that the author can address, with comfort and challenge, a church which is on its way to becoming a martyr-church: the book is 'wholly committed to the great end of strengthening the Church, the bearer of revelation, in its first severe clash with the self-absolutising power of the state'.[16] The book of the Revelation is therefore written out of its time and for its time: the author is not concerned to predict specific historical events in the near or distant future, as is the case with writers of Jewish apocalyptic: rather, he interprets the meaning of the history in which he is involved (with the Church) in terms of a traditional imagery, taken over partly from the Old Testament and partly from Jewish concepts.[17] But if the style and imagery, or some of it, is determined by the apocalyptic tradition, in his interpretation of history and the sensitivity to the actualities of his situation the writer stands in the tradition of prophetic faith and proclamation.

There we may rest our case for the view that the author of Revelation considered himself to be a prophet, and that his writing, while employing much of the traditional apparatus of apocalyptic but lacking many of the most characteristic features of that genre, may justifiably, and probably correctly, be regarded as prophetic in intention and character, especially in its concern with and interpretation of history. 'The profound originality of the Johannine Apocalypse', says A. Feuillet, 'lies in the fact that, whilst making use of the style, imagery and methods of Jewish apocalyptic, it remains faithful to that which creates the greatness of ancient prophecy.'[18]

2. REVELATION: THE FORM AND CONTENT OF CHRISTIAN PROPHECY

In our defence of the prophetic character of the book of Revelation as a whole we have already touched on some general points which belong under this heading. Prophecy can be written down (1.3, 11, 19, 2.1, 8, 12, 18, 3.1, 7, 14, 14.13, 19.9, 21.5, 22.18 f.) and can be included in a letter form. But within this overall form, numerous words and phrases, as well as other formal features, appear to be characteristic of the prophetic mode of speech by reason of their frequent repetition, their occurrence at key points in the book, their similarity to Old Testament prophetic forms, or their particular appropriateness to the prophetic function as it has been defined in the first chapter of this book. These we shall now examine in some detail.[19]

(i) Form

(a) *Vocabulary and Phrases.* (1) We have drawn attention to W. C. van Unnik's suggestion that 1.19 ('what you see, what is and what is to take place hereafter') contains 'a formula describing prophecy': the same applies, in all probability, to the shorter form 'what must take place' (*ha dei genesthai*), a phrase from Dan. 2.28, which is used at three key junctures in the book (Rev. 1.1, 4.1, 22.6) to denote the impending divine will.

(2) We have also alluded to the importance of revelation through audition which is typical of the Old Testament prophetic experience: the formula-like 'I heard' (*ēkousa*) occurs twenty-seven times in the book referring to the reception of prophetic revelation. But even more indicative of the prophetic speech form is the call to hear and heed the inspired utterance (*Weckruf*).[20] While there are numerous other exhortations for the recipients of John's message to hear (1.3, 3.3, 20, 13.9, 22.17 f.) the appearance in each of the seven letters (chs 2 and 3) of the fixed call-formula, 'He who has an ear, let him hear what

the Spirit says to the churches' (the first part of which occurs
in the same or similar form in Matt. 11.15, 13.9, 43; Mark 4.9,
23; Luke 8.8, 14.35) is striking and significant. There is no corresponding appeal for John's audience to 'see' what the writer
has seen, for, although the use of 'I saw (*eidon*)' in the sense
of prophetic vision (cf. Ezek. 1.4, 2.9; Zech. 6.1; Dan. 8.4, 10.5)
is more frequent than 'I heard' and its formulaic character even
more sharply defined, the entire visionary terminology of the
book belongs only to the apocalyptic framework or apparatus
employed by the author. He never uses the nouns *horama* or
optasia and employs *horasis* in the sense of 'vision' only once
(9.17: cf. LXX Isa. 1.1).

(3) Among the most striking of the phrases characteristic of
prophetic speech is the messenger-formula (*Botenformel*) '*tade
legei*' ('the words of' or in the NEB 'these are the words of ...').
Each of the seven letters begins with these words – found
nowhere else in the New Testament except in Acts 21.11, on
the lips of Agabus – which often form the Septuagintal rendering of the Hebrew for 'Thus says the Lord', and which, functionally, form an exact equivalent to the more frequently used
Greek rendering of the Hebrew words, viz. *houtōs legei Kyrios*.
This, says P. S. Minear,[21] is 'John's use of an Old Testament
formula. The Old Testament prophets had established this formula as the appropriate introduction for God's address to his
people. This conventional formula, simple and direct, would
conjure up in a worshipping congregation the fear and trem-
bling associated with standing before God and hearing his
awesome words of judgment and warning.' It is this messenger-
formula or oracular preamble which indicates the authority and
legitimacy of the prophet and his words: through the mouth
of a fully empowered witness the Lord speaks to his community.
We may note in passing here that in the case of both the call-
formula (*Weckruf*) and the messenger-formula the source of the
revelation-word may be the exalted Jesus (characterised by
a variety of christological designations) or the Spirit: this does
not mean that the Spirit and the glorified Christ are simply
identified (cf. 14.13 and especially 22.17), but that the Spirit
is the envoy of Christ who transmits the divine message to the

Church through the inspired prophet. 'The Spirit', says T. Holtz[22] (with particular reference to 22.17), 'is a power which intercedes for the church and pleads, in its place and on its behalf, for the coming of the End, and, at the same time, acts as the representative of Christ in bringing exhortation and encouragement to the whole Church on earth.'

(4) The solemnly recurring 'I know' (*oida*, never *ginōskō*) in each of the letters (five times in the expression 'I know your works') seems to be used as a special form emphasising the absolute clarity of mental vision: indeed, it is very probable that, in respect of both their form and content, these 'I know' sections should be regarded as indicative of the way in which prophecy was directed to a community in the early Christian period. The prophet speaks in the name of the risen Christ who knows and discloses the condition and life-situation of those addressed, and offers suitable encouragement and/or instruction, couched in unmistakably general or standardised terms.

(5) The common word 'Behold' (*idou*), though used frequently in the body of the book to introduce a fresh vision, appears six times in the letters (2.10, 22, 3.8, 9, 20, 4.1) in a way which seems to begin 'a specific word of prophetic revelation',[23] a function it performs in Old Testament prophetic literature as well.

(6) Although John uses *apokalypsis* and the verb *sēmainō* only once each (in the introductory title of the book, 1.1–2), both words have prophetic overtones, as 1 Corinthians 14 and the Shepherd of Hermas show in the case of *apokalypsis*, and John 12.33, 18.32, 21.19 and Acts 11.28 for the verb *sēmainō*. (Cf. Plutarch's description of the oracle at Delphi: *oute legei, oute kryptei, alla sēmainei*, 'it (she) neither speaks nor conceals, but makes known', *de Pyth. Or.* 21.)

(7) John uses *amēn* ('Truly') more frequently than any other New Testament book, apart from the Gospels: this is probably due in part to the liturgical setting of the materials, but some occurrences may reflect the distinctive use of *amēn* as a revelation-formula on the lips of Jesus (see pp. 64–66) and possibly adopted by Christian prophets.

(8) Except for one passage in the Synoptic Gospels (Mark

4.11 and pars.), Revelation is the only book in the New Testament outside the Pauline stream to use *mystērion* ('mystery'). The writer employs it not only in an apocalyptic sense (i.e. the 'symbolic meaning' of some element of a vision, 1.20 and 17.5, 7) but also in the prophetic sense of the 'hidden purpose of God' for and in history (10.7).[24] The writer stands in the long succession of those prophets to whom the 'secret' (*sôḏ*) of the Lord is made known: cf. Amos 3.7.

(9) That John deliberately works with blessings and curses (expressed by the introductory words *makarios* and *ouai*) is evident from their number: seven 'beatitudes' (1.3, 14.13, 16.15, 19.9, 20.6, 22.7 and 22.14) and seven woe-sentences (8.13, 9.12, 11.14, 12.13, 18.10, 16, 19): none of these is adequately accounted for in terms of common-sense wisdom; all seem to be revelations couched in a form characteristic of prophetic speech.

(10) Just as Old Testament prophets were called God's 'servants' (LXX *douloi*), so John uses *doulos* to characterise Christian prophets in 1.1, 10.7 (possibly in conjunction with Old Testament prophets) and in 11.18 where the church-prophets appear to be distinguishable in some way from the general body of Christians ('the saints'),[25] as in 18.24.

(11) We come now to discuss certain words and phrases connected with prophecy whose close association in the Revelation. makes separate consideration of them virtually impossible. These are *logos* and *logos tou theou* and the 'witness' complex of terms (*martyria, martyreō* and *martys*). The word *logos* can bear the sense of an oracular or revelatory utterance in secular Greek, the LXX and in the New Testament,[26] and it is a striking fact that all the occurrences of the term (in the singular or the plural) in the Revelation are probably related to Christian prophecy: indeed, *logos/logoi* are specifically described as *prophēteia* in 1.3, 22.7, 9–10, 18, 19. The repeated 'these words are trustworthy and true' in 21.5 and 22.6 is an asseveration-formula intended to affirm that the oracles are genuine and derived from God, as the addition of *tou theou* in 19.9 makes clear. The plural '(the) words of God' (17.17 and 19.9) is probably an equivalent of the Old Testament *diḇrê ʾelōhîm/Yhwh* and refers to the

disclosure of God's purpose through oracles of the prophets,[27] both those of the old order and those of the Church who see themselves in continuity with the former: this interpretation suits the contexts well and illuminates the texts. The only other instances of *logos* are found in 3.8, 10, where, in the light of what has just been said and of such sentences as 1.3, it probably designates the commandment to exercise patient endurance like Jesus: it is the prophet who is the bearer of the divine word which demands obedience.[28]

Apart from one occurrence of 'the word of God' (singular) to designate the triumphant Jesus (which may be equivalent to 'God's saving purpose in person', 19.13), this phrase is used in Revelation in a way that is distinctive in the entire New Testament, being found exclusively in combination with *martyria* (6.9) or *martyria Iēsou Christou* (1.2, 9, 20.4). The 'and' in each case, if not strictly epexegetical, at least places the two phrases in such close parallelism as to suggest that the author cannot write *logos theou* without linking it to *martyria* (*Iēsou Christou*). In terms of the traditional subjective/objective genitive choices, 'of Jesus Christ' is usually understood as a subjective genitive because of the parallel with *logos theou* and in view of *ho martys* being employed as a christological title (1.5, 3.14). Elsewhere,[29] however, we have argued for an interpretation of the double phrase which allows for objective genitive connotations in the words *Iēsou Christou*: 'the divine word, in the sense of God's divine plan or purpose, and Jesus Christ's attestation or confirmation of it, primarily in his utterances in the visions of this book, but also (for there is no discontinuity between them) in the witness of his life and death'. Those who are later described as having the *martyria* (*Iēsou*) (6.9, 12.17, 19.10) are those who, like John, stand by and preserve Jesus' witness committed to them by declaring it: and what they declare (and suffer for declaring[30]) is not other than what Jesus discloses to his servants and attests (22.16, 20) in this book, namely, the judgments and the sovereign authority of the one, eternal God who is ruler of all and author of salvation, whose purpose will finally triumph over all opposing forces. This witness offers hope as well as warning to the nations, for the goal of the divine judgments is not destruction and annihilation, but repentance and return to God (14.6 ff., 15.3 f.): the victory of the Lamb – achieved once for all in the redeeming death of Christ – will bring to fulfilment the universalistic, prophetic hopes of the Old Testament (5.13, 15.4: cf. Ps. 86.9 and Jer. 16.19).

Now if this is the content of the *martyria Iēsou*, who are those described as 'having' it, and (from the seer's point of view) as enduring persecution to the death in the future because they possess it? According to 12.17 they are all the faithful and obedient Christians and, despite arguments to the contrary, it would seem probable that they are similarly identified in 6.9 and 20.4: the phrases or clauses which follow the references to those who have the witness of Jesus in these verses do not describe different groups but further define the same persons. In short, the *martyria Iēsou* is indistinguishable from the contents of the book – the revelation of Jesus Christ which witnesses to the purpose of God ('the word of God'), and 'those who have the *martyria Iēsou*' describes the body of faithful Christians whose attestation and confirmation of Jesus' witness will eventually, in the circumstances envisaged, bring about persecution and death.

(b) *Extended Formal Elements*. In addition to a characteristic vocabulary, the book of Revelation uses some other, more extended, formal elements associated with the prophetic genre.

(1) Speech in the first-person for the Deity. Although John can speak in his own person (1.9, 5.4, etc.) and can speak of Jesus in the third person (1.1, 5–6, etc.), he repeatedly speaks in the name or in the person of God, Jesus (cf. 'I Jesus' in 22.16) or the angel which represents them both, using 'I' six times and 'I am + predicate' four times. (The Revelation does not contain the formula 'I am' in the absolute, but only with predicate, e.g. 'I am the first and the last', 1.17 etc.) This type of speech in the first person was integral to the ancient Near Eastern messenger-formula in which the messenger 'completely submerged his own ego and spoke as if he were his master himself speaking to the other'.[31] This formula was adopted by the prophets of the Old Testament,[32] whence it comes to the speaker/writer of Revelation. The remarkable feature in comparison to Old

Testament prophetic speech is that the 'I' with which the prophet John speaks belongs almost exclusively, not to God but to the exalted Jesus or the Spirit, as the letters to the seven churches amply show. Incidentally, the corollary of this first-person speech is that the hearer/reader is addressed directly in the second person, and in this respect Revelation is more like Old Testament prophecy than later apocalyptic writings.

(2) Call-narrative. In words borrowed from several Old Testament passages and woven together in a most distinctive fashion (1.10–20) the writer of Revelation describes the vision, almost a 'throne-theophany', which inaugurated this particular prophetic enterprise. Since, however, there is nothing in the vision which indicates that this is the first time that John received prophetic inspiration, and since in chapter 10 he is the recipient of a clear prophetic call or investiture, the vision of chapter 1 may not necessarily be the initial experience which constituted him a prophet. Nevertheless, on the basis of the two passages (10.8–10 and 1.10–20, and especially the words 'I was in the Spirit') we may rightly regard the reception and recounting of such call-scenes as a characteristic element in Christian prophetic experience and activity.

(3) 'Sentences of Holy Law.' E. Käsemann has made familiar the suggestion that 'sentences of holy law' (*Sätze heiligen Rechtes*) which set forth the eschatological *ius talionis* (e.g. 1 Cor. 3.17, 14.38, 16.22) originated in prophetic utterances.[33] In a later chapter we shall deal at some length with this claim – its sources, implications and validity – but we may here simply note that as far as the book of the Revelation is concerned, Käsemann finds the form only in 22.18–19:[34] 'I warn everyone who hears the words of the prophecy of this book: if anyone adds to them, God will add to him the plagues described in this book, and if anyone takes away from the words of the book of this prophecy, God will take away his share in the tree of life and in the holy city, which are described in this book.' F. Hahn, however, claims that the form of the repeated 'Overcoming-words' (*Überwinderspruch*) 'To him who conquers' or 'He who conquers' at the end of each of the seven letters corresponds exactly to what Käsemann terms 'sentences of holy law': but the evidence

for such correspondence eludes us, as it does Ulrich Müller:[35] some elements of the '*Sätze*' form are present in the 'Overcoming-words', as elsewhere in Revelation (14.8–10, 16.5–6 and 18.6), but the participial phrase does not describe an objective, generally valid, state of affairs leading to the expression of an automatic and inevitable judgment: it functions rather as a condition upon which certain promises or consequences depend. The tightly formed chiastic form described by Käsemann is not found except in 22.18–19. It would therefore seem reasonable to claim that the 'sentence of holy law' form – whatever we may think of it – is not a dominant characteristic of John's prophetic speech, although he may have been acquainted with it. It should be added, however, that the 'Overcoming-words', by reason of their eschatological character, may well have been a form used occasionally in early Christian prophecy.

(4) Patterns of instruction (*paraklēsis*) and Repentance-preaching (*Busspredigt*). In the only available, detailed form-critical study of the most obvious prophetic material in Revelation (i.e. the seven letters) Ulrich Müller[36] claims that they reveal one or other (or a mixture) of two basic patterns.

(i) Repentance-preaching (*Busspredigt*) with the following structure:

    (a) A verdict on the Church's life situation.
    (b) An exhortation to remember its reception of the Gospel and a call to repentance.
    (c) A conditional threat of judgment.

(ii) A salvation-word (*Heilswort*) or unconditional announcement of eschatological salvation with two elements: (a) a verdict on the Church (either of praise or blame) and (b) an unconditional proclamation of victory or salvation.

The first pattern is found in Revelation 2.1–7 and 12.17 (in a slightly varied form); 2.18–29, 3.14–22: the second is seen in 2.8–11 and 3.7–13 (in a varied form): both patterns are mingled in 3.1–6. Among the parallels in prophetic speech to the first pattern are the preaching of John the Baptist (Matt. 3.7–10 and par.) and the content of Jeremiah 7.3–15: there are many parallels to the second form in the prophetic salvation-oracles (e.g. Isa. 54.4; Jer. 30.10–11 and 35.18f.).[37]

This analysis is valuable both for its own sake, in calling attention to the undoubted prophetic form and character of the seven letters,[38] and also for the illumination it brings to the question of the prophet's purpose: clearly he spoke to warn, judge, appeal (for repentance) and to encourage.[39] The importance of this for understanding the prophet's role and activity will be dealt with more fully in the chapter that deals with the Pauline material.

(5) The use of traditional material. As far as the prophets of the Old Testament are concerned we cannot, with any claim to accuracy, claim to be able to distinguish traditional material from fresh and original oracles – if indeed any oracle can be regarded as absolutely original and not a new combination of materials of which the prophet was in some sense already aware, even if only subconsciously: but the prophet-like figures of which we learn from Josephus and from the Qumran scrolls certainly did employ, almost exclusively, words, forms and symbols drawn from the Old Testament. There can be no doubt that the seer of Revelation constantly and consciously alludes to the Old Testament, and especially the prophetic books of Isaiah, Jeremiah, Ezekiel, Daniel, and Zechariah, in order to show that the history of the Church unfolds in conformity with the witness of Scripture. This is reminiscent of the way in which certain passages of Scripture were used at Qumran, where the Teacher of Righteousness and those who learned from him stand in the tradition of the Danielic *maśkîlîm* in that they impart to others their insight into the hidden purpose of God, and, in particular, into the time and character of the eschatological events in which they are involved. It is obvious that John was also acquainted with older apocalyptic writings, as almost all critical work on Revelation since R. H. Charles[40] has assumed. He may have had some familiarity with Pauline material, though this does not necessarily presuppose literary dependence, and one or two scholars incline to the view that the Revelation (if dated late) may contain oracles of earlier Christian prophets in the same stream of tradition as John.[41] Is the notoriously difficult oracle containing 17.9 ff. one such? Or is the problem of its dating now settled by J. A. T. Robinson's proposal that the

entire book belongs to AD 68–69?[42] Does John use traditional
words of Jesus? There are in fact no verbatim quotations from
the Synoptic Gospels, but there are some recognisable allusions
(apart from Synoptic passages which themselves, like Revelation, depend on the Old Testament), but they are very few in
number. Only 1.3 (cf. Luke 11.28), the repeated 'He who has
an ear, let him hear ...' (cf. Matt. 11.15, etc.), 3.3 and 16.15
(cf. Matt. 24.43 and par.) and 3.5 (cf. Matt. 10.32 and par.)
would qualify as possible sayings of Jesus: others, like 13.11 (cf.
Matt. 7.15), 18.24 (cf. Luke 11.50 and par.), 19.7 (cf. Matt.
5.12 and par.) are John's own words in reporting a vision, or
an angelic or other heavenly voice. And of the former group
mentioned, only 2.7 (the 'He who has an ear, let him hear ...'),
3.3 (= 16.15) and 3.5, with the possible addition of 3.20, seem
to represent plausible examples of Synoptic sayings being represented in Revelation as *logia* of the exalted Jesus, formally modified only by a process of deparabolisation into paraenetical
exhortations.[43] Thus we may say, with assurance, that in comparison to the Old Testament, the Synoptic tradition of Jesus'
words serves as a *source* for John only to a very minimal extent.
Nor is this surprising: for it was the *kērygma* about Jesus the
crucified and risen one, rather than the historical tradition of
his words and deeds, that was the dominant influence on the
shaping of John's message, just as it was in the case of Paul.
The question as to whether the Revelation contains prophetic
sayings that could have found or did find their way into the
Synoptic tradition as *logia Iēsou* – as some scholars maintain –
is one that we shall examine in detail in a later chapter.

(ii) *Content*

Having reviewed both the language and forms which are
characteristic of Christian prophecy as discernible in the
Revelation, we must now briefly set out the main themes of
the prophetic proclamation which emerge therefrom.

(1) Christian prophecy is the vehicle by means of which
divine judgments and directives are brought to bear upon the
life of the church(es). (*a*) Unfaithfulness and immorality are
rebuked, and a call to repentance offered. These elements are

particularly clear in the letters to the seven churches (as Müller's analysis shows), but they are found elsewhere in the book as well, e.g. 9.20 f., 16.9, 11. Judging from the Revelation, the prophetic message is addressed *directly* to the community of faith rather than to those outside the Church. (b) Exhortations and encouragements are given to believers to remain faithful. These appeals are couched in the form of specific instructions or of promises that a glorious future awaits those who endure (and a terrible judgment the unfaithful). The prophetic preaching may therefore be correctly called *paraenesis*.[44]

(2) Christian prophecy interprets history on the basis of *Heilsgeschichte* (redemptive history). The prophetic message is founded upon the affirmation of God's decisive, saving action in Christ: this event is the source of the prophet's confidence in the power and victory of God in the present time and throughout the short period of time till the establishment of God's final sovereignty. But the interest in the prophetic portrayal of eschatological events (which are regarded as rapidly approaching) is really their significance for John's own time: he offers no review of past history: he is not concerned with predicting events in the near or distant future, but with addressing a church presently involved in a situation of stress and oppression: consequently the message is not speculative (however eschatologically oriented it may be), but is rather designed to meet an existential need for challenge, comfort and hope.[45]

(3) Christian prophecy is characterised by the pronouncement of divine judgment. These judgments fall on both unrepentant, unfaithful Christians and on the enemies of the Church, the persecuting power and institutions of the historical world-order. Some are pronouncements of judgment already accomplished (e.g. 14.8; 18.1–24), but most of them announce, proleptically, a judgment that is soon to come – on unfaithful Christians (2.5, 16, 22, 3.3, 16–19, 14.9–12, 20.11–15, 21.8, 27) and on non-believers (6.1–17, 8.1–9.19, 16.4–7, 17–21, 19.2–3, 20.11–15). 'There is a sense in which all the visions of the future judgment have a *fait-accompli* aspect, for in the visions they are seen as already accomplished. There is thus a combination of "already" and "not yet" in the pronouncements of

judgment: the whole is cast in a "not yet" (but soon!) framework, within which there are declarations that judgment is already accomplished.'[46]

3. REVELATION: PROPHET AND COMMUNITY

The final part of this chapter is concerned with the figure of the prophet 'John' himself and his relationship to the community or communities he addressed.

(i) *The prophet is one who speaks with assumed authority within the congregation(s) he addresses.* Although his activity and message certainly stand in the prophetic tradition, the author of Revelation is nowhere designated as *prophētēs*: he introduces himself simply as 'brother', yet the correctness of his words is unquestionable for they are declared to be reliable and true by the supreme authority, God himself (21.5, 22.6): what he proclaims is of decisive significance (1.3) and cannot be criticised: the eternal destiny of men depends on whether they accept it, or corrupt and reject it (22.18–19). Nevertheless he nowhere has to authenticate or establish this authority, an authority so great that some scholars suggest that he stands closer to Old Testament prophecy than to what we know from elsewhere of New Testament prophecy[47] – a verdict which the vocabulary and content of the book would strengthen. John's consciousness of authority in disclosing divine revelation is such that we may be justified in wondering if his relation to his community is not akin to that of the Qumran Teacher of Righteousness in relation to the sect: the latter saw himself in the role of a prophet of the End-time and a legitimate successor of the ancient prophets who was able to give definitive elucidation of the revelation given to Moses (as 'Interpreter of the Law', CD 6–7) and to the words of the prophets (cf. IQpHab 7.5).[48]

Whether that is a profitable parallel or not, the prophet-author of Revelation seems to claim a distinctive authority for himself over against his brother 'prophets' in at least two respects: (*a*) he wrote a book – a lengthy and closely integrated literary composition – later adjudged to be canonical, and none of them did: this *writing* activity may perhaps be accounted for by the fact of John's geographical separation from the communities he addresses, but it should not pass unnoticed that John wrote in response to the commands by which he was commissioned as a divinely authoritative messenger: and (*b*) his special task is that of mediating the revelation of Christ, and this vocation 'sets him above or at least distinguishes him from his brethren: he is the one by means of whom the other prophets in the Church become sharers in the knowledge and ministry of the divine revelation: they would teach and relate what they had learned, and in this would resemble the *maśkîlîm* of Daniel and at Qumran who were instructed by the prophet-like Teacher in the mysteries of God and their fulfilment. Since it would therefore appear that John is the leader of a prophetic group, rather than merely a member of such a group – a difference in degree, certainly in terms of authority, rather than in kind – it would be unwise to extrapolate too readily from his activity and the content of his prophesying to those of other prophets in the Asia Minor churches.

Whether there were authorities other than the prophets in the church(es) of the book of Revelation is a question on which there is no consensus of opinion. According to Bornkamm, the prophets – the Divine himself and his brethren – together with the apostles are the only authority in the church of the Revelation,[49] since there is no mention of other leaders or officials. Satake goes further and explicitly declares that the prophets are the only office-bearers (*Amtsträger*) in the church or churches pictured in the book.[50] But the evidence on which to form any view of the Church's order is indirect, difficult to assess and of uncertain relevance for the understanding of a book which has no reason to be interested in or to speak directly of ecclesiastical organisation. In that part of the book in which one might expect to discover some hints on organisation – the seven letters – there is in addition to one mention of false apostles (2.2) only one reference to the prophetic function, the Jezebel 'who calls herself a prophetess' (2.20): this phrase imparts no unambiguous information about the currency in the Church of the term 'prophet' or the office so denoted, for the words may serve only to identify the woman by her own peculiar self-designation or they may imply differentiation from true bearers of the prophetic name and gift. It may be said, however, that the series of references which seem to speak of the Church as composed of 'saints and prophets' (1.18, 16.6, 18.24) does not lend support to the view that 'official' ministries other than that of prophets were exercised: it does suggest, as has been observed earlier, that the prophets are in some way separable from the body of believers, but the evidence of the book as a whole is not such as to allow the distinction to be drawn in terms of precedence or position.

(ii) *The prophet addresses a community which itself has a prophetic character.* Earlier in this chapter we argued that the *martyria Iēsou* to which John witnesses (1.2) is Jesus' attestation or confirmation of God's declared plan or purpose, primarily in his utterances in the visions of the Revelation, but also in the witness of his life and death, and that the phrase 'those who have the *martyria Iēsou*' is best understood as a description of the body of faithful Christians whose preservation and confirmation of Jesus' witness will eventually bring about persecution and death. But since this witness is not simply a possession to be kept but also implies the task of communication, is it possible that by the phrase the whole Church is being characterised as, fundamentally, a prophetic community? If, as we would maintain, at 11.3 f. – a notoriously difficult passage – the entire people of God is considered symbolically or ideally (i.e. when utterly faithful to its commission) as 'witnesses',[51] is it also ideally or potentially a church of prophets, as Schweizer has suggested?[52] In this connection the evidence of 19.10 is important. The parallelism between this verse and 22.9 suggests that 'the brethren who hold the testimony of Jesus' are to be identified with the prophets, and the explicatory addition 'For the testimony of Jesus is the spirit of prophecy' (which assures the parallel with 22.9) confirms this: the spirit that inspires prophecy or the prophets is 'the testimony (*martyria*) of Jesus' which they preserve. But elsewhere 'those who hold the testimony of Jesus' is the description of all faithful Christians. What appears to be implied by the collocation of clauses in this verse is that all members of the church are, in principle or potentially, prophets, just as the whole Church presents itself, in exemplary fashion, in the form of the 'two witnesses' (11.3 ff.). The fact that some, like John's brethren to whom he mediates the revelation, are called in a special way to the ministry of prophecy in the churches makes the Christian prophets separable from other Christians (as we have pointed out), but it does not set them in an official position of authority over their fellows: they are carrying out a function which could be – and ideally should be – served by all, that of declaring the word of God and the witness of Jesus, and authority belongs primarily to the message, not to an office.

(iii)   *The Christian prophet exercises his function primarily in the setting of congregational worship.* Although he is separated by imprisonment from the community, it is when the congregation gathers for worship that the revelation comes to the prophet, 'in the Spirit' (1.10; cf. 8.3 f.). The book contains worship materials such as the doxology of 1.5b–6 and the hymns of 4.11 and 5.9b–10: and descriptions of worship in the heavenly sphere abound (chs 4–5, 7.9–17, 15.1–4, 19.1–5). The allusions to Christian believers as 'priests' (1.6, 5.10, 20.6) serve to strengthen the impression that the Revelation is a worship-oriented book, written not for private reading but for public declaration (by the prophets, perhaps) in congregational worship.[53] Cullmann is over-enthusiastic about a valid point when he writes, 'the whole book of Revelation from the greeting of grace and peace in 1.4 to the closing prayer "Come, Lord Jesus" in 20.20, and the benedictions in the last verse, is full of allusions to the liturgical usages of the early community'.[54]

(iv)   *The Christian prophet is a man controlled by the Spirit.* We suggested earlier that phrases like 'I was in the Spirit' (1.10, 4.2) and 'he carried me away in the Spirit' (17.3, 21.10) do not denote ecstatic rapture, but action in the sphere of and under the power of the Spirit (of God or of Christ). And it is the Spirit which inspires the prophet's insight and utterance. Throughout the Revelation the Spirit is regarded as operative (especially in address) in the Church as a kind of *alter ego* or representative of the risen Christ (cf. the Johannine Paraclete). Consequently, as Boring says,[55] 'the original revelatory chain God/Jesus-angel-prophet-church is reduced functionally to Christ-prophet-church. The prophet is the one who stands between the risen Christ and the Church, giving voice to the Church's Lord who is already present as *pneuma* but would be mute without his prophet': or, as Hahn puts it,[56] 'the prophet is the fully authorised witness to Jesus and through his words, provided by the Spirit, the Lord himself speaks to his church'.

(v) *The Christian prophet functions as an interpreter of events in history.* As we have already affirmed, the prophet 'John' speaks sensitively to the actualities of the church-situation he knows. The conflict with the God-opposing political power is interpreted theologically as the prophet understands the Spirit to be instructing him about the meaning of what is *really* going on in the community's struggle, as seen from the divine point of view. Just as the Old Testament prophets were able to place meaningless events within a meaningful framework, so the threatened (or actual) persecution was interpreted by John not as a meaningless tragedy, but as the beginning of the End. Christians could face up to it with courage and hope because of the prophetic word, a word which only a prophet with spirit-inspired insight could provide.

(vi) *The Christian prophet reinterprets the Old Testament in the light of the Christ-event.* The substructure of the Christian prophecy enunciated in the Revelation is formed by the Old Testament, but between the two stands the saving action of God in Christ's suffering and glorification, and it is this that provides the key to what the old Scriptures say to the contemporary situation. But the Christian prophet does not operate in a deductive fashion, quoting the Old Testament and then giving the Christian meaning, but under inspiration (as in the case of the Qumran Teacher of Righteousness) which allows him to perceive the Old Testament texts, not as words merely to be reflected upon but as oracles which form a living unity with his own message.

(vii) *The Christian prophet is not directly associated with miracles and signs.* There is nothing in the book to indicate that supernatural signs accompanied or validated John's own prophetic ministry. There are very few allusions to ecstatic experience and none to glossolalia. The disdain with which he attributes 'great signs' to the false prophets (13.13 f., 19.20?) and the demonic spirits (16.14) would suggest that he sets in opposition the prophetic word of the one who conquered through suffering and the false testimony of signs and wonders. Nevertheless, the difficult passage 11.3–13, relating to the 'two prophets', portrays them as filled with miracle-working power (11.6), even though they died at the hands of their persecutors. If these 'prophet-witnesses' – two, perhaps because that was the minimum number of witnesses required for admissible testimony in Judaism, or because the Church is composed of believers from Israel *and* from the nations – in a variety of figurative reference (which includes the recalling of the exploits of Moses and Elijah) represent or symbolise the messianic remnant-community, and therefore the whole Church in its prophetic or witnessing role, then it would be unduly literalistic to argue on the basis of the Old Testament imagery used that the church(es) to which John ministers *must* possess and exhibit miracle-working power. None the less, it must be admitted that in a church where spirit-inspired prophets played such a dominant role other miraculous gifts of the Spirit *may* have been manifested.

(viii) Finally, *the Christian prophet differentiates between himself and false prophets.* John is aware that there are others in his church(es) who claim to be prophets, whom he does not acknowledge as such, so that *pseudoprophētēs* is a word characteristic of his vocabulary (16.13, 19.20, 20.10): they are also described in allusive terms as 'those who hold the teaching of Balaam' (2.14) and 'those who hold the teaching of the Nicolaitans' (2.15), whose leader (in Thyatira) is Jezebel 'who calls herself a prophetess' (2.20). These designations of false prophets imply that their 'falseness' lies not only in their claim to the prophetic name and title but also, and more importantly, in the teaching (*didachē*) they put forth, which is at least heresy, if not outright apostasy.[57] With his authority as a prophet, John denounces those who are led astray by such purveyors of falsity and by so doing clearly distinguishes from them both himself and his brother-prophets 'who hold the testimony of Jesus'.

Our investigation of the book of the Revelation has yielded a substantial amount of information about New Testament prophecy. Some features to which we have drawn attention may be distinctive to that book: for instance, Revelation is *written* prophecy, whereas most early Christian prophets seem to have delivered their messages orally; and Revelation may well be representative only of a particular strand in the Palestinian-Jewish tradition of prophecy; and the special place the prophet-author of the book holds in the Church may not be a correct indication of the kind of ministry exercised by Christian prophets there or elsewhere. But we have not to build our understanding of the Christian prophetic phenomenon on one New Testament book alone. There are other valuable sources available for consideration, namely Paul and his letters and also the Acts of the Apostles. To the latter we shall now turn our attention.

CHAPTER FOUR

PROPHETS AND PROPHECY IN THE ACTS OF THE APOSTLES

Before turning our attention to the Acts material it is pertinent to observe that in the first volume of his work Luke has much to say about the Spirit, and, in particular, the Spirit of prophecy. The Spirit, as the presence and power of God, is the life-giving agent in the birth of the one who inaugurates the New Age (Luke 1.35): the conviction that the New Age has indeed come is strongly demonstrated by Luke's emphasis on the presence of the Spirit of prophecy throughout his birth narratives concerning John the Baptist and Jesus (1.15, 17, 67, 2.25–27). The third evangelist, more than the other Synoptists, lays emphasis on the role of the Spirit in the Christian life. It is the gift *par excellence* given by the Father to trusting prayer (11.13; cf. Matt. 7.11).

To the promise of the Spirit's assistance in the event of persecution (Matt. 10.20; Mark 13.11) there correspond two Lucan passages. The first (referring to arraignment before authorities) reads, 'The Holy Spirit will teach you in that very hour what you ought to say' (Luke 12.12; cf. John 14.26): in the preceding verse the blasphemy against the Holy Spirit (which cannot receive forgiveness) is best understood as blasphemy against the apostolic preaching which is guided by the Spirit, the constitutive factor in the Church's life. The second (appearing in a context similar to Mark's saying, i.e. in the so-called apocalyptic discourse) affirms that, not the Holy Spirit but 'I (Jesus) will give you a mouth and wisdom' (Luke 21.15). This declaration recalls several narratives relating to prophetic vocation in the Old Testament, in particular Exodus 4.11 ff. where God promises to Moses to open his mouth and speak, and Jeremiah 1.9 where God declares to the prophet that he is putting his words into his mouth. In communicating the Spirit to his own – in circumstances in which they have to defend themselves – Jesus (in Luke's view) is the source of that supernatural wisdom which will render efficacious the witness of his apostles (who are cast in the role of prophets): I, he is saying, am sending upon you the Father's promised Spirit. The action of the Spirit manifests itself in the christological understanding of the Scriptures in accordance with the sense that Jesus himself began to reveal to his own (Luke 24.25 ff., 44 ff.), and that same action of the Spirit underlies and sustains the apostolic witness, as the book of Acts shows.

In the structure of the book of Acts Pentecost holds a place equivalent to that held by the baptism of Jesus in the Gospel and his own affirmation of its significance ('The Spirit of the Lord is upon me . . .', Luke 4.18). The parallelism in the situations is actually mentioned in Jesus' final, post-Resurrection encounter with his disciples: 'John baptised with water, but before many days you shall be baptised with the Holy Spirit. You shall receive power when the Holy Spirit has come upon you; and you shall be my witnesses in Jerusalem and in all Judea and Samaria, and to the end of the earth' (Acts 1.5, 8).

The narrative concerning the strange, revolutionary event of Pentecost presents many problems, both theological and historical. It incorporates many traditions, including that of the confusion of speech at Babel. allusions to the theophany at Sinai: but it makes no explicit mention of the new covenant characterised by the gift of the Spirit upon the people of God (Jer. 31.31–34; Ezek. 36.26–28). Whatever traditions stand behind or are absent from Acts 2 is a matter of secondary importance to the fact that the narrative *as it now stands* is based upon, and intended to create in others, the conviction that the gift of the Spirit to the Church is its empowering for universal mission. 'They were all filled with the Holy Spirit and began to speak in other tongues, as the Spirit gave them utterance' (Acts 2.4). Representatives from every part of the then known world – and the list of peoples is designed to emphasise universality, being derived from an astrological grouping of nations and countries, according to the signs of the Zodiac[1] – who were assembled at Jerusalem heard the mighty deeds of God, each in his own language (or dialect). It is clear that the gift of the Spirit is understood as an endowment which enables the apostles and other Christians to *communicate* with all people: it makes possible and effective the preaching of the word and works of God. Thus equipped to be witnesses of Jesus Christ (1.8), the apostles interpret what has happened in the light of Scripture. The widespread experience of the gift of prophecy foretold by Joel (2.28–32) – an oracle to which late Judaism gave little importance – has been fulfilled 'in the last days', a phrase drawn from Isa. 2.2–4 which speaks of the eschatological pilgrimage of all nations to Zion. Moreover, without it being explicitly said, the ancient desire of Moses has come to fulfilment: 'Would that all the Lord's people were prophets, that the Lord would put his Spirit upon them' (Num. 11.29).

The fact that all the Lord Christ's people, all who have called on the name of the Lord, have received the gift of prophecy is reflected elsewhere in Acts. In a verse which Harnack and others thought was the original and historical account of Pentecost we read, 'When they (the Church) had prayed, the place in which they were gathered together was shaken; and they were all filled with the Holy Spirit and spoke the word of God with boldness' (4.31): 'being filled with the Spirit' would, in Jewish usage, be tantamount to saying 'becoming prophets' (cf. 2.38c), and, in that capacity, with the inspiration of the Spirit, the disciples testify to their faith in the face of hostile opposition. Through its possession of the prophetic charisma the Christian community has the assurance that, in the world in which for the time being it lives, it is not left to its own resources, but experiences help from above in its missionary enterprise.

The second Pentecostal endowment, that of the Gentiles, is recorded in Acts 10.44 ff., and is of the same character as the first: while Peter was speaking 'the Holy Spirit fell on all who heard the word', and the Jewish Christians were amazed that the gift had been poured out on the Gentiles, 'for they heard them speaking in tongues and extolling God'. That Luke is so careful to record the same signs of Spirit-possession on these two great occasions demonstrates clearly that for him the 'prophetic' character of the gift is central: it is the equipment for Gospel proclamation. When the disciples at Ephesus (who had known only of John's baptism) received the Spirit 'they spoke with tongues and prophesied' (19.6).

If these passages make one thing clear, it is this: that all believers had received the prophetic Spirit and could be inspired to prophesy, and that, for Luke, in this kind of context, means to proclaim among Jews and Gentiles the good news of God's grace and action in Christ. But what about the 'tongues'? Is it glossolalia that Luke has in mind? In Acts 2.4 we must not miss the important word 'other' (*heterais*): they spoke 'in other tongues', that is, in various languages ('foreign languages' according to JB) that would be understood by the hearers with a view to the proclamation of the wonderful works of God throughout all the communities of the Jewish diaspora. It seems quite clear that Luke is using *glōssa* and *dialektos* in this passage synonymously for the languages spoken in the countries from which the listeners had come, and the audience was amazed that Galilean Jews could speak languages foreign to themselves but understandable to non-Palestinian pilgrims. In Acts 10.46 and 19.6 there is no reference to 'other' tongues. Does this mean that Luke intends these to be references to the phenomenon of glossolalia (as distinct from xenoglossy), an ecstatic form of intercourse with God, similar to that known at Corinth (1 Cor. 14). Perhaps the Gentiles' 'speaking in strange languages and proclaiming the greatness of God' (10.46 JB) has nothing to do with intelligible communication to others: but, if that is the case, then the parallelism with the Jewish Pentecost has been broken. Perhaps the Ephesian converts' speaking in tongues and prophesying is of the ecstatic kind, but if Luke's understanding of 'prophesying' here is consistent with chapter 2 a legitimate doubt may be raised.

If Luke had been interested in the phenomenon of glossolalia as usually understood (i.e. an unintelligible utterance which does not involve the mind of the speaker), why is it absent from those summaries (e.g. 2.42–47) in which he describes the activities of the primitive Church? Is it not significant that, whereas according to Paul glossolalia occurs in the course of worship among established Christians, Luke's two references (or three, if we include the xenoglossy of 2.4) are related closely to the initial onset and reception of the Spirit? It is the Spirit that Luke is interested in primarily, and only secondarily in miraculous signs, symbolically understood, that authenticate its presence. Indeed, it is possible that in both 10.46 and 19.6 Luke's description of the results of the reception of the Holy Spirit are not to be differentiated from those recorded in chapter 2 (where glossolalia, as normally understood, is not intended) simply because the word *heterais* is absent when it could be implied, and when Luke obviously wants to make his accounts of the three episodes as nearly parallel as possible? That may be a weak argument, but any other view has to take into account the fact that nowhere in Acts (save in 10.46 and 19.6 if these are exceptions) does Luke understand the gift of the Spirit, with or without specific reference to prophecy, in any other terms than as the inspiration or power to *communicate to men*, singly or collectively, truth from God or about God's action.

In support of this claim we may cite the following examples. When Peter declared God's actions in Christ before the Sanhedrin, the Spirit filled him (4.8). Again, when we read that 'the wisdom and Spirit' with which Stephen spoke to his disputants could not be withstood (6.10), 'Spirit' probably denotes inspired speech or prophetic endowment to utter a convincing proclamation. Paul – 'a chosen instrument of mine to carry my name before the Gentiles and kings and the sons of Israel' – is filled with the Holy Spirit to fulfil his task of evangelism (9.17), and Luke says nothing whatever about his speaking in tongues when the Spirit comes upon him. Again, the apostles affirm, after the essential facts of the life of Jesus and of the Gospel have been declared to the Council, that 'we are witnesses to these things, and so is the Holy Spirit whom God has given to those who obey him' (5.32). The gift of the Spirit, the sign of revived prophetism, is essentially concerned with the proclamation of the good news. The phenomenon of glossolalia – in the sense of an ecstatic communion with the divine in which neither the speaker nor the hearer understands the words uttered – somehow seems at odds with this view of the function of the Spirit and the nature of the prophetic gift.

Although it is assumed in the book of Acts that Christian prophecy, as an eschatological power of the Spirit, is a possibility for any Christian – else what would the fulfilment of Joel's prophecy mean? – it appears that some emerged as having the gift of prophecy in a more prominent or more continuing measure: these are called *prophētai*, not because the ability to prophesy was confined to them but because their inspiration and exercise of the gift was more regular and more frequent and thus entitled them to a recognised position in the Church. It is possible that the description of certain individuals as 'full' (*plērēs*) of the Holy Spirit, which Luke apparently derives from a special and primitive source (6.3, 5, 8, 7.55, 11.24) represents an attempt to express the realisation that inspiration was not just an occasional thing which all might experience for a particular occasion – being described therefore as 'filled with the Spirit' (4.8, 31, 9.17, 13.9: cf. Luke 1.41, 67) – but that some seemed to have such sureness of insight and conviction of speech as betokened a more sustained and lasting inspiration.[2] If this is so, then, as Cothenet suggests,[3] Stephen is to be regarded as one of the prophets of the primitive community. One of 'the seven men of good repute, full of the Spirit and of wisdom' (6.3) and himself 'full of faith and of the Holy Spirit' (6.5), Stephen's ministry was marked not only by grace and power but also by miracles and signs, and one is reminded of the same association between the action of the Spirit and signs in the Pauline letters (cf. 1 Thess. 1.5; 1 Cor. 2.4 and 2 Cor. 12.12, as well as the grace-gifts listed in 1 Cor. 12.9 f., 29). Moreover, Stephen's long speech, recounted in Acts 7.1–53, has a strong prophetic ring about it. In the manner of some of the prophets of old Israel, Stephen utters a passionate indictment of unbelieving Jewry and denounces its vain confidence in the Temple. The evident distinctiveness of this speech in the book of Acts and its difference of tone from the associated with Luke clearly imply that it derives from a special source, and a number of scholars have detected in it marks of Samaritan influence.[4] Be that as it may, Stephen's irresistible and inspired interpretation of

Scripture bring vengeance upon him and, as a prophet ('full of the Holy Spirit', 7.55), he receives in his dying moments a vision of the Son of man – a vision which is not merely a consolation in the hour of martyrdom but is also an announcement of approaching judgment on his adversaries – whose prediction, according to Matthew 23.34, he so amply fulfils: 'I send you prophets and wise men and scribes: some of whom you will kill and crucify, and some you will scourge in your synagogues and persecute from town to town.'

Another of the Seven, 'full of the Spirit and wisdom', is Philip, who is the recipient of the rare New Testament title 'evangelist' (21.8). He is the initiator of the mission in Samaria and miracles accompany his preaching (8.5–7). A second narrative, of a literary genre quite different from the preceding one, presents Philip in a manner reminiscent of the inspired men of ancient Israel who were the objects of sudden and dramatic interventions of the Spirit's action (cf. 1 Kgs. 18.12; 2 Kgs. 2.9–12, 16; Ezek. 3.12, 14, etc.). It is the Spirit – the agent of God's purpose in the missionary enterprise of the Church – which tells Philip to go and join himself to the chariot of the Ethiopian (8.29), a directive which gives him the opportunity of winning a convert by means of the interpretation of Scripture. Here again prophetic characteristics are evident. Philip begins from Isaiah 53 (and the length of the quotation recorded may be an indication of the importance of this text in the early Church's scriptural study) and shows how it applies to Jesus of Nazareth. In a manner similar to the actualisation of prophetic Scripture in the *pᵉšārîm* (interpretations) at Qumran, the words of Isaiah are applied to the figure of Jesus – an insight, perhaps, into the way in which the exegetical traditions concerning the function and identity of Jesus came into being at an early stage in the Church's existence. Undoubtedly, this discovery of the 'meaning' of Scripture belonged to the prophetic charism: at least part of the ministry of prophets in the New Testament was the interpretation of the Old.

After having evangelised Samaria, Philip settled at Caesarea (21.8) and he had four virgin daughters who prophesied: the tense of *prophēteuousai* (present, not aorist) indicates that the women exercised the gift of prophecy regularly, not that they uttered a prophecy on one particular occasion. The four prophetesses were destined to enjoy considerable prestige in early Church traditions and the Montanists claimed their patronage, but all that Acts 21.9 suggests is that they were attached to a single community (and therefore not wandering prophets) and that there was a connection between virginity and prophecy (cf. Luke 2.36), consonant with the esteem in which asceticism was held by Jewish-Christian communities.[5] On the content of their prophesying we can only speculate: if it was in the context of the community's meetings for worship, it may have been a kind of liturgical prophecy taking the form of prayer (cf. 1 Cor. 11.4, 5) or spiritual songs (cf. Col. 3.16; Eph. 5.19).[6]

The third prophet of the primitive community 'full of the Holy Spirit' is Barnabas (11.24), concerning whom Luke provides a considerable amount of information, possible because he exercised great influence in Antioch, the city from which, according to tradition, Luke himself originated. It is worth the effort to assemble as well as we can the traditions at our disposal regarding Barnabas, for he best represents the figure of the 'prophet' in the earliest decades of the Church. At Acts 4.36 Luke introduces us to a land-owning Levite, of Cypriot origin, named Joseph who was called by the apostles 'Barnabas', which means 'son of *paraklēsis*'. This designation could be rendered 'son of consolation', in which case it would be more appropriate to Manaen (Menahem, 'Comforter') who is associated with Barnabas in Acts 13.1, but whatever the correct etymology may be, it is intended by Luke to represent Barnabas as 'son of prophecy' (*bar-nᵉbûʾâh* or *bar-nᵉbiyyā*, on the assumption that *paraklēsis* means 'exhortation'. If this interpretation, which has the support of many scholars, is correct, Joseph's 'Christian' name, like Peter's (Matt. 16.18) indicates what his distinctive ministry or function in the Christian community was or was to be ('son of prophecy'=one who is a prophet). It is Barnabas who introduces Paul to the apostles at Jerusalem and assures them of the sincerity of the erstwhile persecutor and the reality of his conversion (9.27). As one who enjoyed the confidence of the mother-church at Jerusalem Barnabas is sent to Antioch

102 NEW TESTAMENT PROPHECY

to make inquiries about the entry of the Gentiles into the Church: being well satisfied with the situation 'he exhorted (*parekalei*) them all to remain faithful to the Lord with steadfast purpose' (11.23). When the first missionary journey begins, Barnabas is the first to be named (13.2, 7) – although he soon takes second place to Paul – and receives, with Paul, the title 'apostle' (14.4, 14). At Antioch Paul and Barnabas are invited to give a word of *paraklēsis* to the congregation (13.15) and Paul obliges with the powerful speech recorded in verses 17–41. Barnabas is again at Paul's side on the occasion of the Council of Jerusalem (15.2; Gal. 2.1, 9) from which emerged the Jerusalem Decree, given through the inspiration of the Holy Spirit and termed *paraklēsis* (15.31). Despite their violent quarrel over John Mark (15.36–39) and Barnabas's compromising with the Judaising faction (Gal. 2.13) Paul always retained in high esteem the colleague of his early days, as 1 Corinthians 9.6 clearly implies.

From this summary of the evidence in Acts concerning the prophet Barnabas – for such he was, according to 13.1 – it is quite clear that the terms *paraklēsis* and *parakaleō* are employed in a quite distinctive way in relation to Christian prophetic speech. 'In Luke's thought', says E. Earle Ellis, '*paraklēsis* is one way in which Christian prophets exercise their ministry and, in this context, is a form of prophecy.'[7] The verb is used by Luke in his Gospel to describe the proclamation of the Baptist (Luke 3.18: cf. 7.26), an utterance which is reminiscent of the warning speeches of the Old Testament prophets: as a description of Peter's preaching (Acts 2.40) it may be an indication of his prophetic character in the Lucan presentation of his apostolic ministry, together with his knowledge of men's hearts (Acts 5.3, 8.21 ff.) and his experience and declaration of revelations in visions and dreams (Acts 10.10; cf. 9.10, 16.9, 18.9, 22.17 ff. and 27.23). As we noted earlier, the letter which made known the Jerusalem Decree, which resolved a matter of urgent pastoral concern relating to uncircumcised believers, is termed *paraklēsis*, issued under the direction of the Spirit (15.28, 31). When we read that the Church throughout Judea, Galilee and Samaria was filled with the *paraklēsis* of the Holy Spirit (9.31) we may be confident that the writer is alluding to its instruction and encouragement through Spirit-inspired prophetic teaching. In Acts 15.32 the phrase 'they exhorted and strengthened (*parekalesan kai epestērixan*) the brethren' is specifically connected with the fact that Judas Barsabbas and Silas are themselves prophets. The same two terms are used at 14.22 with reference to the activity of Paul and Barnabas, both of whom must have been regarded, in certain aspects of their careers, as prophets (13.1): this verse (14.22) offers some insight into their *paraklēsis*: '. . . strengthening the souls of the disciples, exhorting them to continue in the faith, and saying that through many tribulations we must enter the kingdom of God'. The prophetic ministry has the characteristics of pastoral preaching. This understanding of prophetic *paraklēsis* is supported in the Pauline literature (see the next chapter) by 1 Corinthians 14.2 f. where the prophet's ministry of edification (*oikodomē*) is accomplished by means of *paraklēsis* and *paramythia*.

In the essay from which we have already quoted Ellis suggests that the interpretation of Scripture, by methods similar to the Qumran *pesher*-exegesis, was an important activity of the Christian prophet according to the book of Acts, and he takes as his chief example the homily found in 13.16–41. This sermon, set in the context of synagogue worship, is given by Paul in response to the request for a 'word of exhortation (*paraklēsis*)' – a phrase which, incidentally, is used to describe the Letter to the Hebrews (Heb. 13.22) – and Paul (or Saul) is linked with Barnabas among the 'prophets and teachers' in the Antioch church (13.1). Two important and interesting questions are immediately raised. Is the sermon at Pisidian Antioch given by Paul in the capacity of 'prophet', if in fact he was regarded by Luke as such? And secondly, is the interpretation of Scripture its chief characteristic?

It does not emerge unambiguously from the use of the Greek particles in Acts 13.1 that the first three men named (Barnabas, Simeon and Lucius) were prophets, and the remaining two (Manaen and Saul) teachers, although *didaskein* ('to teach') is the term regularly used for Paul's ministry within Christian communities (Acts 11.26, 15.35, 20.20, 28.31): it is probable that both titles apply to all five persons. (It should be noted that attempts have been made to find at Antioch – and if Luke has taken his information from an 'Antioch' source (as many scholars argue) this would take us back to AD 40–50 – not only a twofold ministry, but a threefold, namely, prophets, teachers and, by implication, apostles, since Paul and Barnabas were immediately sent off as missionaries and are called 'apostles' at 14.4, 14: thus we would have the origin of Paul's triad (1 Cor. 12.28) traced back by as much as a decade, and to Antioch.) Luke, however, nowhere else uses the term *didaskalos* and consequently we do not possess in his writing sufficient evidence on which to delimit neatly the functions of the teacher from those of the prophet. In the early stages of the Christian mission clear distinctions of office or function had not been established: we cannot detect an absolute distinction between prophet and apostle, for Barnabas is designated by both terms, and E. C. Selwyn's suggestion (based on Didache 11.3–5) that apostles were 'prophets on circuit' (i.e. sent out as missionaries) in contrast to 'prophets in session'[8] will not account for the fact that elsewhere in Acts apostles reside in Jerusalem and prophets engage in travel. No more can we always distinguish prophets from teachers. The most we can plausibly suggest is a difference between them in terms of the manner and method by which they build up the Church's life, the prophet disclosing the revealed will of God for and in a certain set of circumstances, and the teacher being more concerned with the exposition of Scripture and the transmission of the tradition concerning Jesus.[9] Acts 13.1 does not permit us to say with certainty that Paul delivered his homily at Antioch in his role as prophet or as teacher, or even as missionary-apostle.

Does the content or form of the sermon assist a decision? Some years ago J. W. Bowker[10] suggested that the address at Pisidian Antioch reveals several clear indications of Jewish proem-holily form, the *seder* reading (from Torah) being Deuteronomy, 4.25–46, the *haftarah* (or prophetical reading) 2 Samuel. 7.6–16, and the proem text 1 Samuel 13.14 (quoted in its Targumic form). The case cannot be regarded as conclusive (as Bowker admits), for it was part of the method that the controlling lections governing the pattern were not explicitly quoted and so have to be presupposed from the address itself. Besides, the fact that the introductory verses of the sermon (17–21) will not fit the known formal pattern of proem-homily is embarrassing to the theory. But even if Bowker's case is granted probability, would the form imply the preaching of a prophet or of a teacher? J. W. Doeve argues for the genuineness of the sermon and draws attention to signs in it of Jewish exegetical methods, but adds 'in the argument of Acts xiii the work of a schooled rabbi is quite perceptible'.[11] The form of the homily, then, may represent the exegetical method that is characteristic of the Christian teacher's task, namely, the christological interpretation of Old Testament texts. If, on the other hand, we take the view of Haenchen, Conzelmann and Wilckens[12] that the address is intended by the author of Acts to show how Paul would have spoken to a synagogue audience, beginning with a retrospect of sacred history before coming to the declaration of the decision required in the present and the hope for the future – and Haenchen[13] does observe that 'the speech ends with an Old Testament warning that rumbles with the menace of an earth-tremor and drives home the responsibility of the Jews' – in short, if we look at the content of the sermon, rather than at its formal structure, we may discern the utterance of a prophetic spirit, an exhortation designed to lead to repentance and conversion. But if the address is the utterance of a Christian prophet (in this case, Paul) it is prophetic, not because it interprets Scripture in the way it does (or may do) but because of the exhortation to repentance and obedience, the *paraklēsis*, which it contains.

Ellis's suggestion that similarities exist between the method of biblical interpretation in Acts 13.16–41 and that employed at Qumran, where the community's 'teacher' (*mōreh*) and 'instructors' (*maśkîlîm*) impart their understanding of God's hidden purpose with particular reference to the life of the sect, is less than convincing. The Qumran 'instructors' – with the probable exception of the Teacher of Righteousness or Rightful Teacher – never identify themselves as prophets: they represent the 'wise' of Daniel 11–12 and their activity may form a better parallel for the main function of the New Testament *didaskalos*, that of exposition and the transmission of tradition. On this we shall have more to say in the next chapter.

We return now to the Jerusalem Decree and to the speech of James that precedes its deliverance. Käsemann has noted the similarity of the opening words of the Decree, 'it has seemed good to the Holy Spirit and to us ...' (15.28), to the promulgation of eschatological law elsewhere in the New Testament. He is of the opinion that the latter is the work of Christian prophets – a hypothesis we shall consider later in this book – and that often 'holy Scripture provides the primitive Christian prophet with the stylistic form in which to clothe the sentences of holy law'.[14] But the content and the style of the Decree itself are quite different from those of Käsemann's *Sätze heiligen Rechtes*, and the words 'it has seemed good to the Holy Spirit and to us' are satisfactorily accounted for as an acknowledgment of the Spirit's directing and controlling role in the entire missionary enterprise as well as in decision-making regarding its expansion. Even if the Decree was received at Antioch as prophetic *paraklēsis*, the opening phrase does not necessarily imply that it had its origin in prophetic utterance. In support of Käsemann's view (expressed in the quotation given above) Ellis[15] affirms that the formula *legei Kyrios* in Acts 15.16–18 (from James's speech) actually reflects the exposition of Christian prophets, and observes that the theme of the citation (from Amos 9.11–12) – the inclusion of the Gentiles – is specifically the 'mystery' which, according to Paul, 'has now been revealed to Christ's holy apostles and prophets by the Spirit' (Eph. 3.3–5; Rom. 16.25). But the speech of James contains a number of traces of midrashic style which, in the light of our discussion of Paul's address in chapter 13, might suggest that it was the product of a teacher, rather than a prophet, employing a proof-text (and glossing it) used in the early Church on the subject of the Gentiles: moreover, this *legei Kyrios* quotation (cf. 7.48 ff.) cannot easily be regarded as a distinctively Christian prophetic word since the phrase is included in the Old Testament citation being used. Whether or not the passage from Amos represents the biblical basis and rationale on which the provisions of the Jerusalem Decree were justified, the presence of the *legei Kyrios* formula does not prove that it was derived from Christian prophetic activity.

Finally, we come to the one named prophet in Acts to whom there is attributed the ability to predict future events, Agabus. (Ananias, designated 'a certain disciple' (9.10), received a prophetic revelation concerning the destiny of the newly converted Saul, but this is not really prediction.) Together with a group of prophets from Jerusalem, rather like the bands of early Israelite prophets, Agabus comes to Antioch and prophesies, through the Spirit, that a great famine would take place over the whole world (11.28). Luke has certainly understood the prediction in a historical sense, but it is possible (and in the opinion of many, probable) that the famine which Agabus prophesied (and the verb *sēmainō* suggests some kind of revelatory indication, cf. Rev. 1.1) was an established feature of eschatological preaching, one of the events preceding the End of the Age (cf. Mark 13.8; Rev. 6.5 ff.). Luke may well have de-eschatologised and historicised what was originally an eschatological declaration. The fact that a relief operation followed upon Agabus's prediction may be due to Luke's having combined two quite separate traditions, one about an itinerant prophet, the other about relief brought by Barnabas and Paul from Antioch to Jerusalem.[16] The second prediction by Agabus concerns the fate of Paul – a prediction which was not quite literally fulfilled, a point which some [17] think guarantees Luke's exact preservation of the oracle – and it is accompanied by a symbolic gesture (21.10 f.) reminiscent of the prophets of the Old Testament. Noteworthy in this case are the words which form the introduction to the oracle: 'Thus says the Holy Spirit ...' (*tade legei to pneuma to hagion*): this is not strictly equivalent to the well-known Old Testament formula 'Thus says the Lord', but the insistence on the direct intervention of the Spirit is a feature, not only appropriate to the book of Acts and its understanding of the Spirit but also to Christian prophecy, as the letters to the seven churches in the Revelation show, as well as the later oracles of Montanist prophets. In the case of Agabus, one may be forgiven for wondering if he was not actually trying to cast himself in the role of an Old Testament prophet, but not quite succeeding: for the fact that his word did not strictly come true would have made his prophecy 'false' by Old Testament standards.

Whatever view we take of the Agabus stories – and many scholars assert that both narratives bear the imprint of Lucan formulation and theological *Tendenz* – it is clear that for the author of Acts prediction is not the main function of Christian prophets. In several important passages Christian prophecy, as an eschatological gift or power of the Holy Spirit, is a possibility for any believer, but it is primarily identified with certain leaders (cf. Acts 15.22) who exercise it as a continuing ministry. Although we must be cautious about making a sharp distinction in the earliest period of the Church's life between official and unofficial ministries, it does seem clear that a special position and recognition was conferred upon those who manifested in a prominent and sustained manner the gift of prophesying. Among such 'professional prophets' are the group from the Jerusalem church visiting Antioch, including Agabus (11.27), the Antioch circle (13.1), Judas and Silas who accompanied the Jerusalem Decree to Antioch (15.22, 32) and the daughters of Philip (21.9), together with some other individuals better known to us as apostles (e.g. Paul and Barnabas). The chief function of these prophets appears to be of a pastoral kind: they offer *paraklēsis* to the disciples in order to strengthen them in their faith: thus they are associated with the declaration of the Spirit's guidance and judgment, occasionally accompanied by prediction and symbolic actions and, in the opinion of some, based on the exposition of the Scriptures: in our view, this last function is the mark of the teacher (though the dividing line between teacher and prophet, like that between prophet and apostle, is difficult to draw) rather than of the prophet. Acts distinguishes miracle-working from prophecy (2.17 f., 43, 5.12–16, 10.34, 40, 19.11 f.) and associates signs and miracles with the apostle, though not exclusively so. Peter, who is not called a prophet, has (as we have observed) certain of the marks of the prophet in his insight into men's hearts (5.3, 8.21 ff.) and in the experience and declaration of revelations received in visions and dreams. Paul, who is probably rightly included among the prophets mentioned in Acts 13.1, is never spoken of as prophesying: 'teaching' is the term used most frequently for his ministry within the Christian communities. He too receives revelations and visions, even in an ecstatic state, and the narratives of his conversion and commissioning bear many resemblances to a prophetic call: these features we shall deal with more fully in the next chapter.

At a number of places in Acts the early Christian mission is viewed as a continuation of Jesus' ministry and as a conflict between spirit-powers. The former is expressed most clearly as the immediate action of the exalted Lord himself (e.g. 22.18, 23.11), as well as of the directing power of the Holy Spirit, which is the Spirit of Jesus (16.7). The contest is explicit in the encounter between Peter and Simon Magus (8.9–24) and the encounter of Paul with the false prophet Barjesus (13.6 ff.) and with the medium in Philippi (16.16), two narratives in which Paul's reaction and words are reminiscent of the ancient prophets. The same kind of contest may be implied in the story of the Jewish exorcists (19.13–20). To both of these Lucan themes – the continuation of Jesus' ministry under the direction of the Spirit and the conflict between spirit-powers – the ministry of Christian prophecy is related. Under the direct and immediate inspiration of the Spirit, the prophet exhorts and strengthens the Christian community by pastoral guidance and instruction, and through the power of the Spirit he witnesses to the character of his living Lord, who is himself the Prophet of the End-time (3.22).

CHAPTER FIVE

PAUL AND THE PHENOMENON OF PROPHECY IN THE CHURCH

In this chapter we shall be concerned with two interrelated but distinct topics: whether Paul himself may be legitimately regarded as a prophet and, secondly, what Paul says about the manifestations of Christian prophetism in the congregations to which he addressed his letters. Discussion of the first topic is, in our view, quite straightforward, although certain of the consequences which flow from our answer may have a significant bearing on the entire enterprise of identifying and evaluating correctly New Testament prophets. The investigation of Paul's attitude to the phenomenon of prophets and prophecy in the Christian congregations is a much more difficult undertaking, but we are fortunate that most of what Paul had to say concerning it is found in chapters 12 and 14 of 1 Corinthians, chapters separated by – but not at all separable from – the famous hymn in praise of Christian love (*agapē*), the highest of all spiritual gifts: it is with these chapters and their interpretation that we shall be concerned mainly, though not exclusively, as we seek to set out Paul's assessment – at times, critical and at times, commendatory – of Christian prophets and their functions in the churches to which he wrote. Throughout the chapter we shall treat the evidence from Paul's letters as the primary source of information,[1] employing Acts (where relevant) as corroborative: this approach does not imply that what Acts says about Paul is necessarily incorrect, only that it is responsible to give to what Paul himself says precedence over what Luke, with a different religious experience and writing for another public and for other purposes than Paul had in view, selectively and admiringly tells about the apostle in retrospect.[2]

1. IS PAUL A PROPHET?

Let us recall our characterisation of a Christian prophet: 'a Christian who functions within the Church, occasionally or regularly, as a divinely called and inspired speaker who receives intelligible and authoritative revelations which he is impelled to deliver publicly, in oral or written form, to Christian individuals and/or the Christian community'. If that functional definition is at all adequate, then it would be, in our view, difficult if not impossible to deny that Paul may rightly be called a Christian prophet, although nowhere in the New Testament is he given that title. He himself does not explicitly claim to be a prophet or the possessor of prophetic powers, despite the fact that he obviously held the prophets of the Old Testament in high esteem (Rom. 1.2, 3.21, 16.25 f.; cf. Acts 13.27, 40, 24.14, 26.22, 27) and frequently quoted from them, especially from Isaiah, to support his teaching. (Is this conceivably an illustration of the phenomenon of a prophet drawing upon prophetic traditions? See above pp. 13–14.) The nearest approach to self-designation as a prophet may be Paul's use of 'servant (*doulos*) of Christ' (Rom. 1.1; Gal. 1.10; Phil. 1.1) with reference to himself: in certain books of the Old Testament (2 Kgs. 9.7, 17.13, 23, etc., Ezra 9.11; Jer. 7.25; 25.4, 26.5, 29.19, etc.; Zech. 1.6) the prophets are referred to as 'the servants of the Lord', and almost without exception in these cases the Septuagint renders the word 'servant' (*'ebed*) by *doulos*.

If we wished to give a comprehensive account of Paul's prophetic characteristics[3] we could draw attention to the poetic (and therefore prophet-like) quality of much of his language, but we shall confine ourselves to the features delineated in our working-definition. And there is no doubt that Paul was divinely called and commissioned, that he received revelations, and that he felt himself to be under divine constraint to proclaim, in word and letter, what he had been given. We begin with Gal. 1.15–16, Paul's own testimony to what is usually referred to as his conversion experience: 'When he who had set me apart before I was born (*lit.* from my mother's womb) and had called me through his grace was pleased to reveal (*apokalypsai*) his Son to (*lit.* in) me, in order that I might preach him among the Gentiles ...'. In a context where all the stress is laid on the break that was caused in his life by the direct revelation of Christ, the words about election and call must be interpreted as pointing in advance to the moment when he experienced that revelation. The parallel with an important passage from Isaiah 49.1–6 concerning the calling of God's servant, the prophet, is striking:

The Lord called me from the womb,
  from the body of my mother he named my name....

And now the Lord says,
  who formed me from the womb to be his servant,
to bring Jacob back to him,
  and that Israel might be gathered to him, ...

he says: 'It is too light a thing that you should be my servant
to raise up the tribes of Jacob
and to restore the preserved of Israel;
I will give you as a light to the nations,
that my salvation may reach to the end of the earth.

Here the two ideas of election and call 'from the womb' are linked with the commission to be a light to the Gentiles, and this fits well with Paul's divinely given task, 'that I might preach him (Christ) among the Gentiles'.

Another text may be quoted, in which the parallelism lies not so much in the actual expressions as in the train of thought: it refers to Jeremiah's call as prophet (Jer. 1.4 f.):

Before I formed you in the womb I knew you,
and before you were born I consecrated you;
I appointed you a prophet to the nations.

Paul's description of his call and the commission revealed to him clearly bear the impress of the prophetic self-understanding. The account in Acts which is closest to Paul's own words is 26.12–18 where Christ says that he has appeared to Paul 'to appoint you to serve and bear witness to the things in which you have seen me and to those in which I will appear to you'

– further evidence of continuing revelations – 'delivering you from the people and from the Gentiles' – hinting at the prophetic fate of persecution and suffering, cf. Acts 9.16 – 'to whom I send you to open their eyes ...' (cf. Jer. 1.7, 8; Isa. 42.6, 7, 16). Further prophetic traits in Paul's call may be seen by comparing the Acts accounts of the Damascus road encounter with Isaiah's vision and commissioning in the Temple (Isa. 6), with Ezekiel's call and commission in a throne-theophany (Ezek. 1–2) which has interesting parallels with Enoch's visionary call (1 Enoch 14.8–16.4: cf. also Dan. 7.9 ff.[4]) as well as with Jeremiah 1.[5]

The language of visionary or revelatory experience is explicit in the accounts of or allusions to Paul's conversion-call: the Christophany (Gal. 1.15; cf. 1 Cor. 15.8) or 'heavenly vision' to which he was not disobedient (Acts 26.19) is very probably referred to again (in a context where he discusses 'visions and revelations of the Lord') in 2 Cor. 12.2–4 when Paul speaks of being 'caught up to the third heaven', 'caught up into Paradise' where 'he heard things that cannot be told, which man may not utter'. But other visions were given to Paul: his vision of a man from Macedonia (Acts 16.9–10) was interpreted as a call from God to preach the Gospel to the people there, and, during his stay at Corinth, the Lord spoke to him in a night vision: 'Do not be afraid, but speak and do not be silent' (Acts 18.9). Experiences like these must be among 'the abundance of revelations' which Paul, on his own testimony, witnessed (2 Cor. 12.7).

From our discussion of Old Testament prophecy it will be recalled that the true prophet stood in the intimate council of the Lord (*sôd Yahweh*), thus gaining that knowledge of the divine will, plan and purpose which he had to declare to God's people. It would appear that Paul stood in just such a relationship with Christ. For instance, he points out to the Galatians that the Gospel he preached was 'not man's gospel: for I did not receive it from man, nor was I taught it, but it came through a revelation of/in Christ' (Gal. 1.12). And in 1 Corinthians he asks – and it is not a rhetorical question – 'Have I not seen Jesus our Lord?' (1 Cor. 9.1). Discussing the institution of the

Lord's Supper he affirms, 'For I received from the Lord what I also delivered to you, that the Lord Jesus, on the night when he was betrayed took bread ...' (1 Cor. 11.23): if this does not refer to direct revelation, it acknowledges dependence upon an authoritative tradition which went back (via the Jerusalem church?) to the events of the Upper Room.[6] To the Ephesian elders at Miletus Paul speaks of 'my course and my ministry which I received from the Lord Jesus, to testify to the grace of God' (Acts 20.24: cf. 23.11, 27.23). It was 'by revelation' that he went to Jerusalem 'after fourteen years' (Gal. 2.1 f.) to present his case to the ecclesiastical authorities with whom (as was the case with the Old Testament prophets and the priestly cult) he was frequently in a relationship of tension, yet within *one* Church, the community of men and women freed into discipleship to Christ.[7] Within that community his authority did not come from men (Gal. 1.1), nor even from or through other apostles – for he 'did not confer with flesh and blood' (Gal. 1.16). It was God who had set him apart before he was born, called him through his grace and revealed his Son to him: Christ's appearance to him 'as to one untimely born' (1 Cor. 15.8) was the only credential he needed or claimed for ministry of the Gospel.

The authority exercised by Paul is clear on almost every page of his letters, letters which must be seen as an expression of his missionary preaching: diverse kinds of admonition are urged upon believers and various warrants and sanctions invoked: however much of this may be described as 'tradition' of one sort or another (e.g. *Haustafeln*, or household lists; tables of virtues and vices, words of Jesus, etc.), that is secondary to the fact that they are authoritative within the conceptual framework which assumes that they are part of the larger meaning of 'gospel', the ultimate source of Paul's understanding of authority.[8] Two well-known examples of Paul's authority as a spokesman for the Lord are 1 Corinthians 7.10, 'To the married I give charge, not I but the Lord, that ...' and, even more significant for our purpose, 1 Corinthians 14.37–38 where Paul asserts his authority over the whole Corinthian community, including its prophets: 'If anyone thinks he is a prophet or spiritual, he should acknowledge that what I am writing to you is a command of the Lord. If anyone does not recognise this, he is not recognised', i.e. by the Lord – a pronouncement of divine judgment, rather than a denial of community recognition as an inspired speaker: as G. W. H. Lampe puts it, Paul 'was driven flatly to refuse to admit the possibility that a prophet might be right and he himself be wrong'.[9]

When Paul's exercise of authority – in making pronouncements, etc. – is seen within the framework of gospel- or missionary-preaching, we may in fairness point to 1 Cor. 9.16 as evidence for his sense of being (like the prophets of old) under divine constraint: 'For necessity (*anankē*) is laid upon me. Woe to me if I do not preach the gospel': a divine compulsion – bound up with his calling and election – impels him to proclaim the message of God's grace. It is possible that Paul's words in Phil. 3.12 'Christ Jesus has made me his own (*katelēmphthēn hypo Christou Iēsou*)' – possibly again referring to the Damascus road experience – form a phrase which is open to interpretation as 'Christ Jesus has seized me': in a very forceful expression Paul is saying something not unlike Jeremiah's claim, 'Thou art stronger than I, and thou has prevailed' (Jer. 20.7).

Sufficient has been said to confirm our assertion that Paul may be legitimately defined as a Christian prophet, according to our definition, and yet he is never called by that title, which, in the Pauline corpus, is reserved to the canonical prophets or to certain persons exercising prophetic functions in the Church. Is there any explanation of this strange state of affairs? Teacher, preacher, evangelist, even prophet Paul may be, in fact if not in name, but the chief title which he claims is 'apostle' (a word which, in its New Testament usage, is probably a unique derivation from the verb *apostellein*), possessing the underlying meaning of 'messenger', 'emissary', 'delegate' (on analogy with the Hebrew *šālîaḥ*), or, more generally, 'one who is sent'. Although unanimity has not been reached by scholars on the criteria for apostleship, the nature of the apostolic office, or even on the number of the apostles,[10] there would be general agreement on two fundamental points: (*a*) an apostle must be a witness to the resurrection of the Lord, if not to the earthly life of Jesus as well; and (*b*) an apostle must be called and commissioned by the risen Christ (or by the earthly Lord) to a unique ministry (which will include preaching, teaching the revelation entrusted to him, founding congregations, suffering and perhaps even performing miracles) for which he will be endowed with a special charisma:[11] in short, the apostle is a divinely called and inspired – and therefore authoritative – messenger. It is with good reason that Myers and Freed conclude their essay by saying that, apart from the somewhat broader orientation of the apostle's mission, 'there may be, in the final analysis, not very much difference between the Old Testament prophet and the New Testament apostle'.[12]

That indeed may be so, for the attributes of the apostle were sufficiently extensive to include most if not all of those belonging to the prophet: but, nevertheless, the New Testament distinguishes between the bearers of the two designations and ranks apostles above, or at least before (in terms of usefulness to the community), prophets (1 Cor. 12.28; Eph. 4.11, 2.20, 3.5: cf. Rev. 18.20).

How can this rather ambiguous evidence be treated? We may make Old Testament prophets completely definitive for our understanding of what is meant by 'prophet' in the New Testament: in which case we may have to say that the apostles are the real successors of these prophets – as divinely authoritative messengers – and that the New Testament prophets are inferior or secondary bearers of revelation, and not genuine 'prophets'.[13] This view could be supported by claiming that (*a*) in New Testament times the word *prophētēs* no longer adequately emphasised the status of divinely authoritative messenger, because it had come to mean simply a 'spokesman' or 'one who predicts the future, or has supernatural knowledge', and (*b*) by reason of the fulfilment of Joel 2.28 (promising an outpouring of God's spirit on all flesh which would lead to prophesying) and the widespread expectation of a prophetic revival in the 'age to come' (Num. Rab. 15.25), *prophētai* would have been too broad a term to apply to that limited and special group who were the true successors to the Old Testament prophetic ministry and who were therefore called 'apostles', to the authority of at least one of whom (Paul) the 'prophets' were subject (1 Cor. 14.37–38).

With this approach there are certain weaknesses: (a) it makes the marks, or some of the marks, of the Old Testament prophet absolutely normative for the recognition of prophets and prophecy in the New Testament, and consequently finds that the apostles are the real prophets in the New Testament. Is there not a case (despite Joel 2.28 f. and its fulfilment in a widespread sense on the day of Pentecost) for taking the New Testament usage of the *prophētēs* word-group on its own merits and finding both its continuities and discontinuities with Old Testament prophets and prophecy and its overlap with other functions and functionaries in the New Testament church?

(b) The approach seems to be dominated by the figure of Paul: it is on the basis of Paul's testimony that it is said that there is not much difference between the Old Testament prophets and the New Testament apostles. Perhaps this can be said because we have so much evidence both from and about Paul: but can the same claim be made for Peter? Perhaps. But for James, John, Matthias? Surely this is very questionable. Is it not the fact that Paul is the well-documented apostle *par excellence* that permits us to say what has been said about his Old Testament prophetic characteristics? Admittedly, in the early church the apostles are sometimes connected with Old Testament prophets (Ign., *Phil.* 5.1–2, 9.1–2: *Ep. Polycarp* 6: Hermas, *Sim.* 9.15.4); admittedly, the New Testament itself can sometimes view the apostles as prophets, e.g. Paul (1 Cor. 14.6, 13.9) and possibly Judas and Silas who, though prophets, seem to have been numbered among the apostles or elders; nevertheless, it seems to be the authority of Paul as apostle, as divinely commissioned messenger, that forms the basis for the argument.

But how many apostles were like Paul? If the apostle *par excellence* is made the paradigm for New Testament prophets, by reason solely, or even mainly, of his Old Testament prophetic characteristics, we shall be in danger of recognising only *one* genuine New Testament prophet, or two, if we include the prophet-writer of Revelation in the tradition of Old Testament prophecy! It seems that the New Testament calls Paul and others 'apostles' because their ministry falls mainly, but not exclusively, within what is meant by that term. Paul is evangelist, teacher, preacher and has prophetic features as well, but primarily he is *apostolos*, a term broad enough to include some or all of the other functions mentioned: those who are called 'prophets' in the New Testament primarily exercise the gift of prophecy, though, as in the case of Judas and Silas and Barnabas, they may fulfil other tasks as well, and in their case the name *prophētēs* is indeed indebted to the Old Testament understanding of prophecy, but mediated, through the interpretation of Joel 2.28 f. in Acts, into a milieu in which it was understood in a somewhat less rigidly definable fashion, simply because of its usage in current speech and literature. While apostles might be able, and certainly in the case of Paul were able, to exercise prophetic functions, New Testament prophets, though not called to the apostolic ministry, were, nevertheless, in a meaningful way and consonant with our definition, entitled to be called 'prophets'.

One final point: if the apostle Paul (and perhaps Peter) exercised a prophetic ministry as well, then we cannot easily identify what he says *qua* prophet, any more than we can designate with clarity what he says in his role of evangelist or preacher: it is perhaps only in the matter of disclosing revelations or 'mysteries' that we can point, with any degree of confidence, to 'prophecy' on the part of the apostle. It is in fact very difficult – despite all our certainty about Paul's prophetic characteristics – to say that any particular saying or literary statement is a prophetic utterance from the apostle. With this caveat in mind, we turn to the discussion of what Paul has to say on the subject of Christian prophecy.

2. PAUL ON PROPHECY

'Who the prophets are, what they do and what significance prophecy has for the community – all these questions are answered for Paul at their clearest in 1 Cor. 12–14': so wrote H. Greeven some twenty-five years ago,[14] and few would dispute the correctness of his assertion. Nevertheless, there are a few references to the phenomenon of prophetism outside 1 Corinthians and these deserve some comment before we embark on the study of the chapters mentioned. From Rom. 12.4–6 we learn that 'prophecy' (*prophēteia*) is a grace-gift or charisma given to members of the Church to be used in such a way as to express and maintain the unity of the one Body; that it was a gift either not given to or not exercised by all members of the Church, but by certain individuals; and that those who use the gift of prophecy must do so *kata tēn analogian tēs pisteōs*, and *if* that phrase means 'in proportion to our faith', i.e. in proportion to the quantity of faith given or possessed, it could imply degrees of prophetic ability which varied according to the amount of faith one had, 'faith' being the believer's confidence that God's Spirit is speaking in the actual words he is uttering. What Paul is saying, then, is that the person who exercises the gift of prophecy should speak only when conscious of his words as inspired, and presumably only for as long as he is confident that God is speaking through him.

More interesting is 1 Thess. 5.19–21: 'Do not quench the Spirit, do not despise prophesying (*prophēteia*), but test everything'; and the nearness of verse 20 suggests that the *panta* ('everything') refers primarily, though perhaps not exclusively, to prophecies. In addition to observing that this passage is another witness to the existence of the prophetic phenomenon in the Church and to noting that it is the prophecies, not the prophets, that are to be tested or evaluated, is there anything further to be deduced from this reference? R. P. Martin (with due acknowledgment to J. M. Robinson) has drawn attention to certain interesting features of 1 Thess. 5.16–22: in the original Greek the verb in each of the short sentences stands last; there is a predominance of words which begin with the Greek letter '*p*', thus giving a rhythm; and the order of the injunctions 'Pray, give thanks' and 'do not despise prophesying, but test everything' (i.e. the utterances) is particularly noteworthy. On the basis of these observations he goes on:

When the passage is set down in lines, it reads as though it contained the 'headings' of a Church service. The note of glad adoration is struck at the opening: 'Rejoice always' (verse 16). Prayer and thanksgiving are coupled – a trait which comes into the Church from the synagogue assembly. Christians are counselled to give the Spirit full rein, especially as He opens the mouths of the prophets (verses 19, 20); but cautioned (verse 21) that they must test the spirits (cf. 1 John iv, 1). Above all, nothing unseemly must enter the assembly (verse 22), but all should be done 'decently and in order' (1 Corinthians 14.40). And the closing part of this 'Church order' – if this description is correct – contains a comprehensive prayer for the entire fellowship (verse 23), expressed in the confidence that God will hear and bless (verse 24).[15]

Martin then proceeds to point out that in 1 Corinthians 14 a similar series of apostolic counsels on the subject of public worship meets us – with the exception of the injunction 'do not quench the Spirit', advice which the Corinthian church certainly did not need. If Martin's suggestions about 1 Thessalonians 5 are correct, they confirm (if confirmation is needed) the impression given in 1 Corinthians that prophecy was a gift exercised within the context of congregational worship and closely associated with, if not actually employed in, the activities of prayer and praise.[16]

While the exhortation in 1 Thessalonians 5.20, the allusion to the gift of prophecy in Romans 12.6 and the somewhat ambiguous and not very informative references to Christian prophets in Ephesians (which will be considered later in this chapter) will permit us to assume that prophesying was a common phenomenon in the churches, it is to 1 Corinthians 12–14 that we must look for Paul's views on the subject. The frequency of reference to Christian *prophētai* in these chapters may imply (if it is significant at all) that it was in Corinth that those who prophesied first emerged and were treated as a relatively fixed group within a congregation. That they did form a distinct group seems clear from 12.28 which names the offices or functionaries appointed by God ('apostles', 'prophets', 'teachers', etc.); from the question 'Are all prophets? (*mē pantes prophētai*;)' in v. 29, and from 14.37 'If anyone thinks that he is a prophet

...', which would be meaningless if there was no identifiable position in the church so entitled. The arguments adduced in support of the contrary view (i.e. that prophets were not a distinct grouping) are easily disposed of: 14.5 and 24 refer to an idealised or hypothetical state of affairs, rather than to the actual situation; and 14.31a refers, not to the whole congregation but to all the prophets (the change from the second to the third person plural in the Greek of the clauses in v. 31 suggests a different understanding of 'all').[17] Of course Paul, in common with other New Testament writers, notably Luke and the author of Revelation, is aware that the gift of prophecy belongs potentially to the whole Church (since the Holy Spirit's inspiration was available to all) and that therefore any Christian (including a female one, 1 Cor. 11.5) might *on occasion* prophesy: but this does not mean that all Christians were 'prophets' in the narrower sense, the 'professional prophets' (*die berufsmässige Propheten*[18]), those who came to hold a recognised and authoritative position in a congregation by reason of their prominent and continuing exercise of the spiritual gift,[19] and who, from the evidence of Paul's letters, do not seem to have engaged in an itinerant ministry as the prophets mentioned in the Didache did.

When we seek to discover from 1 Corinthians 14 Paul's view of the prophets and their activity, we find that the information is presented in tension with the Corinthians' understanding of prophecy. Presumably Paul derived his view of the phenomenon from Old Testament/Jewish models and possibly from contact with prophets influenced by such models (like those in Acts), whereas the Corinthians' understanding seems to reflect the Greek ecstatic model: those who practised according to it were employed in the mystery cults and their activities and experience were described (as we pointed out earlier, pp. 29, 33) by terms like *mainomai, mantis, enthousiasmos*, etc., terms which are not used of New Testament prophets. As to the importance of this difference and the tension it created there can be no doubt: Paul, himself possessed of the Spirit for his apostolic ministry of teaching and preaching and therefore a prophet *par excellence*, calls into question the adequacy of the manifestation of religious ecstasy that was accepted among the Corinthians as the legitimising sign of genuine spirit-inspiration: he is on the offensive against the claim that glossolalia[20] was the *sine qua non* of authentic prophetic utterance. That the assault on the Corinthians' lofty estimate of glossolalia is Paul's main concern from early in chapter 12 onwards is indicated by the fact that in the enumeration of spiritual gifts (in 12.8–10, 28, 29–30) glossolalia (with its interpretation) is on each occasion mentioned last, and it is the only one of the three gifts listed after 'healers' (*charismata iamatōn*) in verse 28 that is taken up in verse 30. Because Paul's words about prophecy have this thrust, the information given may well be incomplete, since he may be stressing only (or mainly) what can be differentiated from or contrasted with glossolalia, and it may be lacking in balance, for no phenomenon – religious or otherwise – is quite fairly accounted for by reference to what it is not.

Despite this caveat, we can learn a good deal from 1 Corinthians 14 about prophecy – a spiritual gift which Paul esteemed highly as verse 1 makes clear ('Make love your aim and earnestly desire the spiritual gifts, especially that you may prophesy', cf. 1 Thess. 5.19 ff.), as does the fact that in all the various lists and discussions of charismata in his letters the only constant member is 'prophecy' or 'prophet'. Whereas the man who speaks in a tongue – and his 'inspiration' is not in question – holds a kind of private discourse with the divine which is incomprehensible to others, he who prophesies speaks to (and for) men, and what he utters is intelligible and profitable edification, *oikodomē*. Vielhauer rightly suggests[21] that 'edification' here has both a negative and a positive sense: it expresses the rejection of self-sufficient and over-indulgent religious individualism and egoism which exhausts itself in the production of spiritual phenomena that focus attention on their sources; positively, it denotes the helping of the other person, not only as an individual but as a member of the Church, since the congregation is not edified or built up except through the word intelligibly addressed to another person and received by him as encouragement or admonition and as consolation.

The two words *paraklēsis* and *paramythia* which define or show the nature of *oikodomē* – and the three when taken together provide the nearest approach in Paul's letters to a definition of the prophetic function – are difficult to distinguish: nevertheless, it may be valuable to discover how informative they are in the context of this particular chapter. Verse 31 asserts that the purpose of prophecy is that all members of the congregation may receive 'from speech with the mind (*tō noï*): instruction and exhortation (*manthanōsin kai parakalōntai*) to bring about spiritual growth. The immediately preceding verses (26 ff.) do not provide us with knowledge of the content of the instruction and exhortation. They tell us that, in trying to restore order to proceedings that were potentially very confusing, Paul insists on limiting the number speaking (either in tongues or prophetically) to two or three, and that may imply that the utterances would be longer than those to which the Corinthians were accustomed. They may have expected only a series of short, ejaculatory words of revelation, unconnected with one another: but if only a few prophesy, and one at a time (*kath' hena*), greater orderliness and greater coherence of message will be achieved. Indeed the congregation as a whole will learn only when what they hear is intelligible and coherent. We may therefore reasonably infer that prophetic *paraklēsis* is expressed in sustained utterance.

Something more about the character of the prophetic *paraklēsis* which upbuilds can be learned from 14.24 f. The suggestion that these verses are an example of Pauline irony and nothing more is quite unacceptable. G. Dautzenberg[22] propounds the view that the verses describe an abnormal, or even purely hypothetical, situation and are constructed by Paul in order to prove (by means of the presence of the phenomenon of cardiognosis) the apocalyptic character of prophecy in the Church (cf. 1 Cor. 4.5[b]). But charismatic insight into and disclosure of the innermost hearts of individuals is not something that belongs to the End-time alone: it was characteristic of Jesus' prophetic ministry and indeed is a characteristic of the phenomenon of prophecy wherever it appears in the history of religions.

Much more convincing, in our opinion, is the generally held view that by including, intentionally, outsiders and non-believers in his discussion, Paul demonstrates his desire to affirm the missionary function of the word, even of the inspired prophetic word spoken in worship. According to 14.24 f. the effects of prophesying, not on members of the congregation but on an unbeliever who happens to visit a service of worship, will be to bring about conviction, conversion and the acknowledgment of the divine presence in the midst of the assembled congregation. The chance hearer of prophecy is convicted (*elenchetai*):[23] his sin or unfaith is exposed and repentance demanded. Secondly, he is in some sense judged or examined (*anakrinetai*), either in the court of conscience or by God, speaking and acting in the prophet(s), who is calling the unbeliever to account, in anticipation as it were of the final judgment. Thirdly, 'the secrets of his heart are disclosed'. Although many have suggested it, this does not refer to the practice of mind-reading: if that part of the prophet's stock-in-trade was being exercised, Allo's wry comment would be in order: 'What profane person would have wanted to expose himself to risk in such meetings?'[24] It is much more likely that what is meant is that, on the basis of the prophet's utterance (cf. 2 Cor. 4.2), the unbeliever is made aware, for the first time perhaps, certainly in a comprehensible manner, that his life has been under the power of sin. 'The moral truth of Christianity', says C. K. Barrett,[25] 'proclaimed in inspired speech' ... the prophetic Word of God which is sharper than any two-edged sword (Heb. 4.12) are sufficient to convict the sinner. God's word effects its entrance through the conscience and then creates religious conviction.' When the convicted unbeliever demonstrates his sense of unworthiness and confesses his awareness of the immediacy of God's presence ('God is really among you', v. 25), the eschatological promises of Scripture (Isa. 45.14 and Zech. 8.23) are fulfilled. In the conversion of the unbeliever there is a genuine sign for believers that God is effectively present in the assembly through the prophetic ministry, rather than in showy, ecstatic performances that benefit only the performer. Bornkamm's comment is strikingly relevant:

Without wanting to ignore the peculiarity of the speaking

in tongues, we will have to see in this passage the passionate attack of Paul on all irresponsible speaking in worship that does not concern itself with those on the fringe and those outside, and that with self-satisfied skill makes use of an esoteric language or even a Christian 'jargon', by contrast with which a stranger must feel himself hopelessly on the outside.[26]

E. Schweizer[27] makes the same point and observes that in the last resort Paul would allow no distinction to be drawn between prophetic proclamation to Church members and to those from outside: what happens to the latter, according to 14.25, is not fundamentally different from what happens to every Church member when he really hears God's word afresh and accepts again what he has already learnt. In this way the individual believer is edified by the prophetic utterance whilst the congregation as a whole is edified by the response to the word by the outsider.

Prophecy edifies also because it serves as 'a sign for believers' (14.22). The polemical thrust of this verse suggests that the Corinthians maintained that glossolalia serves as a sign for believers, i.e. as a proof of high pneumatic status and authority.[28] This Paul refutes and, with the help of Isaiah 28.11–12 – the only relevant passage in the Old Testament which mentions unintelligible utterance – asserts that the incomprehensibility of glossolalia is a sign, not for believers but for unbelievers – a sign of divine judgment, not of divine pleasure – a sign, that is, not of closeness to God but of their distance from God.[29] What can be described as a 'sign' (for believers) is prophecy (the word 'sign' is demanded by the balance of the sentence, though it is lacking in the Greek), but a 'sign' in what sense? Hardly a 'sign' of judgment as in 22a, for Paul could not then deny it that role in respect of unbelievers (22b), since, as we have just seen, in verses 24 f. prophecy serves primarily as a sign of judgment, bringing conviction to unbelievers in their lack of faith. The parallel between glossolalia and prophecy at this point means only that each functions as a sign, not a sign of judgment, but a sign. 'Prophecy is a sign, as glossolalia is a sign', says J. D. G. Dunn,[30] 'in that both reveal God's attitude – the one God's attitude towards wilful unbelief (hence a sign of judgment), the other God's attitude towards faith. Prophecy by its inspiration *and* content reveals that God is present in the midst of the assembly – even the unbeliever confesses this (vv. 24 f.). As glossolalia confirms the unbeliever in his unbelief (v. 23 – "You are mad" = God is *not* here), so prophecy confirms the believer in his faith (v. 25 – God is here).' 'Sign for believers' is, in the context, simply a way of affirming that prophecy is of edifying value in the assembly, whereas glossolalia in itself has no value in the assembly since it is merely self-edifying (14.4).

Prophecy builds up or edifies the community because it often came as a word of revelation. It seems likely from 14.26 and 30 that the possession and public declaration of a revelation was the characteristic, if not exclusive contribution of a prophet to the assembly's worship. But what is meant by 'a revelation' (v. 26) or 'a word of revelation' (v. 6)? In the light of the list of spiritual gifts in 12.8 f. it may be related to 'the utterance of wisdom' mentioned there, i.e. mature, insightful, practical instruction and exhortation: but it could go further and include the intelligibile communication of some supernatural disclosure of God's purpose, or even of some ecstatic auditory experience (2 Cor. 12.1, 7). Whatever precise content we attempt to give to 'a revelation', the mere reception of an *apokalypsis* does not constitute a prophecy until it is publicly and intelligibly proclaimed: only then does it build up the church, exhort and console, for the 'word of revelation' may also be (perhaps we ought to say, should also be) a challenging or comforting word.

Now if conviction and conversion (14.24 f.), disclosure of 'revelations', as well as encouragement and comfort are all associated with prophetic speaking in worship, what kind of utterance is it? It is not simply teaching (*didachē*), though all intelligible communication has a teaching element in it: nor is it simply preaching, in the sense of proclamation (*kērygma*) to believer and unbeliever alike. Elsewhere[31] I have suggested that the category of *pastoral preaching* may be a useful designation for the Christian prophet's speech, and we have seen signs of its appropriateness when discussing prophecy in Acts. This suggestion owes its inspiration to two significant observations made by M. A. Chevallier and F. J. Leenhardt. At the end of his examination of 1 Corinthians 14 the former writes: 'Prophecy has as its function the illumination by the revelation of God of the life of Christians, whether as a community, or as individuals';[32] and with reference to Romans 12.6 Leenhardt says, 'The prophet is not the man of predictions, but of preaching who implants the Word of God into the life of a community, who gives words or orders that are concrete and precise.'[33] Do not these two statements point in the direction of classifying prophetic utterance as pastoral preaching which by its very nature offers guidance and instruction?

Support for this view can be found in the book of the Revelation, if not in its entirety, then certainly in the circular letters of chapters 2–3 (see chapter Three above, pp. 83–84) and from the relevant material on prophets in Acts (see chapter Four): but it can be defended from the chapters in 1 Corinthians we are considering. Already we have noted that when he is describing the effects of prophetic speaking Paul uses terms like 'upbuild' (*oikodomē, oikodomein*), 'learn' (*manthanō*) which refer, at least in part, to instruction. To these we may be justified in adding the verb *katēchein*. In 1 Corinthians 14.19 Paul says, 'In the assembly I would rather speak five words with my mind (*tō noï mou*) in order to instruct others (*hina kai allous katēchēsō*) than ten thousand words in a tongue.' In the context of a chapter in which glossolalia and prophecy are contrasted in terms of the unintelligibility of the one and the comprehensibility of the other, speech with the mind (i.e. intelligent and intelligible speech) may well refer, implicitly, to prophetic speech:[34] if so, its aim is instruction. The rare word *katēcheō* is normally used with the meaning of giving instruction in the content of the faith,[35] and Galatians 6.6 suggests the presence in the congregation of a (professional) teaching ministry carried out by *katēchountes*, the equivalent of the *didaskaloi* of 1 Corinthians 12.28.

Is there any idea of instruction inherent in the terms *parakaleisthai/paraklēsis* and *paramythia* which are also used by Paul with reference to the purpose or the effects of prophetic speaking? It is, as we have said, difficult to draw any sharp distinction between the meanings of *paraklēsis* and *paramythia* in 1 Corinthians 14.3: both are characterised by the twofoldness of admonition and comfort, and these, in turn, are grounded in the gospel itself, which is both gift and task, consolation and demand. However, if we confine our investigation of the meaning of *paraklēsis/parakaleō* to Paul's usage, we may sum up its varied nuances (plead, admonish, console) in the words of H. Schlier: 'The word which we translate as "exhort" designates, in the vocabulary of the Apostle, a kind of recall to order, which is at one and the same time a request and an encouragement.'[36] The request may be for men to accept the gospel (2 Cor. 5.20; 1 Thess. 2.3), but it may also be admonitory, addressed to those already within faith and designed to lead them to conduct worthy of the Gospel, and here Phil. 1.1 (where *paraklēsis* and *paramythion* are found together) is important, for if the verse is correctly interpreted as referring to the presence of *paraklēsis* and loving consolation in the common life of the Body of Christ, we may then ask whence these are derived. Is it from worship, from the ministries of preaching and teaching, as well as from the spiritual fellowship?

But even more significant is 1 Thess. 2.12 where Paul describes his work in relation to the Thessalonians as individual Christians in these words: 'we exhorted each one of you and encouraged you (*parakalountes hymas kai paramythoumenoi*) and charged you to lead a life worthy of God, who calls you into his own kingdom and glory'. This is the outworking of the charisma of pastoral exhortation (cf. Rom. 12.8 where the charisma of *paraklēsis* may fall within the scope of prophetic activity), and, indeed, Paul's letters are examples of this *paraklēsis*. It is exhortatory preaching; it constantly refers back to the work of salvation as its presupposition and basis; its locus is normally in the worshipping congregation and it contributes to the guidance, correction, encouragement – in short, the *oikodomē* of the community. The purpose of *paraklēsis* overlaps with that of intelligible *prophēteia* and that of *didachē*; and Ellis may well be right in suggesting that *paraklēsis* has a special connection with Christian prophecy, even when that connection is not explicitly expressed.[37]

In asserting that New Testament prophecy functions, at least in part, as what might be called 'pastoral instruction', and that the term *paraklēsis*, so closely connected with prophetic speaking, is to be interpreted often in terms of exhortatory teaching, we become immediately aware of its special continuity with one strand of the Old Testament understanding of prophecy. A view of New Testament prophecy that allows it to include a broadly paraenetical function has a significant precedent in the Deuteronomistic conception of prophecy (cf. pp. 15 ff. above) in which the activity of prophets is largely concerned with (legal) instruction and with warning people to change their ways (cf. 2 Kgs. 17.13 f.; Zech. 1. 4–6, and in later Judaism, Jub. 1.12; 1 Enoch 89.53 f.; Jos., *Antiq.* x.60). It is this kind of understanding of the prophetic role that is carried forward when the New Testament attributes to prophets in the Church the task, not only of kerygmatic proclamation but of warning, instructing and correcting the congregation and individuals on the fringe, of guiding Christians towards conduct more worthy of the Gospel by the communication of the *paraklēsis* that upbuilds. As *pastoral* preachers the New Testament prophets teach and give instruction on what the Christian way requires of individual believers and of the community as a whole. As an objection to this view it may be argued that a teacher or instructor works with materials already known and makes them relevant to his hearer's needs, whereas a prophet's utterance cannot and should not be dissociated from the impartation of knowledge not already available and which does not come to him by the application of rational thought, but only by 'revelation'. Can a prophet exercise a teaching function and still fulfil his prophetic calling? The claim made earlier (pp. 13 f.) that divinely inspired and authoritative Old Testament prophets could and did employ traditional materials points in the direction of an affirmative answer: in the case of New Testament prophets that answer may be confirmed, for the prophet is not the only leader in the Church whose speech is inspired by the Spirit, nor does his every word have to convey truth hitherto unknown if it is to be genuinely prophetic. One important restraint upon the prophet is the demand that he should exercise the gift *kata tēn analogian tēs pisteōs* (Rom. 12.6), i.e., as von Campenhausen and Käsemann and others interpret the phrase, 'in agreement with the faith as proclaimed by the apostles', the *fides quae creditur*.[38] Moreover, Paul is emphatic in his demand that what the prophet says must be intelligent and intelligible and what he utters 'with the mind' may be 'teaching' for those who hear. It is the glossolalist, not the prophet, who *speaks* mysteries (i.e. hidden secrets or riddles with no solution) in the spirit (14.2): and the ecstatic has his 'revelations' (2 Cor. 12.1, 7). But these are private experiences and do not edify the community. The prophet *knows* 'mysteries' (13.2) but he must convey or proclaim them to the community 'with the mind', and their *communication* can surely be described, in some sense, as 'teaching'.

If we ask what kind of 'mystery' could be revealed by the prophet that would build up the community and offer *paraklēsis* and *paramythia*, 1 Corinthians 12–14 provides no information. The possibility that 1 Corinthians 2.6–16 was, in origin, a prophetic revelation of a mystery is explored by G. Dautzenberg[39], but, despite its attractive features, the suggestion depends on the virtual identification of *pneumatikoi* with prophets, and that cannot be assumed and is, in our view, incorrect.[40] The term *pneumatikoi* seems to be a general designation of those endowed with spiritual gifts and perhaps, in particular, the gift of inspired speech (to sing, pray, teach, interpret), whereas *prophētēs* has a more restricted connotation.[41] It is frequently claimed that 1 Thessalonians 4.15 ff. is an example of a prophetic revelation which would bring comfort: 'for this we declare to you by the word of the Lord (*en logō Kyriou*) that we who are alive, who are left until the coming of the Lord, shall not precede those who have fallen asleep ...'. But is this 'word of the Lord' a new revelation received from the risen Christ and prophetically announced? May it not mean, as Rigaux and others maintain, that Paul goes back, not to a single saying of Jesus but to his apocalyptic teaching as a whole, in order to validate his message and clarify the issues which agitated some of his correspondents?[42] It is with much greater assurance that we may point to Romans 11.25 f. and 1 Corinthians 15.51 as examples of Paul's prophetic unveiling of *mysteria*. The disclosure of the latter mystery – 'We shall not all sleep, but we shall all be changed...' – does, without detriment to its function in the context, offer comfort to the reader. The mystery 'that all Israel shall be saved' is the climax of Romans 9–11, but especially of 11.16–24, which warns Gentile Christians not to be arrogant or complacent. The revelation of this *mystērion* is not simply proclamation: it depends on inspired insight into the meaning of Scripture (Isa. 59.20 f.) and is prophetic instruction 'I do not want you to be ignorant...', (11.25) which builds up the Church, giving warning and, as in the case of 1 Corinthians 15.51, comfort as well. If Christian prophets revealed mysteries in the manner of the Apostle – and we cannot know whether that was the case or not – then that activity belonged to their ministry of *paraklēsis* and *paramythia*: their inspired knowledge and intelligible communication of the eschatological secrets – and prophets in Paul do not predict earthly events of the future – is turned to the service of the community in advice, encouragement and warning. G. Friedrich has summed up well this aspect of the role of Christian prophets in the Pauline churches:

> The prophet is the spirit-endowed counsellor of the community who tells it what to do in specific situations, who blames and praises, whose preaching contains admonition and comfort, the call for repentence and promise.[43]

That, we submit, may be legitimately called a ministry of pastoral teaching and instruction.

If it is argued that Christian prophets exercised a teaching ministry in the Church, which included pastoral preaching and instruction in Christian living, have we not trespassed into a description of the functions associated with *didaskaloi* ('teachers'), another fairly fixed circle in the communities (1 Cor. 12.28 f.; Rom. 12.7)? The presence in the Church of 'teachers' is not in doubt, but certainty about their function is lacking. They are spirit-endowed; their teaching must be intelligible if it is to be profitable (1 Cor. 14.6). But what did they teach? The view associated with Dibelius that the specific activity of the 'teacher' was the provision of *paraenesis* requires modification. If *paraklēsis* – which is certainly part of the prophet's task – includes guidance in the Christian way of life, then *paraenesis* cannot have been the exclusive ministry of 'teachers'. Admittedly, 1 Corinthians 4.17 states that the content of what Paul taught in every church was 'my ways (*hodoi mou*) in Christ', and when the rabbinic background of the phrase is accepted (i.e. that Greek *hodoi* is the equivalent of the Hebrew *h^alākôth*, from *hlk* 'to go, walk') this comes to denote the *rules* for Christian living (cf. also Rom. 16.17). But should one presume to describe the Christian teacher's function on the basis of what Paul says *he* always and everywhere taught? No: and one ought to be equally wary of describing the Christian prophet's role and activity solely on the basis of Paul's prophetic experience and characteristics. It is exceedingly doubtful that all Christian teachers and prophets were gifted with an authority and an inspiration like Paul's.

Recent scholarship is correct in claiming that the characteristic feature of the 'teacher's' work is to be found in his relation to tradition.[44] In the words of H. von Campenhausen, 'teaching is concerned with handing on and expounding the Christ-tradition, with impressing on men the precepts and propositions of the faith, and above all with the exegesis of the Old Testament as understood by the young Church'.[45] The teacher was preeminently the interpreter of the Old Testament with reference to the meaning of the Christ-event for the Church (cf. Rom. 15.4), in much the same way as the Teacher of Righteousness or Rightful Teacher of Qumran expounded the prophecies of the Old Testament with reference to the situation and life of the sectarian community. Obviously the meaning of *didaskein* and *didachē* has a certain fluidity in Paul's usage, and it would be wrong to make a too neat differentiation between the functions of teacher and prophet. Both instruct and preach, but the characteristic emphasis of the teacher may be found in his expository work: that is different from, but not opposed to, prophetic revelation (even of Scripture's meaning, as in the case of Rom. 11.25 f.) and to the ministry that builds up the congregation by offering correction, guidance and pastoral exhortation. If these are in fact part of the prophet's task in the Christian assembly, then we are provided with not only a line of continuity with one strand of the Old Testament under-standing of the prophetic function, but also with a line of conti-nuity between the classical prophets of the Old Testament and Christian prophets in the New. New Testament Christianity must have been aware, not only of those prophetic words in its Scriptures that could be interpreted in relation to the com-ing, the fate and the significance of Jesus but also of the utterances of Amos, Jeremiah and others who delivered a message to the life-situation of the people they addressed, in words of consolation, judgment, guidance or exhortation. In their pastoral preaching the prophets of the New Testament continue this aspect of the ancient prophetic task and ministry.

It would, however, be quite wrong and unfair to the evidence to claim, or even to give the impression, that the role of pastoral preaching was the only role allotted to Christian prophets by Paul. In 1 Corinthians 14.29 Paul says, 'Let two or three pro-phets speak, and let the others weigh what is said' (*diakrinetōsan*). Who are 'the others'? Although a strong case can be made out for regarding them as the other members of the congregation, i.e. the hearers in general,[46] it seems more probable that in this particular context 'the other prophets' is meant:[47] the observa-tion in verse 31 that 'you can all prophesy one by one' cannot mean everybody present, but 'all upon whom the spirit of pro-phecy comes'. Now in 1 Corinthians 12.10 'the ability to distin-guish between spirits' (*diakriseis pneumatōn*) is regarded as a gift of the Spirit, a charisma not given to all, but in the sequence it forms a pair with 'prophecy' (*prophēteia*) and cannot be regarded as independent of that gift: in fact, 'distinguishing be-tween spirits' provides a test of prophetic utterance and a con-trol against its abuse, and, as such, would probably have been exercised mostly, if not exclusively, by prophets. But what does 'distinguishing between spirits' or 'discerning of spirits' mean?

An unusual view is offered by G. Dautzenberg[48] to the effect that *diakriseis pneumatōn* means 'interpreting the utterances of the Spirit'. In order to show that *diakrinō* can mean 'explain' or 'interpret', he uses, primarily, examples from related words such as *synkrinō*, as if a verbal root could be expected to carry the same meaning everywhere. His examples of *diakrinō* and *diakrisis* from Philo (and LXX Symmachus Gen. 40.8) reveal that the terms could be used with reference to interpreting (or perhaps understanding, even evaluating) dreams: but this is not their usual sense for the biblical writers. Dautzenberg does not provide a single example of this meaning for *diakrinō* or *diakrisis* from the New Testament, the Septuagint, or the Apostolic Fathers (Hermas, *Sim.* 2.1 is scarcely convincing). Furthermore, to give *pneumata* the sense 'utterances of the Spirit' would require much stronger defence than is provided. Dautzenberg's argument must be judged unconvincing. Ulrich B. Müller is surely correct in observing that since Paul insists that prophecy must be intelligible and understandable, what would be the need for the exercise of a gift of explanation![49]

In company with most scholars we interpret *diakrinō* and *diakrisis* in terms of distinguishing, evaluating or discerning (with a view to separation): but what are the *pneumata* so evaluated? It is very unlikely that they are angelic beings,[50] for Paul nowhere speaks of angelic mediation (except in unequivocally negative tones; cf. Rom. 8.38; 2 Cor. 11.14, 12.7; Gal. 1.8; Col. 2.18) now that the Spirit has been given in its fullness: it is probably too precise to claim that by *pneumata* (in 1 Cor. 12.10) Paul means *pneumatika*, 'spiritual gifts': it seems best to allow the word its more general, unrestricted sense – 'distinguishing between spirits', i.e. between the Holy Spirit and various other spirits at work in people claiming to be inspired. This could include the evaluation of (supposed) prophets, as well as of miracle-workers, glossolalists, teachers, etc. The plural form (*diakriseis*) supports this interpretation, indicating the ability to make discriminating judgments in various types of situation. A particular instance of the exercise of this gift of evaluation, in our view, is 1 Corinthians 14.29: there prophecies are tested, weighed, evaluated in order to determine their source of inspiration, their genuine or counterfeit quality. It may be that 14.34–36 (the command for women to keep silence in the assembly) also has to do with the need to test prophetic inspira-

tion, if the women members of the Corinthian church were –
like the daughters of Philip in Acts 21.9 – in possession of the
prophetic gift. Perhaps some women had abused the gift and
Paul warns against unseemly behaviour in an assembly where
the worship was liable to get quickly out of hand (11.17 ff.) and
notably where women were concerned (cf. 11.5–16).[51] If this
interpretation is plausible, it brings 14.33b–36 – often regarded
as an awkward interpolation – into the flow and theme of the
chapter. That 1 Corinthians 12.3 provides *a* test of inspired
speech can hardly be doubted, but it is not a test for true and
false prophecy: Paul is concerned to correct the ignorance of
the Corinthians concerning spiritual gifts in general (including,
of course, inspired utterances), an area which was unknown to
them when they served idols.

Before we leave 1 Corinthians 12–14 a few more points regarding 'prophecy' may be made.

(1) If our argument that 14.29 allows prophets to evaluate
or test the inspiration of other prophets is correct, then it is
implied that utterances of New Testament prophets (at least
those in Corinth) are not always accorded the unchallengeable
authority which the 'Thus says the Lord' of the Old Testament
prophets possessed. Indeed, in certain circumstances, one prophet has to make way for another (14.30). The reason for this
regulation is the desire for orderliness and the fact that 'the
spirits of prophets are subject to prophets'. When we interpret
'spirits' here, not as angelic spirits, nor as the individual, human
spirits of the prophets, but as the manifestations of the Spirit
at work in prophets, we see again a kind of restraint upon the
exercise of the prophetic gift such as would have been inconsistent with the Old Testament view of prophetic declaration. But orderliness in worship was not an issue for those who
were impelled to affirm 'Thus says the Lord'! In respect of self-
restraint, as in the matter of evaluation, the prophets of the Old
Testament – with their indisputable authority and sense of compulsion to speak – are not in the same class as New Testament
prophets: nevertheless, we cannot deny the name 'prophet'
to those to whom Paul gives it: we may note that he himself,
rather than the prophets he speaks of, stands more firmly in the

tradition of those who declared 'Thus says the Lord'. But never does Paul despise the prophets in the Christian community, even if they do not possess the divinely authorised messenger status oᶠ the Old Testament prophets: on the contrary, he affirms that the ministry of prophets edifies the Church and that the gift is to be zealously sought (14.1).

(2) Paul urges the Corinthians to use the gifts they have or want (especially the gift of prophecy) in such a way as to build up the Church. Why should they do this? Because speaking intelligibly and worshipping in an orderly way reflect the best gift of all, love (*agapē*) the love which 'is patient and kind ... not jealous or boastful ... (and) does not insist on its own way'.

Whether written before or composed specifically for this letter to Corinth, chapter 13 is necessary to Paul's purpose before he can introduce the content of chapter 14.[52] And chapter 13 itself indicates some interesting things about prophecy. (*a*) It is distinct from ordinary human language ('tongues of men') and from speech in the language of angels: the latter (cf. Test.Job 48–50, where Job's daughters speak in the dialects of various classes of angels) may have been the original label for what came to be called *glōssais lalein*, under the influence of the use of *glōssa* to mean 'incomprehensible words'[53] (*b*) 'Prophecy' is co-ordinated with 'understanding all mysteries and all knowledge', that is, with insight into the hidden purposes of God made known in the Gospel and with awareness of 'the moral and other implications to be drawn from the data of the Christian revelation'.[54] This coincides with much of what we have already said about prophecy upbuilding the Church through revelation and pastoral preaching. But it would be unwise to put too much emphasis on the language of 1 Corinthians 13.2: Paul may simply be piling up an argument on the basis of hypothetical superlatives. (*c*) Prophecy will cease (13.8) – and Paul uses a strong word *katargeō* which means 'to render ineffective, and therefore useless or obsolete' – because it is imperfect (v. 9, *ek merous*), that is, fragmentary, giving only a partial knowledge of the subject it treats, viz. the truth about God: full and complete knowledge will be attained in the consummation. And prophecy is 'imperfect' because 'we see in a mirror dimly'. This phrase seems to be an allusion to Numbers 12.6–8 which concerns God's method of speech with Moses ('not in dark speech', *ou di' ainigmatōn*). Dautzenberg claims[55] that the use of Num. 12.6–8 here is similar to the way it was employed in Jewish apocalyptic literature and therefore asserts that early Christian prophecy must be understood largely in the light of Jewish apocalyptic.

But to draw such a far-reaching conclusion from what may be no more than a coincidental similarity of usage is unjustifiable. 'We' – and that includes Paul himself, prophet *par excellence* though he may be – are now in the position of prophets who see *di'ainigmatōn*, in riddles or dark speech, and perhaps 'in a vision or mirror' (Num. 12.6), but 'then' we shall see face to face (as Moses did), a reference to seeing God at the consummation. The mirror imagery suggests both the indirectness and the incompleteness of the revelation or knowledge presently received, but need not imply that the image is distorted. If we apply this to prophecy (as is legitimate, in view of the allusion to Moses in Num. 12.6–8, and because v. 12 in 1 Cor. 13 is a ground for v. 9) it means that the prophet receives revelation from God in some kind of indirect manner, that what he sees and learns is not the whole picture, but only a glimpse into reality which may be difficult to understand and interpret. Only at the End, when the perfect comes (i.e. at the parousia) will he – and all men – see 'face to face' (cf. Deut. 34.10, concerning Moses whom the Lord knew 'face to face'), i.e. with complete clarity and certainty: *then* there will be no need for the gift of prophecy. Important though it is for the life and up-building up of the Church the gift is both limited and temporary.

From the evidence set forth so far in this chapter we may draw the following conclusions. (i) In Corinth there was a fairly well defined circle of recognised prophets (1 Cor. 12.28, 14.29 ff.): from this, and from Romans 12.8, we may presume that there were a number of prophets in each or most of the Pauline congregations. (ii) Whereas only an apostle might exercise apostolic authority, anyone might prophesy: indeed, Paul expected that members of the Corinthian assembly other than the prophets would be inspired to prophesy (14.5, 24, 31 [?]), the only difference between the prophets and other members of the church being that the former prophesied regularly and the latter only occasionally. (iii) Prophetic authority derived only from prophetic inspiration, not from an official community choice of particular individuals, and, unlike Paul's apostolic (and prophetic) authority, the prophet's authority in speaking was subject to evaluation and assessment (by other prophets) in terms of its genuinely inspired (i.e. by the Spirit of Christ) quality. (iv) Paul gives to prophecy a key role in the building up of the community, and the terms he uses in connection with it suggest that it may be regarded as functioning, at least in part, as pastoral preaching or exhortation. (v) Prophecy must always be intelligible and intelligent speech: even 'revelation' is not prophecy until it is publicly declared in an understand-able manner. (vi) Prophecy is partial and temporary: its use-fulness – though second only to that of apostles – will cease when the consummation, the parousia, comes. (vii) Prophecy was exercised in the context of the worship of the Christian assembly.

Now we turn to the references to prophets in the letter to the Ephesians, the Pauline authorship of which is still in doubt, de-spite recent arguments to the contrary.[56] In Ephesians 4.11 we have a clear reference to 'prophets' as one of the gifts of Christ to his church: the fact that they are preceded, in the list, by 'apostles' is in accordance with general New Testament usage; but that they are followed by only 'evangelists, pastors and teachers' may suggest a post-Pauline tendency to look to regular offices as the guarantee of ecclesiastical unity, rather than to the ability of the charismatically endowed community to regu-late its own life. On the other hand, the obvious parallels between Ephesians 4.3 and 1 Corinthians 12.13, between Ephesians 4.7 and Romans 12.3 and 1 Corinthians 12.11, and between Ephesians 4.12 ff. and Romans 12.4 ff. and 1 Corin-thians 12.14–27 may be taken as evidence of the parallel between the situations envisaged in Ephesians 4, Romans 12, and 1 Corinthians 12; in which case, the 'gifts' of Ephesians 4.11 are less likely to be offices than regular ministries (within a charismatic community) like the 'prophets and teachers' of I Corinthians 12.28 and the 'overseers and deacons' of Philippians 1.1.[57]

In Ephesians 2.20 and 3.5 'apostles and prophets' are mentioned together, in the first case as 'the foundation (*themelion*) of God's household' (which could suggest a second-generation veneration of first-generation leaders), and, in the second passage, as those to whom the 'mystery' of the inclusion of the Gentiles was made known by the Spirit, and nowhere in the New Testament is there any indication that such a revelation was made to (New Testament) prophets: it was a revelation given to apostles, Peter and Paul (cf. Acts 1.8, 10.15, 34 f., 47 f., 11.9–18, 15.7, 14–20, 28, 22.21, 26,17 f.; Gal. 1.16). In view of the fact that there is no definite article before 'prophets' in the phrase 'the (holy) apostles and prophets' in these two verses, it is quite possible that two distinct groups (apostles and New Testament prophets) are not implied by the 'and': 'the apostles who are also prophets' is a possible translation and, in our view, the correct one.[58] J. Murphy-O'Connor observes that the term 'apostle' signifies the mission and the term 'prophet' the character of that mission and the means by which it is exercised.[59] In other words, what we have in Ephesians 2.20 and 3.5 is a twofold designation of the founders of the church and of those to whom there was revealed the 'mystery' of the Gentiles' inclusion therein: they are 'apostles' in that they are the authoritative witnesses to, indeed the representatives of, Jesus; and they are 'prophets' by virtue of the fact that they are the authentic messengers and agents of the revelation they received. Although this manner of speaking of apostles (and of prophets) is unusual in Paul, and although there seems to be a change or development of view between Ephesians 2.20 and I Corinthians 3.10–11 (where Christ is the 'foundation' of the Church), these are not decisive reasons against the authenticity of Ephesians: after all, in I Corinthians 3.10 Paul claims to have laid the foundation ('Christ'), presumably by his preaching, and that is tantamount to uniting in himself the functions of apostle and prophet, as well as being quite consistent with what Ephesians 2.20 asserts.

Finally, in the Pastorals – which seem to bear witness to a situation in which both Spirit and charisma have become in effect subordinate to office, to ritual and to tradition – it is not surprising that 'prophetic utterance' (*prophēteia*) appears to belong to the past (1 Tim. 1.18) and was part of Timothy's ordination service (4.14), perhaps in the sense of the 'liturgy of the Word'.[60] Is prophecy on the way to becoming, or has it already become, a formalised part of good ecclesiastical order? The phrase 'The Spirit expressly says ...' (1 Tim. 4.1) might imply continuing prophetic activity: but more probably it is an appeal to a prophetic word from the past, that is, before the 'later times' which are present to the author:[61] indeed the phrase may already be an established formula to introduce a word from tradition, like the regular rabbinic formula 'The Holy Spirit cries and says ...' which always introduces scriptural quotations. Paul's understanding of the Spirit was far more dynamic than that, and his conception of prophecy much less institutionalised: prophecy, for Paul, was a vital, widely available, edifying charisma, as the main portion of this chapter has amply shown.

CHAPTER SIX

OTHER BOOKS AND TRADITIONS ASSOCIATED WITH CHRISTIAN PROPHETISM

With varying degrees of assurance, claims have been made for the emergence from Christian prophetic circles of certain New Testament books, in whole or in part, as well as for the presence of a deep interest in Christian prophecy on the part of the editors or compilers of Synoptic tradition.

In 1947 H. A. Guy made a strikingly forthright claim about the authorship of the two books which are still most often considered to have close connections with Christian prophetic activity.

> Although a rigid distinction cannot be drawn, it may be said that the work of propagating the Christian message to the outside world and extending the bounds of the Church was the preaching' (*kerygma*), while 'prophecy' (*prophēteia*) was primarily 'a sign to them that believe' (I Corinthians 14.22). The fact that *prophēteia* had a wide connotation justifies us in including among the Christian prophets such men as the writer of the Epistle to the Hebrews and the author of the fourth Gospel. The ordinary eschatology and apocalyptic had little value for them, but they nevertheless felt that they were the recipients of a revelation, the utterance of which assisted in the *paraklēsis* and the *oikodomē* of the Christian community.[1]

In addition to the two very general considerations noted about the authors by Guy, viz. the possession of revelations and their disclosure for the upbuilding of the Christians addressed, what other evidence may be adduced to support his hypothesis?

I. HEBREWS

In many ways the letter to the Hebrews presents 'the riddle

of the New Testament', and it is often regarded as, among early Christian writings, 'without father, without mother, and without genealogy'! So far as its structure is concerned, some scholars have attempted to find the rhetorical scheme of later Greek hortatory speeches, with a prologue (1.1–4.13), two expositions concerning Jesus as high priest (4.14–6.20 and 7.1–10.18), and an epilogue (10.19–13.25): but there are only a few phrases in Hebrews which would justify the supposition that the rhetorical pattern underlies the letter. Though christological sections are regularly followed by paraenetical or hortatory ones, the author occasionally includes admonitions even inside the dogmatic parts (2.1 ff., 3.7 ff., 5.11 ff.): indeed it seems as if christology is being used as a means of supporting the exhortation. Despite the fact that the theological and christological parts are of great interest and significance, as is an older tradition of confessional formulae (1.3, 4.12–13, 7.3, 26, 13.14), the letter is structured around the paraenetic passages (2.1–4, 3.7–4.11, 4.14–16, 5.11–6.12, 10.19–39, 12.1–13.17) and the whole can be thus called a 'word of exhortation' (*logos parakleseōs*). And we have seen earlier, in the chapters on Acts and Paul, how characteristic of New Testament prophets was the delivery of *paraklēsis* or 'pastoral preaching'.

In its literary character Hebrews is unique in the New Testament canon. The word 'letter' never appears, nor does the term 'to write'. Instead, we find the terms 'word', 'speech', 'proclamation' (*logos*). No specific references to the concrete situation of the original readers – certainly none that is necessarily to be interpreted as such – are present in the book. Indeed one is obliged to say that Hebrews is not a real 'letter' at all,[2] but rather a literary composition or essay meant for general reading. The final salutation (13.22–25), which alone speaks against such a literary evaluation (and which cannot seriously be attributed to another hand), could and probably should be explained as the attempt to convert the literary piece into a 'letter'.

But must we remain content to describe Hebrews as a 'literary composition' or 'essay'? No: there are one or two features which may suggest a better definition. The remarkably good style and the acquaintance with the modes of expression of Greek rhetoric – features which Hebrews has in common with Philo and the Wisdom of Solomon, for instance – suggest the teacher or preacher. The frequent changes from 'we' to 'you' and to the individual 'I' point in the same direction. The possibility, even the probability, is that we have before us a written sermon, which in form and style is akin to the Jewish–Hellenistic homily of the synagogue. Now if our earlier contention that Christian prophets engaged in 'pastoral preaching', exhorting, encouraging, warning and so forth, is correct, then it is not at all inconceivable that in Hebrews we have an example of that activity: of course it is in written form, but may it not have been uttered, under inspiration, before being committed to writing? It is not a particularly long homily: it can be read aloud in slightly less than one hour.

This is not the place to discuss the repeated attempts which have been made to bring the evidence of the Qumran documents into some kind of relation to the letter to the Hebrews[3] – and it is easy to be carried away by their real or imagined affinities – nevertheless we should observe that in its exegetical use of the Old Testament Scriptures (in the Septuagint version) Hebrews displays certain similarities to the *pesher*-technique employed at Qumran.[4] As the Qumran writers believed that they were witnessing the beginning of the fulfilment of the purpose of God revealed to the prophets, according to the understanding of the prophetic oracles divinely granted to the Teacher of Righteousness, so in Hebrews the Old Testament writings are treated by the author as a parable or mystery which awaits its explanation: and the explanation given takes the form of messianic typology. For example, the oracle regarding the son of David, 'I will be his father and he shall be my son' (2 Sam. 7.14), is applied to the Davidic Messiah both in Hebrews 1.5b and in 4QFlor; but in Hebrews, of course, the Davidic Messiah is identified with Jesus. The quotation in Hebrews 1.6 from the Song of Moses, Deuteronomy 32.43 ('and let all the angels of God worship him') – applied to the introduction of the first-begotten into the world – comes from the longer text of the Song hitherto known only from the Septuagint but now attested in Hebrew in one of the fragments from Qumran Cave 4.

Probably the most striking biblical parallel between Hebrews and the Qumran texts relates to Habakkuk 2.3 f., expounded in the Habakkuk-*pesher* (1QpHab) of those who will experience deliverance because of their enduring loyalty to and trust in the Teacher of Righteousness, and in Hebrews 10.38 f. of those who believe and win through to life by patient and faithful waiting for the advent of the Coming One. Markus Barth has aptly claimed that in Hebrews 'exegesis is the endeavour to help people in need by telling them what the Bible says of their shepherd Jesus Christ'.[5] If that is so, and it is indeed very plausible, then the question arises whether this type of exposition falls within the functions which we tentatively ascribed to teachers in the Christian community (see above, p. 132) or belongs to the activity of 'pastoral preaching' (*paraklēsis*) which was characteristic of the Christian prophet's ministry. It is extremely difficult to answer such a question with any degree of certainty, but the overriding intention of the exegesis in Hebrews – to offer paraenesis that upbuilds, or as Barth puts it, 'to help people in need' – may just tilt the balance in favour of its being the work of a Christian prophet.

The problem of the authorship of Hebrews will probably never be solved. But of the various candidates suggested through the centuries for the honour, one name has occurred from time to time which is of interest in relation to the possible prophetic origin of the book. In *de Pudicitia* 20 Tertullian names Barnabas as the author of the epistle, and in such a way as to suggest that this was not a private opinion of his own, but a commonly agreed ascription in his circles. Admittedly this view of the authorship is not without problems: could Barnabas have so completely abandoned the position of the primitive community with regard to the law and the cultus? could he have been so rhetorically trained and Hellenistically oriented as to become the author of this document? Questions like these remain, and assume greater or lesser importance to different scholars, but a strong defence of Barnabas's authorship of the letter has recently been offered by J. A. T. Robinson,[6] who dates the composition of the book to *c.* AD 67.

The case runs as follows: (i) Barnabas can be associated with

Rome (*pace* W. Manson[7]), having accompanied Peter on a visit to that city after they left Corinth, following Claudius's death in 54. (ii) What the writer himself calls his 'word of exhortation' (13.22) fits admirably the Greek-speaking Cypriot Jew, Barnabas, who was a Levite by descent and was well known and highly regarded in Jerusalem. The 'nickname' given to him by the apostles meaning 'son of exhortation' (Acts 4.36) betokens one with a gift for the kind of synagogue exposition which is the literary character of Hebrews. At Antioch (Acts 11.23) Barnabas 'exhorted them all to hold fast to the Lord with resolute hearts' (NEB): that is very much the tenor of Hebrews. (iii) The situation addressed by the letter to the Hebrews requires that it be written by someone who had already proved himself a mediator in the church, and this Barnabas had certainly done (Acts 9.26–30; 11.22–30; 15.22–39). (iv) The statement in Hebrews 2.3 that the message of salvation 'was attested to us by those who heard him [the Lord]', would suit Barnabas admirably. He was among those in Jerusalem who had heard the message from Peter and John (Acts 4.4), and in those pentecostal days had seen it confirmed by God who, as the writer says, 'also bore witness by signs and wonders and various miracles and by gifts of the Holy Spirit distributed according to his own will' (Heb. 2.4). (v) The author of Hebrews belongs to the Pauline circle, as the traditional attribution of the letter attests and as the references to Timothy as his travelling companion shows (13.23), but the writing of the document is later than Paul's active career: ' ... the mantle of the Apostle has in part fallen upon the writer himself. He can address his readers with a pastoral authority superior to that of their own leaders and with a conscience clear of local involvement (Heb. 13.17 f.), and yet with no personal claim to apostolic aegis. There cannot have been too many of such men around. With the entirely proper desire of the church to see that his work had a place in the canon, the crucial test of apostolicity subsequently required its ascription to Paul himself – though the churches of the west that knew it best knew otherwise. In compensation perhaps he himself became credited with that equally anonymous but much inferior homily on the same theme [the relationship of Christianity to the ritual ordinances of Judaism] which we now know as the Epistle of Barnabas.'[8]

If this case for the authorship of Hebrews by Barnabas may be regarded as cumulatively more convincing than that for any other of the suggested authors, then it is a strong pointer towards the Christian-prophetic origin of the book, for, as we have seen in the chapter on Acts, Barnabas was one of the prophets of the early Christian community (Acts 13.1). Is it a mere coincidence that in Acts 13.15 the rulers of the synagogue at Pisidian Antioch sent a message to Paul and Barnabas inviting them to pass on any 'word of exhortation' (i.e. a homily) that they had to the assembled company and that the author of the homily or sermon which we know as the letter to the Hebrews designated his work as a 'word of exhortation' (*logos paraklēseōs*)? A reasonably good case can be put forward for regarding the letter to the Hebrews as an example of the (written) 'pastoral preaching' of a Christian prophet, possibly Barnabas, which contains both reprimand and encouragement designed to upbuild the community.

2. THE FOURTH GOSPEL AND THE JOHANNINE EPISTLES

In spite of considerable differences in literary genre, style and theological outlook, the writings traditionally attributed to John contain sufficient affinities to allow us to speak of a Johannine *corpus* which, among other common themes, presents a developed theology of the Holy Spirit as the gift of the risen Christ to his Church. We are not here concerned to offer an exposition of that theology, but only to consider such themes and aspects of it as relate directly to prophetism, and in particular the prophetic origin of the writings. We have already devoted a chapter of this book to the Revelation: we shall now confine our attention to the Gospel and the Epistles of John.

The prophetic character of the Johannine writings (including the Revelation) has been affirmed by numerous scholars in terms of Harnack's thesis, by means of which they interpret these books in the context of the conflict between a charismatic, itinerant ministry and a ministry that has become localised and institutionalised. For instance, G. Bornkamm claims that 2 and 3 John reflect 'the open conflict between the holder of a congregational office viewed in terms of monarchical episcopacy and the representative of a free authority not restricted to any locality'.[9] The 'elder' (*presbyteros*), who is the author of the letters, does not denote his age, nor his apostolic dignity, nor his membership of a directing body in a local church: he is 'outside any ecclesiastical constitution: he is to be regarded, not as an office-bearer but as a specially valued teacher or as a prophet of the older period', who was to be the mediator and a guarantor of the authentic or apostolic (Johannine) tradition. In point of fact, however, his kind of dignity was discredited and the authority of local officials or monarchical bishops (of which the conduct of Diotrephes offers an example) developed and carried the day in the age which followed.

This approach to the prophetic concern of the Johannine *corpus* of material has been employed, in an intriguing way, with reference to the Fourth Gospel by A. Kragerud in his book *Der Lieblingsjünger im Johannesevangelium*.[10] According to Kragerud, the Beloved Disciple is the representative of the Johannine school of thought, the symbol of the charismatic ministry in the church, of the prophetism cultivated in Johannine circles, and therefore he is opposed to Peter who is the representative of ecclesiastical organisation and the institutional ministry. Although this hypothesis rests upon thorough literary and theological analysis, it suffers from major weaknesses. Although it is obvious that in the Fourth Gospel the Beloved Disciple has a figurative dimension, that does not exhaust his significance. Mary and Peter also possess a symbolic dimension, but that does not reduce their characters to pure symbols. The clear import of the passages in the Fourth Gospel that describe the Beloved Disciple is that he is a real person whose actions are significant on the Gospel scene: his possible symbolic value must remain secondary to his real historical identity. Moreover, it is doubtful if the Beloved Disciple does represent (on John's second level of meaning) the charismatic spirit active in prophecy: it is much more likely that he symbolises the disciple or believer *par excellence*, the example to be followed by the reader of John's book,

and as such is presented as superior to Peter (cf. 20.4, 8). Kragerud's attempt to make the Fourth Gospel a kind of manifesto
for the charismatic freedom and prophetism of the Johannine
circle against bishops and presbyters who wanted to direct the
Christian communities cannot be judged successful.

In recent criticism the homiletic view of the making of the
Fourth Gospel has been steadily gaining ground, and Barnabas
Lindars is persuasive in its defence.[11] In his commentary
on John's Gospel he illustrates from chapter 5 (with which
there must be included 7.15–24) John's literary method and its
homiletic basis.[12] An opening sign (2–9a) is followed by a tran-
sitional dialogue (9b–18) which rather artificially paves the way
for the discourse (19–47) which is concluded in a closing
dialogue (7.16–24). In connection with the discourse he writes
as follows:

> The discourse is not really based on the Sign, but has its own
> text in the form of a parable stemming from non-Synoptic
> traditions of the words of Jesus. . . . Though other traditional
> material can be discerned in verses 24, 30, 32–6, the whole
> is really a Johannine composition in the form of a speech by
> Jesus himself. Some may feel that John is morally wrong to
> do this, but it is to be explained simply as his homiletic
> method. He is using the device of the dramatic monologue;
> all preachers know how gripping this can be – it is a method
> which can be illustrated from Christian homiletic works
> down the ages, e.g. Thomas à Kempis in the fourteenth cen-
> tury and R. M. Benson in the nineteenth. The preacher feels
> that he has the mind of Christ (cf. 1 C. 2.1–16), and that
> what he says is a legitimate extension of his teaching. It is
> likely that John was held by his fellow Churchmen to be a
> prophet (cf. 1. C. 14.1–5).

This paragraph includes certain quite massive assumptions
concerning the authority of a prophet's utterances and their
intermingling with sayings of Jesus in the Gospels. These matters will engage our attention in a later chapter of this book:
for the moment, let us stay with the Johannine discourses and
their composition. Homilies or sermons they may be, uttered

under inspiration at eucharistic celebrations perhaps: but does that require the speaker to be a prophet? 1 Corinthians 14.1– 5 will not of itself provide a conclusive answer. Were Christian prophets – speaking to men for their upbuilding and encouragement and consolation – the only preachers or homilists in the first-century Christian communities? Is it not every bit as likely, if not more so, that the discourses in the Fourth Gospel emanate from inspired *teachers*, able to discern the profound theological significance of traditional material concerning the earthly Jesus? The theological teachers of the second-century Church would suggest a positive answer. Of course, the sayings of Christ, uttered by the prophet under inspiration, in the book of Revelation, are often quickly drawn in to support the view that the Johannine tradition of Jesus-speech was prophetic in origin:[13] to do so is a mistaken procedure. In the first place, the author of Revelation identifies himself as a prophet: the composer of the Johannine discourses does not. Secondly, in the 'I'-words of Revelation the exalted Lord speaks, whereas the discourses of the Fourth Gospel are presented as sayings of Jesus. To sum up thus far: the view that the homilies or discourses in John's Gospel derive from a Christian prophet, presumably within the Johannine school or circle, remains at best a hypothesis, and a hypothesis dogged by some difficult questions.

Concerning the prophetic role of the Paraclete in John's Gospel there can be very little doubt. In the *logia* which describe the functions of the Paraclete – a word which is virtually untranslatable if all its nuances are to be preserved – two other titles are employed, the Holy Spirit and the Spirit of truth, the latter being reminiscent of Qumran terminology. In an important essay entitled 'The Paraclete in the Fourth Gospel'[14] R. E. Brown observes that 'it is because the Paraclete is very carefully patterned on Jesus that the figure of the Qumran Spirit of Truth ... has also become part of the Johannine picture of the Paraclete. If John calls the Paraclete the Spirit of Truth, we suspect that the primary factor that made this title seem fitting was that in Johannine thought the Paraclete is the Spirit of Jesus and Jesus is the truth.... Whatever is said about the

Paraclete is said elsewhere in the Gospel about Jesus.'[15] This is not surprising, for if the Paraclete is 'another Paraclete' (John 14.16) this would imply that Jesus was the first Paraclete, an observation which gains credence from 1 John 2.1. In opposition to those who may have dreamed of an age of the Spirit which would be superior to that of Christ, the evangelist is at pains to stress that the Spirit receives from Christ what he proclaims (16.14) and that he will witness to Christ (16.8 ff. and 1 John 5.7).

To express the action of the Paraclete the following terms are used: teach (14.26), bring to your remembrance (*hypomimnēskein:* 14.26), bear witness (15.26), convince (*elenchein:* 16.8), guide (*hodēgein*: 16.13), declare (*anangellein*: 16.13, 14, 15) and glorify (*doxazein*: 16.14). Such a list is sufficient in itself to prove that the Spirit acts in the manner of a prophet during the time of the Church. In connection with 'remembering' one recalls the care with which the evangelist distinguishes between the time of Jesus and that time when the disciples will *understand* the signifance of what has taken place or of what Jesus said (2.22, 7.39, 12.16). Likewise the Spirit makes possible the understanding of the Scriptures whereby their christological import is discovered (Acts 8.31 : *hodēgēsei*).

The verb 'bear witness', with which is associated 'convince' or 'convict' (cf. 1 Cor. 14.24 f. where *elenchein* appears) takes us into the forensic sphere. Whether we interpret John 16.8 ff. in terms of the accusation of the world by the mouth of the disciples, since it is by the mouth of the disciples that the Paraclete bears witness to Christ, or of an inner witness that the Spirit bears to the disciples by convincing them of the unrighteousness of the world, it is clear that in this hostile engagement with the world the Paraclete will assist the disciples just as Jesus had promised in the event of their being persecuted (Matt. 10.19 f.; Mark 13.11; Luke 12.11 f.). He will bear witness along with them (cf. John 15.26–7 with Acts 5.32) and, at the same time, 'he will declare the things that are to come' (16.13). Since only the Son has knowledge of the future, he transmits it to the Paraclete who, in turn, communicates it to the disciples. The prophetic charisma, spread abroad through the Church by the Spirit (1 Thess. 5.19f.; 1 Cor. 12 and 14, etc.), goes back ultimately to Christ, the revelation of the Father.

The promise of John 16.13 has a particular relevance to the book of Revelation (cf. Rev. 1.19): the message of the Spirit to the churches is not other than the witness of Jesus, Son of man (Rev. 1.12–16), finding its voice through the prophet-author of the book. As Boring points out,[16] the revelatory claim with which the book of Revelation begins (God, the exalted Christ, his angel, the prophet, the community and the world) has a close similarity to that found in John (Father, Jesus, Paraclete, apostolic community, world: 14.16), and this constitutes an important datum linking the Gospel with the Revelation and with Christian prophecy.

But what is the link? It is far too sweeping to suggest that the author of John – the Beloved Disciple – is in some way an 'incarnation' of the Paraclete:[17] the most that can be said with any assurance is that by reason of the way in which the Fourth Gospel portrays the two central figures which represent divine revelation – the Paraclete and Jesus – the Gospel and the other Johannine literature emerged, at different points in time, from a community in which Christian prophecy played a significant role. That the author of the Gospel, or parts of it, was himself a Christian prophet, must remain very hypothetical.

At this point we may make a few comments on 1 John. This letter – which has no real epistolary characteristics save the use of the verb 'write' – is directed against heretics who are compromising the faith in Christ and who appear to be the precursors of the Docetism that was later combated by Ignatius. In opposition to this threat John solemnly reaffirms that Jesus is indeed the Christ (2.22), the Son of God (4.15). In the doctrinal confusion created by the subtle theories of the new teachers the discernment of spirits is necessary: 'Beloved, do not believe every spirit, but test the spirits (*dokimazete ta pneumata*) to see whether they are of God: for many false prophets have gone out into the world' (4.1). These false prophets are analogous to the 'false teachers' of 2 Pet. 2.1: it is not stated that they laid claim to special visions or revelations, but only that they were spreading a teaching that was contrary to the truth: being under the domination of the spirit of darkness or error, they were attempting to draw away the faithful from the truth they had received 'from the beginning' (2.7, 24, 3.11; cf. 2 John 5, 6) and they are identified with the anti-Christ (2.18, 22, 4.3: cf. 2 John 7), i.e. a manifestation of resistance to God.

It has been suggested that 1 John reflects a situation in which spirit-inspired prophets, uttering words of the risen Lord, have become a real problem in the church which reacts by emphasising tradition and the traditional commandment (1.1–4, 2.7),[18] but this theory seems less than adequate as an explanation of the danger the writer of 1 John confronts. The teaching of the false prophets was doctrinally erroneous in regard to the incarnation, morality and eschatology: it is this serious threat that evokes from the writer insistence upon adherence to the original apostolic witness. It is necessary to be in a communion of trust and love with those whom Christ chose as his witnesses in order to enter into communion with the Father and his Son, Jesus Christ (1.3). The false prophets have separated themselves from the former and therefore cannot participate in the latter: they have gone out into the world because they did not abide in the orthodox doctrine (cf. 2 John 9) which the apostolic tradition, witnessed to by the Spirit, alone conserved.

We have just considered the claim that certain New Testament books were written by Christian prophets or emerged from prophetic circles: it is now time to consider briefly three strands of Synoptic material which some scholars link with Christian prophetic activity – the Q source and the redactional or editorial work of the writers of Matthew and Luke.

3. THE Q TRADITION

For the investigation of the prophetic features, forms and themes of the Q tradition we are most indebted to R. A. Edwards's book *A Theology of Q: Eschatology, Prophecy and Wisdom*.[19] Well aware of the difference of opinion among scholars as to the extent of Q, even on the part of those who accept the hypothesis, Edwards is unwilling to propose that material which looks like Q tradition but is recorded by Matthew or Luke (but not both) should be employed in describing Q theology: for him, Q material resides in (a) words which agree precisely between Matthew and Luke alone, and (b) words which are very close, but because of the context may be in a different case, person or tense. Having identified what belongs to Q tradition (which he thinks arose in Northern Palestine or Syria in the decade 40–50) by means of this minimal definition, Edwards suggests that the theology of Q, or of the Q community which collected, used and preserved the material, may be described under three heads: eschatology, prophecy and wisdom.

Several different types of evidence point to the presence of a prophetic dimension. (i) Prophets are mentioned in six pericopae in Q (Luke 6.22 f. and par.; Luke 16.16; Luke 7.26 and par.; Luke 10.23 f. and par.; Luke 11.47–51 and par.; Luke 13.34 f. and par.; Luke 16.16 and par.). (ii) The *legō hymin* introductory formula, which is often considered to be indicative of prophetic speech, is quite prominent in Q, occurring fourteen times. (iii) Proclamation or announcement – a traditional characteristic of prophetic speech – is to be found in Q in a variety of judgment and warning sayings (Luke 10.12 and par.; Luke 10.13–15 and par.; Luke 12.8 f. and par.; Luke 3.17b and par.). (iv) There is a definite interest in John the Baptist and his preaching of judgment: and (v) there are quotations from Old Testament prophetic books. On the basis of this evidence Edwards suggests that 'some, if not all, members of the Q community saw their role in the End-time in a way similar to that of the prophets of Israel. They announce the will of YHWH by repeating the words of Jesus, the Son of Man'[20]: but he does not think these announcements necessarily imply any creativity on the part of the prophet-like members of the community. This is not self-contradictory: Edwards is content to seek an understanding of the Q community – the contours of its thought and self-understanding – and finds that it has a great interest in sayings which contain prophetic features, forms and themes: he is far too well aware of the problems and difficulties involved in attributing the creativity to Christian prophets that makes them responsible for the origin of a particular saying or group of sayings – not the least of which is, in his own words, that 'one must argue that a saying is not from Jesus in order to argue that it comes from a Christian prophet'[21] – to claim that his Q community, for all its theological interest in prophetic material (and almost half of the Q pericopae evince some such interest), did more than prophetically announce God's will by repeating *logia Iēsou*. Those who have no difficulty in attributing creativity to Christian prophets in respect of words of Jesus will view substantial tracts of the Q tradition quite differently.

4. MATTHEW'S REDACTION

Redaction-critical studies of Matthew's gospel have produced many suggestions about the author's interest in Christian prophets and prophecy. In his essay 'Observance of the Law and Charismatic Activity in Matthew'[22] Eduard Schweizer considers as not impossible the idea that Matthew intended to describe Jesus as an itinerant prophet, the prototype of all future Christian prophets, but the basis for this hypothesis – the infancy stories and in particular 2.15, 23 – is extremely tenuous. He goes on to suggest, admittedly in a very tentative way, that the use of some of the Old Testament quotations by Matthew (8.17, 12.17–21, 27.9 f.) serves to urge the disciples to imitate the ideal of a charismatic, itinerant prophet, following Jesus in perfect obedience: that these are the marks of discipleship is proved, he thinks, by the collocation of 10.41 and 42, where the disciple is described as 'prophet' and 'righteous man', that is, one who engages in charismatic activity and who obeys God's law as interpreted by Jesus. But neither this interpretation of Matthew 10.41 nor that of E. Käsemann – 'The community consists of the prophets who obviously exercise leadership in it and the righteous, as the general body of members call themselves, carrying on the Jewish nomenclature'[23] – pays sufficient attention to the other occasions (13.17 and 23.29) where Matthew links 'prophets' and 'righteous (men)' and where *dikaios* has the specific sense of 'one who teaches righteousness' (cf. Dan. 12.3).[24] Therefore in 10.41 'prophet' and 'righteous man' are in synonymous parallelism; both exercise a preaching or teaching function. In the Matthean composition of the missionary discourse 10.41 is placed at the end in order to suggest the link which should exist between the initial mission of the Twelve and that of the itinerant Christian preachers of his own day. There is no other message to be made known than that which Jesus had himself already proclaimed.

In addition to the messengers of old who have been unable to bring about the repentance of the chosen people there are sent forth envoys by Jesus, according to Matthew (23.34, 'I send you ...'), by the Wisdom of God, according to Luke (11.49). Generally speaking scholars prefer the Lucan introduction: 'Therefore the Wisdom of God said, "I will send them prophets and apostles ..."'. But, as É. Cothenet observes, [25] this formula has overtones of Lucan theological *Tendenz* with its desire to emphasise the unity of salvation-history, and Matthew's list, 'prophets and wise men and scribes' may, by reason of its uniqueness, have a strong claim to be regarded as primitive. Even if one hesitates about which form of the introduction to the *logion* is original (Luke's 'Wisdom' or Matthew's 'Jesus'), the intention of Jesus to send out envoys has already been expressed in the missionary discourse. But here the circumstances are different: in this list of functionaries who will act in the community, Jesus characterises the different forms of witness that his envoys will have to bear against the unbelieving Jews: prophetic denunciation of the wrongdoing of the people (cf. Stephen's discourse in Acts 7); the manifestation of the secrets of divine wisdom (the role of the 'wise' (*maśkîlîm*) in Daniel); and right interpretation of the law (the role of Christian scribes, cf. Matt. 13.52).

Without pretending to find here a precise list of ministries, one cannot help but note that Jesus himself is at the source of the new *prophēteia* and the new *didachē*. And from his perspective (if the logion is authentic), as well as from Matthew's, the apostles are the first to fulfil this witnessing role. The other *logia* which affirm that they are more blessed than the prophets and righteous men of the old order show quite clearly that they themselves are considered as prophets.

Paul Minear[26] extends this insight that Matthew thought of Jesus' disciples as prophets and suggests that the relation between the congregation and the Christian prophets in Matthew's own day was roughly analogous to that between the crowds and the disciples in Jesus' day. Matthew, in his view, thought that Christian leaders (i.e. prophets) faced a double danger: they might become either false prophets or hypocrites, and Matthew was more concerned with the hypocrisies of church leaders than with those of synagogue leaders. Matthew 7.22–3 condemns prophets who prophesy and perform miracles in the name of Jesus, but do not observe God's law. Whether these are to be identified with the 'false prophets' of 7.15, and who exactly the latter are, remain debated questions,[27] but are not strictly relevant here. Sufficient to say, on the basis of 7.22–3, that Matthew is opposed to any charismatic enthusiasm that is not under the constraint of obedience to God's law as interpreted by Jesus: but he is far from being opposed on principle to charismatics (i.e. men inspired by the Spirit to prophesy and perform miracles). According to 10.1 the charismatic deeds of Jesus continue on in the community of Jesus and are God's signs that the Old Testament prophecies have been fulfilled; and the very warning against false prophets presupposes the activity of genuine prophets in the church. What they actually were doing is probably best implied from what has just been said above on 23.34: they engaged in a ministry of preaching, warning, revelation and teaching – all features of Christian prophetism which have already been stressed in foregoing chapters of this book.

5. LUKE'S REDACTION

In our discussion of the prophetic characteristics of Jesus' teaching and ministry we had occasion to draw attention to a number of phrases in the Lucan tradition which imply that the third evangelist understood Jesus as a prophet. There is the spontaneous exclamation of the people of Nain, 'A great prophet has arisen among us' (7.17), the words of the Pharisee, 'If this man were a prophet . . .' (7.39), the Emmaus disciples' description of Jesus as one 'who was a prophet' (24.19) and the telling

affirmation made by Jesus himself, 'I must go on my way ...
for it cannot be that a prophet should perish outside Jerusalem'
(13.33), a *logion* which has a strong claim to authenticity in view
of its form and its agreement with the generally accepted teaching of Judaism that prophets had to suffer or even undergo martyrdom.[28] The 'keynote speech' of 4.18–27 – which many
scholars regard as Lucan, either in location in the Gospel or
in content, or both – also contains a reference to the unacceptability of the prophet.

Recently J. A. Sanders[29] has studied this passage by the
method of 'comparative midrash' and argues that Jesus'
midrash on Isaiah 61 constituted the offence, and particularly
the question of who the poor, the captives and the blind would
be. For 11QMelch (in which Isa. 61 is the central text) they
are representatives of what Sanders calls the 'in-group', and
the same expectation confronted Jesus in his home town synagogue. But by referring to Elijah and Elisha's reaching out
beyond the 'in-group' Jesus insists that these words apply to those
to whom God wishes them to apply. He thus plays the role of
a true prophet in the classical tradition of the Elijah, Amos,
Isaiah, Jeremiah type who cannot be accepted (*dektos*) by his
countrymen because his message must always bear in it a divine
challenge to Israel's covenantal self-understanding in any
generation.

Although Sanders may give too much prominence in his
interpretation to Isaiah 61, interpreted from the perspective of
11QMelch, his comments about Jesus' prophetic function are
extremely valuable: a prophet is indeed that kind of person who
will, virtually by definition, achieve unacceptability because his
message involves the radical questioning of his hearers' self-
understanding before God: rejection, even where he might
have expected acceptance (in his home town), is a form of verifi-
cation of the authenticity of his role. From this scene – whether
editorially placed or constructed, or not – Luke seems to de-
velop his understanding of the Jesus who will function in his
Gospel as a prophet-martyr.

In 1976 Paul Minear published an original and lively book
entitled *To Heal and to Reveal: The Prophetic Vocation according*

to Luke.[30] In the first part of this book he tackles the problem of getting from a contemporary consciousness (or world-view) to an understanding of that consciousness within which prophetic language makes any sense at all. Using the text of Luke 10.1–16 he shows how exegesis can reach into the implicit presuppositions of the prophetic language and uncover its structures of consciousness. Luke's concept of authority, his symbolism of heaven and his understanding of human need in which both material and spiritual lacks are supplied by God, are all shown to be foreign to our 'world-view', but Minear also demonstrates how exegesis can help discover analogous structures of human experience which might bridge the gap.

The second part of his book concentrates on the prophetic vocation in Luke-Acts and shows how the concept of prophets/prophecy is significant for Luke's understanding of John the Baptist as the prophet like Elijah, Jesus as the prophet like Moses, and the apostles as prophets like Jesus. Concerning this typology and succession of prophetic figures questions may rightly be raised as to the availability of convincing evidence: for example, Luke omits Mark 9.11–13 and Mark 1.6 where the identification of John and Elijah is either explicit or implicit; and Jesus as the prophet like Moses is a Matthean theme far more obviously than it is a Lucan one. Nevertheless Minear has sound things to say about Luke-Acts and provides a corrective to works on that tradition which pay little attention to the prophetic element. One observation of interest relates to what we said in an earlier paragraph: it may be that Luke's presentation of Jesus as a prophetic model to the disciples explains why Luke plays down the element of atonement in Jesus' sufferings: as prophet Jesus must face suffering and a martyr's death as an example to those (the disciples) who are called to carry on his prophetic ministry.

Sufficient has been said in this chapter – and more could have been included in it – to show that interest in the phenomenon of Christian prophecy is not confined to one or two books in the New Testament: there is scarcely a significant strand of tradition in the New Testament *corpus* that has not – in the view of some scholar – a greater or lesser measure of relatedness or indebtedness to Christian prophetic activity. The question of the correctness of the various claims will go on being asked, if not definitely answered, for a long time to come.

CHRISTIAN PROPHETS AND
THE SAYINGS OF JESUS

I. THE TRADITIONAL EVIDENCE FOR THE CREATIVE ROLE OF PROPHETS

It is almost a commonplace in contemporary New Testament scholarship to attribute to Christian prophets in the early Church a creative role in respect of sayings which the Gospel tradition presents as dominical utterances. Among modern scholars the authority for this view is to be found in the form-critical analyses and conclusions of Rudolf Bultmann.[1] Christian tradition, he affirms, took over certain Jewish materials and put them on the lips of Jesus (e.g. the Marcan apocalypse): the Christian community also revised or reworked elements from older traditions (e.g. the interpretation of the Sign of Jonah in connection with the person of Jesus, Matt. 12.40) and even formed *logia* which reflect its own interests and concerns. Such *logia* are 'inauthentic' (in the sense that they are not genuine dominical sayings) and, according to Bultmann, they may originally have gained currency as utterances of the Spirit in the Church, without their ascription to Jesus being initially intended. Sayings like Rev. 16.15 (in which the risen Christ speaks) and Rev. 3.20 show clearly, in his opinion, the process of the creation (or, reformulation) of such *logia*. These sayings would only gradually have been regarded as prophetic words of the historical Jesus. 'The Church drew no distinction between such utterances by Christian prophets and the sayings of Jesus in the tradition, for the reason that even the dominical sayings in the tradition were not the pronouncements of a past authority, but sayings of the risen Lord who is always a contemporary for the Church.'

It is noteworthy that in this sentence Bultmann discloses for the first time the identity of those who created or reformulated *logia*, namely, Christian prophets. Unless he assumes that because these *logia* were eventually considered as prophetic sayings of Jesus they must have been uttered originally by prophets in the Church, it would seem that his attribution of the creative role to this particular group or class depends on the authorities he refers to in the accompanying footnote, which reads as follows:

> Cp. H. Gunkel, *Reden und Aufsätze*, 1913, p. 173, 'One can suppose that not a few sayings, which have come down to us in the New Testament as utterances of Jesus, were originally spoken by such inspired men (like the singer in Od. Sol. 42) in the name of Christ.' H. von Soden had already made the same point, *Das Interesse des apostolischen Zeitalters an der evangelischen Geschichte*, 1892, p. 153. He refers to the circular letters of Rev. And Rev. in general provides, like the Od. Sol., quite clear examples of this phenomenon. Od. Sol. 42.6 gives clear expression to it:
>
> For I have risen and stand by them
> And speak through their mouth.

Bultmann's view that Christian prophets originally produced certain *logia* later attributed to Jesus is followed by such influential scholars as P. Vielhauer, H. Conzelmann and E. Käsemann,[2] whose special extension of the theory will receive consideration later; and Käsemann is followed by, among many, N. Perrin.[3] So widespread is the acceptance of Bultmann's view that J. Jeremias refers to it (without acknowledgment) in the first volume of his *New Testament Theology* in such a way as to suggest that he regards it as one of the assured results of form-critical study of the Gospels: 'The seven letters of Christ to the seven churches in Asia Minor (Rev. 2–3) and other sayings of the exalted Lord handed down in the first person (e.g. Rev. 1.17–20; 16.15; 22.12 ff.) allow the conclusion that early Christian prophets addressed congregations in words of encouragement, admonition, censure and promise, using the name of Christ in the first person. Prophetic sayings of this kind found their way into the tradition about Jesus and became fused with the words that he had spoken during his lifetime.'[4] This view is echoed, as we have seen in earlier chapters of this book, by many of those who are engaged in the study of early Christian prophecy.

But Bultmann's original statement has been subjected to significant criticisms and modifications in the course of time and research. For instance, the other great exponent of the form-critical method, M. Dibelius, suggests that, since Paul in 1 Cor. 7.10, 12, and 25 distinguishes between commands that come from the Lord and the opinion which he himself offers, we may assume that there was a wing within the primitive community which attached authority to acknowledged authenticity and preserved *logia* explicitly as words of Jesus, although another wing, characterised by *Enthusiasmus*, did not (or was not able to) differentiate in Christian exhortation between sayings of Jesus and words regarded as having been uttered 'in the Spirit' or 'in the name of the Lord'; but Dibelius is ready to admit that 'this stringing together of genuine sayings of Jesus with other Christian words of exhortation could become a source of error'.[5]

F. Neugebauer is also opposed to the theory that the early Christian community did not recognise any difference between words of Jesus and the sayings of anonymous charismatics.[6] In addition to pointing out that no similar transformation of *logia* occurs in Jewish or New Testament writings, Neugebauer observes that if Bultmann can say that words of prophets only 'gradually' became words of the historical Jesus, this in fact presupposes that the community was able to make and did make a distinction between the two: moreover, if words of the risen Lord uttered by prophets had the same value as *logia Iēsou* there is no reason for the projection of the former into a pre-Easter setting.

In putting forward their view of the creative role of prophets in respect of *logia Iēsou*, Bultmann and his followers have not taken with sufficient seriousness the part played by tradition in the early Christian community and the importance of the Twelve as witnesses of the tradition of Jesus' words.

Although the thesis of B. Gerhardsson[7] may be criticised for having claimed too great a degree of fixity in tradition and for having assumed too much about first-century rabbinic methods of teaching, there is much of value in his contention that the followers of Jesus accorded to his remembered teaching a very definite authority and that they therefore took care about its accurate transmission. Nor should it be forgotten that H. Schür-mann has argued that the pre-Easter teaching and preaching activity provides a probable 'setting-in-life' (*Sitz im Leben*) for the initial collection and systematisation of the Logia-tradi-tion.[8] Prophets and other teachers in the community may have played a part in the process whereby *logia* of Jesus were adapted to the post-Easter situation of the Church (cf. the detailed explanations of certain parables) in a manner similar to the *pesher*-technique at Qumran, whereby the authoritative message of Scripture was applied to the situation of the sect: but that is not the same thing as ascribing to them the creation *de novo*, indeed *ex nihilo*, of sayings of Jesus. The place given by Bultmann and others to the Christian prophets is precisely that occupied by the Gnostic authors of apocryphal Gospels: in these works it is not the Jesus of history who teaches by action and by word, but the resurrected Lord who conveys truths and revelations to this or that privileged individual disciple. Had the Christian community fallen into this dangerous position in the first few decades of its existence?

These are serious criticisms of the view of Bultmann and his disciples on the role of Christian prophets in the formulation of 'sayings of Jesus': they require an answer from those who promulgate the theory as if it were an assured fact. 'General statements that Christian prophets contributed to the tradition continue to be made, but works which attempt to document this hypothesis in particular cases, with specific evidence, have been extremely rare.'[9]

Let us consider the evidence which has been adduced by Bultmann and others to support or validate the theory. Apart from references to prophetic words in the book of Revelation, the supporting evidence for Bultmann's case comprises reference to the work of two earlier scholars (Gunkel and von Soden) and to Odes of Solomon 42.6 which, Bultmann asserts, gives clear expression to the phenomenon of inspired speech in the name of Christ by inspired men: 'For I have risen and stand by them/And speak through their mouth'. Vielhauer refers to the same verse as being illustrative of the prophetic conscious-ness of Palestinian Christian prophets.[10]

Despite attempts to provide the Odes with a Jewish-Christian origin and a date in the first century AD, the view is still widely accepted that we have to do with a Gnostic hymn-book from the second century. If so, should we seek or expect to find in it evidence on which to base a theory about the consciousness and activity of primitive Christian prophets? In any case, what-ever be the date and character of the Odes, the verse in question from Ode 42 does not specifically refer to prophets, but to be-lievers in general: as J. H. Bernard commented many years ago, 'the Risen Christ is with his faithful ones who speak in his name'.[11] More recently W. Bauer has said of the passage, 'The Redeemer rejoices that his persecutors are dead, whilst he is resurrected and can speak through those who seek their life in him', and he draws attention to parallels in Matthew 18.20 and 28.20 (for the presence of Christ with his own) and in Acts 18.9 f. (for speech through the mouth of believers). He might have referred also to Luke 21.15 where, in what may be a genuine *logion*, Jesus promises to give 'mouth and wisdom' to his disciples when they are persecuted. We may interpret Odes of Solomon 42.6 of prophets only if we are prepared to admit that all believers are (potentially or actually) prophets, and that view then robs the verse of its relevance for any argument about 'Christian prophets', for these are normally regarded as having formed a distinct class or group within the Christian community.

Bultmann enlists in support his theory about sayings of the risen Lord entering the Gospel tradition the views expressed by H. Gunkel and H. von Soden. The earlier of the two, von Soden, observes (in the essay referred to) that in Matthew and Luke the narrative material remains, on the whole, as it had been established by Mark, but the sayings material undergoes adaptation: parables are inevitably expanded in the interests of edifying the community; their emphases are altered and, as a result of exposition, they are changed into allegories; words of the Lord are adapted to problems and conditions which emerged later and thereby transformed and 'many a thing that was considered in time as a saying of the Lord was not so originally, but was rather a happy expression of some truth that was dawning on Christianity' (*eine glückliche Fassung irgend einer Wahrheit, welche der Christenheit aufgegangen war*). Produced in the manner of the circular letters in Revelation, sayings might come into circulation which could properly be traced back to the glorified Lord, but which were gradually placed on the lips of the earthly Jesus. The conviction that the Spirit of Christ was active in Christians and that the thoughts of Jesus must have coincided exactly with those of the Christians enables us to understand this assertion which results, inescapably, from sober and conscientious consideration of the material handed down in the Synoptics. To pursue this view and prove it, says von Soden, would require detailed work that would take him far afield from his purpose: but, he adds, 'it is significant to observe the extent to which the utterances already fixed in the sources of Matthew and Luke have remained free of this influence'.[12]

In spite of this final observation (which leaves a very substantial amount of the *logia Iēsou* untouched by prophetic creativity), von Soden's general argument is open to the same kind of criticism as is directed against Bultmann. Some will wish to question the unexamined and undefended progression from adaptation of sayings of Jesus by the Church to the ascription to Jesus of truths that were dawning upon Christian faith. What can be the justification for this step on the part of a scholar who, in 1892, had not recourse to the presuppositions and 'results' of the form-critical method? The only supporting evidence mentioned is the production of the circular letters in the book of Revelation. But as we have stated, these letters, whether from the end of the first century AD or earlier, are still acknowledged to be what they are, utterances of the risen Lord: contrary to what is often claimed, explicitly or implicitly, on the basis of them, these passages from Revelation suggest nothing about the attribution to the historical Jesus of words of the exalted Christ spoken through the Spirit.

Again, one may note that, according to von Soden, the plausibility of this theory of ascription rests on the conviction that the Spirit of Jesus was active in Christians and the thoughts of Jesus coincided precisely with theirs. Why then is Paul careful to differentiate between his own opinions and the teachings of Jesus, although he too claims to have the Spirit, just as the Corinthians do (1 Cor. 7.40)? Moreover, there is evidence that the early Church distinguished between the Spirit addressing a man (cf. Acts 10,19, 11.12, 13.2, 21.11) and utterances of the glorified Lord (cf. Acts 9.4ff., 10f., 18.9, 23.11), and nowhere in the Pauline epistolary material is there presupposed or implied an identity between a revelation received in encounter with the Spirit and words of the historical Jesus. 1 Thessalonians 4.15 (*en logō kyriou*) does not necessarily refer to a saying of the exalted Lord or to a revelation in the Spirit: it may refer to a saying of Jesus, or more probably to the apocalyptic message of Jesus as a whole. There is no likelihood that the 'mystery' in Romans 11.25 ff. and 1 Corinthians 15.51 f., even if it be a revelation, is thought of as having derived from the earthly Jesus.

It remains to point out that von Soden does not attempt to identify those who formulated sayings which eventually were regarded as *logia Iesou* as prophets in the primitive Christian community: to say that they were 'produced in the manner of the circular letters of Revelation' is not really informative unless and until we have reached firm conclusions about the character of the author of that book and the nature of these letters in particular (see above, pp. 87–90). All in all, one confesses to the impression that Bultmann's view does not gain much in authority or conviction by his appeal to the work of von Soden.

In our criticisms of the use of Odes of Solomon 42.6 we have partly disposed of Bultmann's appeal to the work of H. Gunkel. The essay in *Reden und Aufsätze* to which Bultmann alludes is concerned with the Odes of Solomon and the quotation he gives is from Gunkel's comments on Ode 42. He observes that in vv. 4 ff. Christ speaks in the first person through the mouth of the inspired singer, and goes on:

As the prophet of Israel's God says 'I' and means 'Yahweh', as the demon-possessed man, when asked what the demon is called, answers 'I am called Legion', so the inspired person dares to say 'I' and mean 'Christ'; such revelations of the Divine in the first person, in which God speaks through the servant who is dedicated to him, also appear in the syncretistic religions. One can suppose that not a few sayings, which have come down to us as utterances of Jesus, were originally spoken by such inspired men in the name of Christ. (p. 173, translation mine)

On this we make two comments. The point being made here is different from the one which the usual interpretation of the appeal to Odes of Solomon 42.6 appears to make. It is not speech by the risen Christ 'through their mouth' which denotes prophetic consciousness; rather, it is the use of 'I' when the speaker or singer means Christ (and this is quite common in the Odes) which is a sign of prophet-like inspiration. Gunkel does not say that all who speak thus are prophets, only that they are inspired men, as the prophets were: and in any case the prophet was not the only person to use 'I' with reference to Yahweh (cf. Deut. 32 and Ps. 2). Yet, immediately after his reference to Gunkel, Bultmann speaks of 'utterances of Christian prophets' and later on he says: 'The I-sayings were predominantly the work of the *Hellenistic churches*, though a beginning had already been made in the *Palestinian church*. Here too Christian prophets filled by the Spirit spoke in the name of the ascended Lord sayings like Revelation 16.15.'[13] Bultmann's appeal to Gunkel does not give him the right to speak so definitely of 'Christian prophets', only of inspired men. It cannot be assumed that all inspired speech in the early Christian community emanated from prophets: were not 'teachers' and 'evangelists' also inspired by the Spirit? In the second place, Gunkel proceeds immediately from the consciousness of inspiration expressed in what he considers as an excerpt from a second-century Gnostic hymn-book, and from parallels found in the utterances which result from ecstatic union between an individual and god(s) in the mystery religions, to an assumption about the formation (or creation) of sayings of Jesus in the Gospel tradition. Surely this requires supporting arguments. It receives none and therefore the supposition carries little conviction. Again we must admit that Bultmann's case does not gain much strength from his appeal to the work of Gunkel.

In the course of his assertions about the creative role of Christian prophets in relation to *logia Iēsou* Bultmann seeks confirmation from the book of Revelation. In so doing he is following von Soden: and Bultmann is followed by, among many others, Vielhauer and Jeremias. These last-mentioned scholars appeal to the letters of Revelation 2–3 (and to other specific verses) as evidence of the activity of Christian prophets addressing the community and using the name of Christ in the first person, and they go on to suggest that prophetic sayings of this kind found their way into the tradition of Jesus' words. But, as we have already observed, no evidence for this process can be drawn from these passages: the letters are clearly acknowledged as sayings of the exalted Lord spoken through the Spirit. The same may be said of the specific verses to which Bultmann appeals: Revelation 3.20 ('Behold I stand at the door . . .') and Revelation 16.15 ('Lo, I am coming like a thief . . .') are unmistakeably presented as words of the living Christ through the Spirit to the Church. In both these cases, it should be noted, one might plausibly suggest that what the Lord says by the Spirit (through the prophet-author) is in fact a development or adaptation of something already present in the tradition of Jesus' sayings: Revelation 16.15 echoes a *logion* of Jesus, preserved in a life-setting which is perfectly appropriate (Luke 12.39; Matt. 24.43); and when Revelation 3.20 is taken with the immediately following verse there appears to be an echo of Luke 22.29 f. and Luke 12.36. Instead of inferring that these prophetic utterances have become part of the tradition of Jesus' words, we might suggest that prophetic utterance in the name of Christ has taken up genuine *logia* and pointed them to the current situation – hardly a surprising use of the authentic Jesus-material in the teaching and preaching ministry of the church.

However that may be, a much more radical question must

be raised in connection with the appeal to the book of Revelation for evidence of the activity and consciousness of Christian prophets. Is the prophet-author of Revelation typical of the prophets in the Christian community? In an earlier chapter we have expressed support for the view that his position is unique in that he is the one by means of whom his 'brethren' (the prophets in the Church) become sharers in the knowledge and ministry of the divine revelation: all other members of the community, including the prophets, are subordinate to his authority; the community-prophets are the bearers and keepers of the words of the author and they do not make any independent contribution to the prophecy; like the *maśkîlîm* of Daniel (and at Qumran) their function may be that of transmission through teaching.

Now if it is the case that the prophet-author of the Revelation has a special role in his community (and that not simply because he is absent from it), then it cannot be said, without other evidence, that Christian prophets in the primitive communities spoke as he did in the name of the risen Christ, nor that their prophetic consciousness may be discerned by simply examining his. And other firm evidence is in fact lacking. We cannot draw upon the so-called 'words of Christian prophets' in the Synoptic gospels, for the legitimacy of this characterisation is what has to be proved. Nor can we confidently appeal to the discourses in the Fourth Gospel: these may indeed be homilies composed around sayings of Jesus and presented in the form of a speech by Jesus himself, but, as we have seen, there is no certain evidence that they emanated from a Christian prophet. The quite extensive information provided by Acts on the activity of Christian prophets does not include any evidence that would support the view that they spoke in the name of the risen Christ: indeed evidence to the contrary lies in the fact that Agabus introduces his oracle with 'Thus says the Holy Spirit' (21.11) and is described as speaking 'by the Spirit' (11.28). And so far as the evidence from Paul is concerned, neither what he says about the function of prophets and prophecy in the Church (1 Cor. 14.3) nor his own activity in word and writing suggested that he considered the production, in the Spirit, of sayings of the

Lord in the first person to be characteristic of prophets of the Christian era: the use of the well-known epigraph *legei kyrios* (Rom. 12.19; 1 Cor. 14.21; 2 Cor. 6.16 ff.) ought not to be produced as contrary evidence: it is only an assumption that these Old Testament citations were introduced with Christian prophetic consciousness, and, in any case, *kyrios* probably denotes the Lord God (cf. 2 Cor. 6.16b). Although Paul, called to apostleship, in a manner clearly reminiscent of a prophetic vocation, is a man of the Spirit (1 Cor. 7.40) and possesses the gifts of the Spirit, i.e. is a charismatic and a prophet, there is no trace in his writings of his having addressed his readers (or hearers) using the name of Christ in the first person. To sum up: the relevance and value of the appeal to the book of Revelation in connection with the supposedly creative role of Christian prophets may be very much less than is commonly imagined.

Of those who have developed Bultmann's view on the role of Christian prophets in the Church, E. Käsemann has made what is probably the most distinctive contribution.[14] According to Käsemann, there was an enthusiastic movement in both Gentile and Palestinian Christianity which was rooted in the Easter experiences. To this movement prophecy – under the inspiration of the Spirit – gave direction and leadership: prophets were in fact charismatic leaders in the community (cf. Matt. 10.41, and p. 154 above). Apocalyptic theology – and for Käsemann apocalyptic was the mother of all Christian theology – was combined with enthusiastic piety, for the prophets saw in the possession of the Spirit within the community the pledge of the imminent parousia in which the return of Jesus, the Son of man, is awaited. In this situation the Christian prophets spoke directly in the name of the risen Lord: to them belong those sayings which begin 'I am come' (*ēlthon*) which look back over and sum up the finished work of Jesus, as well as many, if not all, the *logia* relating to the coming Son of man.

Basic to Käsemann's view are the results of the influential study in which he isolated in the Pauline letters and in the Synoptics 'Sentences of Holy Law (*Sätze heiligen Rechtes*)'.[15] Examples of such expressions of the eschatological *ius talionis* are 1 Corinthians 3.17, 'If anyone destroys God's temple, God will destroy him', and Matthew 10.32, 'Everyone who acknowledges me before men, I also will acknowledge before my Father who is in heaven, but whoever denies me before men, I also will deny before my Father who is in heaven'. These 'sentences of holy law', in strict chiastic form, are attributed by Käsemann to the Christian prophets, the leaders of the community, who in expectation of the imminent Last Day themselves proclaimed the verdict of the ultimate Judge without recourse to any other sanction.

This theory of Käsemann has not gone uncriticised. Klaus Berger[16] has argued that the *form* of the so-called 'sentences of holy law' – so noteworthy for Käsemann – belongs to the genre of sapiential exhortation in which the sanction corresponds to the action, according to a law of imminent justice; that is, the 'sentences' are actually conditional relative clauses of wisdom origin having nothing to do with legal norms. Such formulations could be transposed into the realm of eschatology, but by themselves they do not require us to assume the existence in a Christian community of prophets who promulgated the eschatological *ius talionis*. It is extremely hazardous to extrapolate from a literary feature (whose precise classification is uncertain) to a judgment concerning the identity of those who may have employed the form: form criticism cannot demonstrate the prophetic origin of the 'sentences' investigated: indeed, as used by Berger, the same critical method suggests that the sayings had their setting in church instruction (especially for new converts).

There is, however, an even greater weakness in Käsemann's position. While it has been claimed by Perrin that Käsemann's case for the attribution of the 'sentences of holy law' to Christian prophets is clearly and convincingly argued,[17] it is our impression that the position and the necessary presuppositions are simply affirmed, or reaffirmed, virtually without argument of any kind. In the essays of Käsemann which were published (or delivered) prior to the appearance of 'Sentences of Holy Law in the New Testament' (1954) there are only two references to prophets or prophecy of the Christian era. In connection with the interpretation of 2 Peter 1.20, it is asserted that 'primitive Christian prophecy was one of the most dangerous instruments, if not indeed the determining factor, in the increasing hold which Gnosticism was gaining on the Church' by the time of the writing of this epistle, a trend which was thwarted by the adoption of an institutionalised ministry conferred by ordination.[18] Secondly, in an essay entitled 'Is the Gospel Objective?' (delivered and published in 1953)[19] the following statement is made concerning the part played by prophets in early Christianity:

> As we can see clearly in the Revelation of John, they clothed their own epigrammatic words in the form of 'I' sayings of Jesus, speaking as Spirit-filled men with the authority and in the name of the exalted Christ. When these words were handed on, the distinction between the exalted and the earthly Lord very quickly disappeared, more especially as primitive Christianity was not particularly interested in the latter. Thus it came about that countless 'I' sayings of the Christ who revealed himself through the mouth of prophets gained entry into the Synoptic tradition as sayings of Jesus.

This assertion amounts quite simply to a restatement of what Bultmann had said thirty years earlier, and for which, if our examination thus far has any validity, support – even when sought in the Revelation – is proving very feeble. There is no argument, no justification, offered by Käsemann. As far as the other reference to Christian prophecy is concerned, if early Christian prophets were in fact allowed to be so freely creative as Käsemann asserts, it is little wonder that he has to blame them for assisting the spread of Gnosticism within the Church! As we observed earlier, the Gnostic authors of apocryphal gospels fulfil the function given by Bultmann and his followers to Christian prophets in respect of the teaching of the Lord. Many, however, will not be convinced that the primitive Church (as early as AD 50) had opened the door to this dangerous development by failing to distinguish between the earthly and the exalted Lord speaking! In any case, the links Käsemann makes between Christian prophecy and the Gnosticising of the Church are too sharply drawn. Much more certain knowledge – not just suppositions and hypotheses – is needed about Christian prophecy, and much more about the origin and nature of Gnosis, before affirmations of this kind may be made.

These two references from earlier essays form the total preparation that Käsemann offers for the introduction of Christian prophets in the discussion of the 'sentences of holy law'. The opening paragraphs of this essay are concerned with the structure of these 'sentences' and with their expression of the talion motif, which is located on the eschatological level because the Last Day is imminent in which God will vindicate his own honour and make good his own justice. Men serve God in this 'only in so far as they are already proclaiming in the earthly present the criterion of his *ekdikēsis*'.[20] The next sentence is revealing. 'Admittedly, this is only possible for those who, *being endowed with charisma*, have knowledge of this criterion and are therefore able to proclaim it *with prophetic authority*.' (Italics mine.) Does it require charismatic endowment to recognise the criterion of the divine judgment and proclaim it? And why has it to be proclaimed with prophetic authority? Were there not others in the Church, besides prophets, to speak, instruct and warn? These questions become even more embarrassing to the case if the form of the judgment-declaration belongs to the genre of wisdom-exhortation. It is hard to avoid the impression that the italicised phrases are added – without argument or justification – in order to introduce what is affirmed from that point onwards, that those who deliver the 'sentences of holy law' are charismatics and, in particular, prophets of the Christian era. The following extracts show how the case develops.

> The word of the one who is endowed with charisma, who discloses within the community the criterion of the divine action, anticipates the verdict of the ultimate Judge ... The prophet's sole task is to open up the vista towards this tribunal and thereby to set the guilty man in the place of decision ... (p. 68).

> The eschatological law of God, mediated through charismatic men ... (p. 73).

And, with reference to Revelation 22.18 ff.:

'Here we see that it is prophetic proclamation which is the original *Sitz im Leben* for sentences of this kind' (p. 76).

It would seem that the attribution of the so-called 'sentences of holy law' to Christian prophets is really presupposed by Käsemann: at best it is only a hypothesis, but one which has been elevated to the level of assumed fact by reason of its frequent reiteration. Indeed, the evidence produced by the Bultmann school in support of the contention that the Christian prophets played a creative role in respect of sayings later attributed to the earthly Jesus proves, on examination, to be lacking in substance and authority. The information we can glean from the New Testament (especially from Paul and Acts) does not lend much credibility to the suggestion that the Christian prophets were the leaders in the Christian communities: that honour and authority surely belonged to apostles in the primitive church, and they were witnesses to the ministry of Jesus and therefore capable of exercising control on what was accepted as dominical teaching: another group, however important, can hardly have possessed the authority to speak in the name of the risen Lord and have their declarations accepted – even eventually – as words of Jesus. If it is to merit further consideration, the case for the attribution to Christian prophets of a creative role in respect of *logia Iēsou* requires validation by fresh and convincing arguments. Repetition of the evidence so far adduced cannot establish the theory.

2. A NEW CASE DESCRIBED AND APPRAISED

In a paper delivered to the 1975 meeting of the SBL Seminar on Christian Prophecy[21] Gerald F. Hawthorne set out a number of considerations which he regards as cumulative evidence for attributing a creative role to Christian prophets in respect of some sayings which the Gospels present as dominical utterances. Important to his case – which we shall present in abbreviated form, though as far as possible in his words – is Hawthorne's definition of a Christian prophet as 'an unusually powerful figure in the early church, who spoke the Word of the Lord with authority, who was a receiver and proclaimer of divine revelations, as well as one who was a preacher of the Good News in the more traditional sense' (p. 105). The meaning of 'authority' and 'Word of the Lord' in this definition is clarified when the author describes what he calls the 'higher dimension' of prophecy: this is related directly to a special work of the Spirit upon the prophet by which the Spirit revealed to him a word from the risen exalted Christ: 'under these circumstances, when the prophet spoke, this word became *the command of the Lord* for either an individual Christian or for the whole Christian community (1 Cor. 14:29–30, 37).... Like OT prophecy this prophetic message was an immediate communication of God's (Christ's) word to his people through human lips. There are times in fact when the risen Christ speaks in the first person and the figure of the prophet fades into the background –"Behold," says Christ, "I am coming as a thief" (Rev. 16:15; 22:7), so that it is clear that the words that are spoken are indeed the words of the heavenly Lord (Rev. chaps. 2 and 3)' (pp. 107–8). It is highly significant that the New Testament passages alluded to in support of this view of prophetic authority are from Paul and the author of Revelation: we must again question the correctness of an appeal to these figures. Were Paul and the prophet-author of Revelation typical of Christian prophets, or was not theirs a unique consciousness and authority?

Let us now turn to the evidence Hawthorne lists for the possibility that some sayings of Christian prophets became intermingled with sayings of Jesus in the Gospel tradition.

(1) Although the early Church may have been concerned to distinguish between the 'Jesus of history' and the 'Christ of faith', it believed firmly that these two titles belonged to the same person: cf. Acts 2.36, 'God has made him both Lord and Christ, this Jesus whom you crucified'. Hence, the risen Lord of the Church was not a different person from that of the Jesus who lived and taught in Palestine, but one and the same.

(2) The early Church regarded itself as a community of the Spirit, living in those last days when God would pour out his Spirit on all flesh so that men and women would rise up and

prophesy (Acts 2.16–21). 'This meant that the church *expected* people to prophesy, to speak the word of the Lord to them, and that therefore they not only looked back to a past time when Jesus *was* with them, but to the exciting present moment of Jesus' immediate presence as their living Lord-Christ-with-them-today' (p. 110).

(3) Therefore the interest of the early Christians lay not only in what their Lord had once said to a basically Jewish audience, but also in what the living Lord of the Church was saying to them (Palestinian and Hellenist) in the present. 'It is a fact of Scripture that these Christians took for granted that the heavenly Christ *would reveal* to them further truths about himself' (pp. 110–111), John 16.12–15 being, as it were, the 'proof-text'.

(4) The prophet in the pneumatic community spoke with the authority of one especially inspired by the Spirit, 'that all important identifying power which made the prophet's words one and the same with the words of Christ. He was the earthly voice, so to speak, by which the heavenly Lord expressed in propositional form those promised relevations of himself and of his will to individuals and/or groups in the early history of the Christian church' (p. 111).

(5) The words of the exalted Jesus spoken through his prophets are very similar in form and content to the words of Jesus recorded by the evangelists: cf. Revelation 2.10 and Matthew 10.28, 22; Revelation 16.15 and Matthew 24.43–44/Luke 12.39; Revelation 3.5 and Luke 17.7–9, etc. 'Surely it is not too much to say that *all* words of the Blessed One, whether spoken in Galilee by his own lips or from heaven through his prophet, would be heard by the church as instruction, encouragement, chastening or promise from the ever-living Lord. . . . If this is so then is it impossible to imagine that some of the risen Lord's words could have been included perhaps unconsciously among the pre-resurrection sayings of Jesus?' (p. 112).

(6) *a.* Although Paul appears to distinguish the words spoken by the earthly Jesus and preserved in the tradition of the Church from those that were not (that is, from those spoken

by the risen Lord through a prophet, even through Paul himself), we should not forget that the apostle vigorously asserted his independence from tradition (Gal. 1.11–12, 2.6): consequently, when he says that he received something from the Lord he may have meant that he received it directly from the risen Lord through revelation (cf. Gal. 2.2 and perhaps Rom. 14.14 and 1 Cor. 7.12). *b.* Paul's general instructions to the churches contain elements of what have been thought of as traditional sayings of Jesus, or at least allusions to them, but in these cases Paul felt no compulsion to point out this fact or to distinguish between them and his own demands as apostle-prophet for the conduct of the churches to which he wrote. In the liturgy of the Eucharist there are commingled traditional words of Jesus with prophetic words of the risen Lord, viz. the Pauline exposition of the Jesus-words, 'For as often as you eat this bread and drink the cup, you proclaim the Lord's death until he comes' (1 Cor. 11.26). *c.* The well-known *en logō kyriou* (1 Thess. 4.15) could be (among other acknowledged possibilities) a reference to words of Christ spoken through a prophet (Paul himself) by revelation: at any rate, the saying was regarded by the early Church as dominical as any of the sayings of Jesus in the Gospels. *d.* Could the eucharistic command 'Do this ... in remembrance of me', found only in Luke and in Paul – where it is claimed to have been received from the Lord (1 Cor. 11.23) – be 'a concrete example of a word received from the risen Lord, transmitted to the Corinthian church by the prophet Paul, which found its way into the gospel narrative as a word of Jesus through Paul's close associate, Luke'? (p. 114).

(7) The interpretative treatment of Old Testament Scripture by early Christian prophets may provide a model for the prophet's working with the traditional sayings of Jesus in the period before they took written form in the Gospels. 'Is it not possible that a *peshered* saying of Jesus (or even a saying *de novo*) from a Christian prophet would readily have had an authoritative status and as such been given a place within the gospel tradition?' (p. 114), for example, the dual divorce terminology in Mark 10.11–12.

(8) The author of the letter to the Hebrews is a Christian prophet, and Hebrews 2.11–13 and 10.5–7 show him taking Old Testament words, quoting them (exactly or freely) and placing them in the mouth of Jesus so that they become his words.

(9) Sayings of Jesus which are today not considered part of the text of the traditional four Gospels were accepted as authentic *logia* and therefore canonised by certain segments of the early Church, for example, the ending(s) of Mark and the passage John 7.53–8.1. Such sayings could have been drawn from oral tradition, but is it not also possible that they were oracles of Christian prophets which solved particular problems faced by the early church and which supplemented the tradition available?

(10) In John's Gospel there are places where it is extremely difficult to say where the words of Jesus end and the words of the evangelist begin (cf. John 3.10–21). This may be explained by viewing the Fourth Gospel as the work of a Christian prophet guided and validated by the Spirit of truth in his creative handling of tradition.

(11) That the words of the risen Lord are equally authentic with those of the earthly Jesus is evidenced in the early centuries of the Church's history by the Didache, the writings of Justin Martyr and of Melito of Sardis. In his sermon *On the Passover* Melito the prophet fades out, as it were, like the prophet in Revelation, and the risen Lord speaks through his mouth: 'I am the Christ. I am the one who destroyed death ... and bound the strong one. ... Therefore, come unto me all families of men ... and receive forgiveness for your sins. I am your forgiveness ...'. And Hawthorne asks: 'How would Melito's audience have heard these words? Would they, could they, have been in a position to distinguish them from any sayings of Jesus they perhaps may have read in or heard from the gospels – assuming, of course, that the gospels were regularly and universally read alongside the OT in the liturgy of the church? (I rather think this is a twentieth century question – one that never would have occurred to them)' (p. 117).

Such is Hawthorne's cumulative case in favour of the view

that Christian prophets did have a part in the creation of dominical sayings. His concluding remarks show that he does not think that more than a small number of Jesus-sayings were so created, and that the early Church was incapable of or uninterested in distinguishing between the words of Jesus and the words of its exalted Lord, 'but it seems that, if there was a situation in which the words of the earthly Jesus and the words of the risen Lord existed side by side and circulated together, there was bound to be (at least there was the possibility of) a mingling of the two together – unconsciously if not consciously' (p. 117): moreover, sayings originating with Christian prophets (considering their credentials and inspiration) and later attributed to the earthly Jesus should not be regarded as inferior or secondary to 'genuine' *logia*, for 'authenticity' has to do with the authority by which a word comes to us, not with its place on the scale of historical probability.[22]

What response can be made to this case, presented carefully by a cautious and conservative scholar? On certain details of his theory we have reservations: for instance, on his interpretation of Acts 2.16–21 (see Chapter Four above); on his use of the Johannine doctrine of the Spirit to validate what early Christians in general might assume or do. And we would want to offer alternative explanations of some of the New Testament passages which form bricks in the building of his hypothesis, e.g. Mark 10.11–12, and on the ending of Mark.

But there are two features of his case which lead us to pass upon the whole the verdict 'Not proven'. The first concerns the measure of authority he attributes to the Christian prophet – 'a pneumatic and awesome figure within the early church, ... What he said was accepted by the community as the command of the Lord to be obeyed without question' (p. 109). This is true of the Old Testament prophet, but is it true of New Testament prophets, with the exception of Paul and the prophet-author of the Revelation? When discussing the Church prophets' activity in Corinth Paul does not give the impression that their words were divinely authoritative: if they had been, why should they have required testing and control? Congregational prophets did not enjoy the authoritative status of Paul or of the unknown 'John' who wrote Revelation.

The second important point is that Hawthorne's case does not provide one absolutely certain prophetic word which became a part of the tradition of Jesus' utterances. In each of the crucial sections of his argument (points 5 to 11) he either presents a question, 'Is it not possible that . . .?', 'Could not such and such be the case . . .?', or he builds upon an assumption – about the prophetic character of John's Gospel or about the prophetic origin of Hebrews – which does not necessarily command the widespread assent of scholars. In short, imaginative guesses, speculation and unproved assumptions – to which different scholars will react differently – take the place of concrete proof for his case. In our view, Hawthorne has not decisively proved that any single utterance of the risen Lord spoken by a prophet actually became part of the tradition of dominical sayings. What he has done – and perhaps he was attempting to do no more – is to provide a very reasonable case for the *possibility* of some intermingling.

One very difficult and important question now remains for discussion. Once we admit the possibility of a mingling of words of the earthly Jesus and words of the risen Lord spoken through prophets, by what criteria may we decide which sayings belong to the latter category? Käsemann's criteria, based on form (a precise chiastic structure) and content (a concern with eschatological judgment), are much too uncertain to be valuable: the 'I-sayings' – on the analogy of Odes of Solomon 42.6 and Revelation 16.15 – do not form a satisfactory distinguishing feature of the Christian prophet's creative work: the *amēn*-formula is proof to V. Hasler[23], but Jeremias, as we have seen above (pp. 64–65), argues against this and claims that the *amēn*-formula is a most important key in discovering the *ipsissima verba* of Jesus. In his unpublished Oxford thesis (1973), entitled *New Testament Prophecy and the Gospel Tradition*, W. J. Houston uses functional and formal criteria to distinguish prophetic sayings: they must have a 'paracletic' function, be based on an apocalyptic midrash of Old Testament words or words of Jesus, and use eschatological language. But just why an evangelist or apostle or even Jesus himself, rather than a Christian prophet, could not have spoken most of the passages Houston isolates is never made clear.

Perhaps the most serious and systematic attempt to formulate criteria by which to identify the contributions of Christian prophets to the Synoptic tradition has been made by M. E. Boring in his essay, 'How May We identify Oracles of Christian Prophets in the Synoptic Tradition? Mark 3.28–9 as a Test Case'.[24] Having gathered together the sources available for describing the Christian prophet Boring seeks to discover a characterisation of Christian prophets prior to any of these sources. This he attempts to do (i) by projecting as far as possible the available data about Christian prophetism backwards and into Palestine; (ii) by constructing a list of the characteristics of the prophet which are common to several of the sources, or which, though unique, provide some typical trait of Christian prophetism; and (iii) by comparing this characterisation with those Synoptic *logia* of Jesus which (*a*) *originally* existed independently of a narrative context and (*b*) on other grounds are regarded as secondary (i.e. church products) rather than words of the historical Jesus.

Some of the evidence and presuppositions embodied in this methodology are open to criticism (e.g. the desire to provide a Palestinian home for prophecy, even in the case of Revelation: see Chapter Three, note 2): but it is with Boring's application of his criteria to Mark 3.28–29 that we shall concern ourselves. He makes six assertions about this *logion*. (i) It is an independent saying which rests uncomfortably in all its present contexts; (ii) it possesses formal indications of prophetic speech, the initial *amēn*, chiasmus, and legal form; (iii) the saying is eschatological in content and tone – a characteristic of all early Christian prophecy; (iv) the saying was uttered with the authority fitted to the Christian prophet rather than to the Christian scribe; (v) the *logion* is considered as a *pesher* on Isaiah 63.3–11, and interpreting Scripture was an important function of Christian prophets; and (vi) the association of the Holy Spirit with the Spirit of prophecy (common to such sources as Revelation, Acts, the Didache, Hermas) is evident here.

These are indeed interesting suggestions for deciding the prophetic origin of 'dominical' sayings, but each one is open to question. (i) Does the fact that a saying rests uncomfortably in all its contexts necessarily mean that it is not genuinely dominical? It may point in that direction, but we must not forget that the evangelists may well have experienced difficulty in 'locating' items of remembered tradition. (ii) The formal indications of prophetic speech in Mark 3.28–29 include the *amēn*-formula and, while many are disposed to regard this as clear evidence of prophetic utterance, others claim it as a sign of Jesus' own authoritative speech. (iii) There is no valid reason for claiming that all Christian prophecy was eschatological and that therefore only eschatologically oriented sayings can have originated with Christian prophets. There are shades of Käsemann's arguments and assumptions here. Undoubtedly prophecy could be eschatological, but it is noteworthy that Paul describes prophecy, not in eschatological terms but in terms of exhortation, building up and strengthening the church (1 Cor. 14.3). (iv) Whilst the saying investigated was authoritatively uttered, that does not *per se* decide its prophetic origin: did not Jesus himself speak with authority? (v) If the exegesis of Old Testament Scripture (in this case Isa. 63.3–11) underlies this saying, was such exegesis confined to Christian prophets? Are there not adequate grounds for claiming that Jesus too interpreted the Old Testament with reference to himself and his mission (i.e. in a *pesher*-ising way)? (vi) This last criterion is of significance only if the others have all been shown to be operative.

By raising these questions we do not wish to give the impression that we are not taking serously the possibility that some sayings of Jesus preserved in tradition originated from Christian prophets: on the contrary, it is because we do take it seriously that we have to draw attention to the immense difficulties that belong to the attempt to decide which sayings derive from prophets, as well as to the numerous presuppositions that underlie Boring's decision in the case of Mark 3.28–29.

Further evidence on these presuppositions may be gathered from a short paper Boring read to the 1976 meeting of the SBL Seminar on Christian Prophecy in which he offers a test exegesis of Matthew 10.23 in order to establish its prophetic origin.[25] Here he again uses the *amēn legō hymin* formula as an indication of prophetic speech, and argues that the oracle, in its *original* meaning (i.e. apart from Matthew's understanding of it), must have referred to the parousia at the end of history, that is, it must be eschatological! He also adduces the 'wandering' motif and the persecution theme (23a) as indicative of prophetic speech and experience, and offers the opinion that 'in the early post-Easter enthusiasm it was Christian prophets who first identified Jesus as the Son of man and ... the whole tradition of Son of man sayings depends on this early prophetic speech event. The transition from the proclaimer to the proclaimed was facilitated by Christian prophets who spoke in Jesus' name as the Son of man' (p. 130). The saying as a whole, Boring thinks, is a reformulation and representation by a Christian prophet, seeking to speak to a specific missionary problem, of a Jewish tradition (Sotah 9.15) that in the days immediately before the Messiah's advent 'the people of the frontier (or, Gebul) should go about from city to city with none to show mercy on them'.

Is not hypothesis being built upon hypothesis in order to demonstrate the prophetic origin of a *logion*, whose genuineness (not simply by reason of its unfulfilled content) as a dominical utterance is confidently affirmed by many scholars of great distinction. If, in the case of Käsemann's argument, repetition fails to persuade, so will the assertion of inherited presuppositions in Boring's exegetical investigations. We find it almost incredible that Boring thinks he can dispose of the origin of the Son of man sayings in the cavalier fashion indicated by the quotation given above: when New Testament critics of the stature of Bultmann, E. Schweizer, M. Black and C. F. D. Moule argue for the genuineness of this or that group of Son of man sayings, or indeed (in the case of Moule) for the genuineness of many in each group (those relating to the ministry, to the Passion and, thirdly, to the *eschaton*), to say that 'the whole tradition of Son of man sayings depends on an early prophetic speech event' smacks of irresponsibility: one wonders what next will be claimed for 'Christian prophetic speech'!

To return to Hawthorne's cautious conclusion that perhaps

a small number of Jesus-sayings were created by Christian prophets because 'if there was a situation in which the words of
the earthly Jesus and the words of the risen Jesus existed side by
side and circulated together, there was bound to be (at least
there was the possibility of) a mingling of the two together –
unconsciously if not consciously':[26] in principle, this commands
our assent, but the problems of distinguishing between the two
(which we consider necessary, but not on the grounds of difference in their authority or inspiration), are still pressing. To
be open to the possibility of having an origin in inspired Christian prophetic speech in the name of the risen Lord a Jesus-
saying must (i) fail to pass all the linguistic, environmental and
other criteria for genuineness; (ii) be proved to be no part of
the evangelists's editorial work; and then (iii) be shown to be
consistent with what we know of the characteristics of Christian
prophetic speech in the first century (which, unless we are too
heavily dependent on Paul and Revelation, is not really very
much). In our opinion, not many sayings of Jesus in the Synoptics will pass these tests.

Some may think that the expositions of some of the parables
derive from Christian prophets, though they could equally well
be ascribed to Christian teachers: others will think of at least
some of the words of Jesus after his resurrection, and in particular of Matthew 28.18–20 which is an expansion over similar
sayings in Luke 24.48 f., John 20.21 and Mark 16.15(?) to include the only trinitarian baptismal formula in the New Testament; and yet others may think of the words of Matthew 18.20,
'where two or three are gathered together in my name, there
am I in the midst of them', in which the speaker is the risen
and glorified Christ whose presence is a reality in the community of his followers. Luke 11.49–51 may well reveal another
kind of prophetic activity, viz. the modification and expansion
of *ipsissima verba* to bring out their meaning for the Christian
prophet's own era and audience. On this passage E. E. Ellis
comments: 'The present passage seems to be best understood
as an oracle from the exalted Jesus or, more likely, a saying
from his [Jesus'] pre-resurrection ministry "*pesher*-ed" and
given detailed application by a Christian prophet to the

judgment on "this generation" in the siege and destruction of Jersualem (AD 66–70).'[27] Of how many more passages this could be said with any degree of confidence we do not know: possibly Luke 21.20–24 could be included, but there is no evidence that the liberty of adaptation – which, be it noted, is not the same as the creation of sayings *ex nihilo* – was taken casually. Even with regard to what we have just suggested, very little though it may appear to some, we must admit that we are dealing only with possibilities, not with certainties or assured results.[28]

CHAPTER EIGHT

THE DECLINE OF PROPHECY

Before considering the eventual decline of prophetic activity in the Church and the reasons for it we must acknowledge that at the beginning of the post-apostolic period Christian prophets were still held in high esteem. The document which shows most clearly the great repute they enjoyed is the Didache, which, despite attempts to date it around the middle of the first century, seems most appropriately located somewhere in the years between AD 70 and 110.[1] Chapters 11–13 of this book contain virtually all of the information that is relevant to prophets. Like all itinerant missionaries they are to be received if their teaching conforms to the Church's doctrine: indeed they are to be received 'as the Lord'. But if a prophet (or apostle) remains three days or, on departing, asks for money, he is a false prophet (11.1–6). Contrary to Paul's insistence that prophets be examined, the Didachist asserts that it is an unforgivable sin to test or judge any prophet speaking in the Spirit. Nevertheless, objective criteria are given for discerning the genuinely inspired: disinterestedness in reward, consistency between what he practises and what he preaches, and, above all, 'having the ways of the Lord' (11.7–12). Whereas any ordinary Christian traveller should be prepared to earn his living by manual work while he stays with a group of his brethren in any place, a prophet who wishes to settle permanently in a community is worthy of his maintenance by virtue of his highly prized prophetic ministry as the congregation's 'high priest': he is to be given permission to offer the eucharistic thanksgiving as much as he wishes (10.7), since, as a pneumatic, he is not tied, as other Christians are, to the wording or the extent of the usual prayers: he is to be treated somewhat like the Levite in the book of Deuteronomy (Deut. 18.6ff., 26.12ff.) and given the first-fruits of the wine-press and threshing-floor, of oxen and sheep, of baking, of wine, oil, of money, clothes and every possession, as seems appropriate, so that he need not have any material worries (13.1–7). But the Didache seems to imply that the number of prophets was already dwindling and the 'office' becoming obsolescent. It is assumed that there will not be a prophet in every church, for bishops and deacons are to be appointed to perform the service of prophets and teachers, and the former are not to be despised – an indication of how highly the prophets were still respected in this period of transition from a pneumatic to an institutional ministry.

> The attitude of the *Didache* towards prophecy is comparable to that of Paul towards speaking with tongues. Paul entirely allows that speaking with tongues is a gift of the Spirit; but for the sake of edification and good order in the church he prefers coherent prophecy. Just so the author of the *Didache* allows the supreme value and unique prestige of a true prophet; but experience has by this time proved that self-authenticated wandering prophets are a doubtful blessing.... The aim, therefore, of the author of the *Didache* is to create, wherever it did not yet exist, *a resident ministry of episcopoi and deacons.* Where this already exists, he tries to raise its status; congregations are bidden to regard these as their 'honourable men along with the prophets and teachers'. Evidently one main object of the *Didache* is to secure that the resident ministers shall *no longer be treated as of subordinate importance.*[2]

Something of genuine prophetic character appeared in Hermas's *Shepherd* (of uncertain date between *c.* AD 90 and 130), but the author, despite his reception and transmission of revelations, does not lay claim to the position or title of prophet, nor does he number the prophets among the dignitaries of the Church, apostles, bishops, teachers, deacons (*Vis.* 3.5.1.). Nevertheless, he is still acquainted with those who have the divine Spirit and who speak as filled by the angel of the prophetic Spirit. The Eleventh Mandate – the subject of an important monograph by J. Reiling[3] – is devoted to the discernment of spirits, and the criteria offered are moral. A man inspired by the divine Spirit will give proof of that by his life and character.

The difference between a false prophet and a true one will be obvious from their behaviour before the assembled congregation. The former will act like a soothsayer or oracle-monger (*mantis*), but the true prophet will speak only when God decides.

> When the man who has the divine Spirit comes into a synagogue of righteous men, who have faith in the divine Spirit, and intercession is made to God by the synagogue of those men, then the angel of the prophetic Spirit, who is in contact with him, fills the man, and the man, filled with the Holy Spirit, speaks to the congregation as the Lord pleases (*Man.* 11.9).

An ambitious, self-assertive, talkative or mercenary 'prophet' betokens inspiration from a very different source.

Although Ignatius of Antioch and, to a lesser extent, Polycarp may be rightly considered as having possessed prophetic gifts, the chief manifestation of prophetism in the post-apostolic age was the rise of the Montanist movement which appeared about AD 156 (or AD 172) in Phrygia and spread quickly to other parts of the Christian world, including Gaul, Rome and North Africa, where it gained its most illustrious convert in Tertullian. Montanus, the leader of the movement – which called itself the 'New Prophecy' – taught that, as the dispensation of the Father had given place to the dispensation of the Son when Christ came to earth, so now the dispensation of the Son had given place to the dispensation of the Spirit. For (he claimed) Christ's promise of the coming Paraclete had now been fulfilled and he, Montanus, was the Paraclete's mouthpiece. The coming of the Paraclete was the immediate prelude to the second coming of Christ and the establishment of the New Jerusalem in Pepuza, one of the towns of Phrygia.

Montanism could have been a valuable revivalist movement within the Church for it had some admirable features, without which it would surely never have attracted the allegiance of Tertullian. Its adherents believed in the present work of the Holy Spirit in the individual, stirring up charismata, prophecy and enthusiasm; and they affirmed a rigorous standard of

Christian morality and discipline. Thus they wanted to revive, with great urgency (in view of their belief in the imminent second Advent of the Lord), some of the things which had given power to primitive Christianity.

Very probably such a revival seemed necessary in view of the growth of rigid ecclesiastical organisation. The Church was acquiring a stiffer framework of law and order, a fixed canon of Scripture, an authoritative hierarchy, an aspiration after uniformity, a retrospective eye and an increasing respect for tradition. This institutional shell – a defence against the chaos of Gnosticism – was valuable, but it might come to stifle the freedom and warmth of the Gospel and might tempt the average Christian to be content with good churchmanship – believing and doing what he is told to believe and do, and, when he fails, taking his punishment and receiving his absolution, thereby becoming once more safe in the bosom of the Church. No doubt there was awareness of this danger and therefore Montanist enthusiasm received a widespread welcome for a short time.

But Montanism was soon found out. Its enthusiasm was not purely and specifically Christian, but was tainted with the fanaticism of the old Asiatic cults of which Montanus had once been a priest: the Holy Spirit seemed to be saying nothing of any religious or intellectual value to his ecstatic prophets and prophetesses (Prisca and Maximilla) – a judgment which any study of the authentic prophetic sayings preserved[4] would confirm; and the asceticism was so extreme as to be virtually dualistic. Moreover, the glorification of Pepuza as the New Jeruslem was a threat to all the ancient sees, and, what is even more important, just when the formation of a defined canon of Scripture seemed the right way to check Gnosticism, the Montanists were teaching men to expect new and authoritative revelations. Furthermore, the movement did not stay within the Church: it became sectarian, a group of Christians who are visibly spiritual, a congregation of saints (cf. Tertullian, *de Pudicitia*, 21). If some criticism of authoritarianism and institutionalism might have been wholesome, the tendency of Montanism was to repudiate the existing hierarchy altogether and, by its emphasis on prophets acting and speaking under immediate inspiration, to deny the whole principle of order and authority which the bulk of the Church had welcomed, as well as the particular idea of apostolic succession which was at this time coming into prominence as the basis of episcopal authority.

Although the dogma that there are Christian prophets survived rather longer than prophecy itself, the repudiation of Montanism marks the effective end of prophecy in the Church. Its disappearance was due, in the main, to two factors, both of which have been suggested in the preceding paragraphs. The number of people possessing prophetic powers grew less and less (cf. Did. 13.4) – perhaps with the waning of the imminent expectation of the End – and appointed office-bearers and Scripture took the place of pneumatic inspiration: as G. Friedrich says: 'Montanism was the last great flare up of prophecy in the Church. When it was resisted and vaniquished, the institutional office gained a decisive victory over the *charisma*'.[5] A similar point of view is expressed by Käsemann: 'A ministry conferred by ordination is bound to be the natural opponent both of Gnosis and of primitive Christian prophecy. Thus it was no accident that the latter either died out gradually within the ranks of orthodoxy or was crowded out into the sects. II Peter has lost all knowledge of it: prophecy is now confined to written prophecy as recorded in the Old Testament'.[6] Fr. von Campenhausen's observations in his essay 'Prophets and Teachers in the Second Century',[7] are more nuanced. While admitting that the element of 'office' became more and more prominent in the course of the second century, he is of the opinion that it is not office as such, i.e. as a legal and institutional fact, that is the real focus of interest, but rather the traditional body of truth, the truth of God's Church, which it is the duty of the office to serve and to preserve. In the service of that truth both office-holders and the old free men of the Spirit continue to play their part.

To start in every case from a supposed opposition between two separate blocs, the official and the charismatic, is a typical modern misunderstanding. Not only do office-holders possess the Spirit, but the spirituals, for their part, to the extent that they rightly belong to the Church, derive the power of their teaching from traditional apostolic truth.[8]

Consequently, when the era of the prophets closed, with the condemnation of Montanist enthusiasm and ecstasy, the increasing hellenisation of the Church – with its emphasis on the spirituality and rationality of the faith – created the tendency to rely more and more on rational and didactic forms of spiritual utterance: therefore the place of the prophets, as witnesses to the living truth, was taken by the 'teachers' of both the free and the official Church, that is, by catechists, preachers, scholars and theologians (e.g. Clement of Alexandria), men who were the first conscious champions of an individualist and personal spirituality in the Church, but whose authority was based not on any revelation directly received but on the exposition of existing traditions, and very particularly of the Scriptures, at first those of the Old Covenant, but later those of the New and of the apostles.

Whereas Friedrich and Käsemann attribute the decline of prophecy primarily to the increasing authority of an official ministry in an institutionalised Church, von Campenhausen sees the matter more in terms of a dogmatic principle: the proper transmission of apostolic truth. When prophets could no longer be found or depended upon to fulfil that function, their place was taken by exegetes and teachers of the authoritative tradition. It is not necessary, in our view, to judge either of these approaches wrong: in all probability the two factors emphasised – office and the transmission of truth – were jointly responsible for the rapid disappearance of prophetic activity in the Church. After all, were not bishops appointed to be custodians of the apostolic truth and tradition?

The other main reason for the decline of prophecy was that false prophets were present – from a quite early stage in the Church's life (cf. 1 John and the Pastoral epistles) and in growing numbers in the second and third generations (cf. the Didache and Hermas) – and these undermined the position and authority of genuine prophets. Unfortunately the Church was not easily able to safeguard prophecy from the excesses of charlatans, since it did not possess or (if it possessed it) did not effectively use the charisma of discernment. As we have pointed out, various criteria for the 'testing of spirits' were from time to time enunciated and presumably employed in the unmasking of fraudulent prophets: they certainly were in relation to Montanism. But ability to discern and repudiate the false seems not to have been balanced by ability to discern and retain the true. The result was that the apparently large number of false prophets abroad not only undermined the authority of the decreasing numbers of true prophets, but also brought the whole phenomenon of prophetism under suspicion, thus aiding its decline and eventual disappearance. Irenaeus did issue a warning to his contemporaries that true prophecy was being driven out of the Church as a consequence of the battle against false prophets (*Adv. Haer.* 3.9.9): but his warning was in vain and the Church lost the immensely valuable contribution to its life that comes from genuinely inspired prophetic utterance.

CHAPTER NINE

PROPHECY TODAY

When confronted by the title of this chapter many will think of the expectations and hopes expressed, sometimes privately, sometimes through the media, that archbishops, bishops and other church leaders will utter a 'prophetic' word in the contemporary situation: such words are usually sought at times of real or supposed national crisis, and those who call for them seem to desire an ecclesiastical pronouncement that will condemn some threat to the national fibre or morale, that will expose injustice, discrimination or exploitation, that will give the Church a 'lead', that will recall the citizens to the central verities of the Christian faith, thus restoring hope, vision, integrity and direction.

It would probably be true to say that no generation has failed to produce a person or persons of this 'prophetic' stature: the renowned William Temple was certainly one such, and in recent times Dom Helda Camara, Martin Luther King and Bishop Trevor Huddleston may justly be regarded as men of comparable power and influence. Of course, not only church leaders are expected to speak 'prophetically': parish clergy and ministers are looked to as well for the declaration of a 'word from the Lord' on pressing social problems and inequities: and men and women have not been lacking to speak out thus, sometimes at considerable cost to themselves. As Paul Tillich has said:

The prophetic spirit has not disappeared from the earth. Decades before the world wars, men judged the European civilisation and prophesied its end in speech and print. There are among us people like these. They are like the refined instruments which register the shaking of the earth on far-removed sections of its surface. These people register the shaking of their civilisation, its self-destructive trends, and its disintegration and fall, decades before the final catastrophe occurs. They have an invisible and almost infallible sensorium in their souls; and they have an irresistible urge to pronounce what they have registered, perhaps against their own wills. For no true prophet has ever prophesied voluntarily. It has been forced upon him by a Divine Voice to which he has not been able to close his ears. . . . Most human beings, of course, are not able to stand the message of the shaking of the foundations. They reject and attack the prophetic minds, not because they really disagree with them but because they sense the truth of their words and cannot receive it. They repress it into mockery or fury against those who *know* and dare to say what they know.[1]

However, this kind of prophetic utterance – whose value and relevance at certain times cannot be impugned – stands in the succession of Old Testament prophetic speech, and especially in the tradition of the denunciations of Amos and Micah, rather than in the succession of New Testament prophets, in so far as we are able to discover their activities and oracles. The exception is, as we have observed several times in this book, the prophet-author of Revelation who by what he writes, and especially in his messages to the seven churches of Asia Minor, seems to stand closer to the prophets of the Old Covenant by virtue of the authority he claims and exercises to praise or, more often, to condemn the life of the communities to which he addresses himself. He resembles the apostles like Peter and especially Paul who function in relation to the early Church in an authentic prophetic manner 'in the name of the Lord', rather than the community-prophets who, according to the book of Revelation, seem to be the guardians (and exponents?) of the prophet-author's words, and who, in the Pauline churches, seem to have played a secondary, though significant, role. It should be noted that in the case of Old Testament prophets, New Testament prophets, and the successors of both in the eras to follow and up to our own time, they are men (and women) who speak from *within* the community of faith (Israel or the Church) to both 'church' and 'nation' or 'society'. That there are figures outside the Church today who speak in 'prophetic' tones or act 'prophetically' is, in our view, undeniable; but with their activities, authority and value we cannot concern ourselves here, save to say that God's mouthpieces need not always be church-members.

Some, perhaps only a few nowadays, will, at the mention of the word 'prophecy', immediately think of prediction, and especially of the prediction of the End or the Second Coming. For a long time the enigmatic and abstruse symbols of the book of Daniel and the Revelation have been used as 'time-tables' by which one may identify how far along the road we are towards the parousia. This misuse of the books mentioned rests on a misunderstanding of their nature and purpose and of Scripture's function in general: it often leads to identifications and predictions which are, to say the least, bizarre. How is it that, for many decades, those who specialise in such 'interpretations' of Scriptural passages always arrive at the conclusion that the very moment in which they are speaking or writing is the immediate prelude to the imminent parousia? If the biblical authors cannot be wrong – and the proponents of this type of Bible-reading are doughty defenders of Scripture's infallibility – then something must be wrong with the interpretation! It is not with this kind of understanding of prophecy that we intend to deal here. Prediction does not seem to have been an important function of the New Testament prophet, and certainly not datable prediction of the End.

What we shall attempt to consider in this chapter is the revival of the phenomenon of prophecy in Pentecostal Churches and in Neo-Pentecostal circles. By 'Pentecostal' we mean those churches (and their members) which claim, not always in their titles, to be Pentecostal. 'Neo-Pentecostal' refers to groups and persons within the traditional churches (both Protestant and in the last decade or so the Roman Catholic Church). The phrase 'charismatic renewal' has become more common usage than 'Pentecostal' among Neo-Pentecostals. But behind the various names there stands the same central reality, the theological raison d'être of Pentecostalism – the Pentecostal or charismatic experience of the Holy Spirit in a life- and speech-transforming event in the career of the Christian. Only when the Holy Spirit permanently, personally and fully enters the believer's life does that person become eligible for endowment with one or more of the nine gifts of the Spirit listed in 1 Corinthians 12.8–10 (*lit.* 'a word of wisdom, a word of knowledge, faith, gifts of healings, operations of works of power, prophecy, discernment of spirits, different kinds of tongues and interpretation of tongues').

In classical Pentecostal belief, and in some Neo-Pentecostal teaching, 'baptism' in the Spirit' – the experienced event of being filled with the Spirit as the apostles were 'filled' on the day of Pentecost (Acts 2.4) – is quite distinct from and subsequent to conversion to Jesus Christ and distinct from, though not necessarily subsequent to, 'water-baptism': it normally has as its outward sign or evidence a breaking into tongues (glossolalia) by the one 'baptised' (Acts 10.44–47). But the New Testament texts which are adduced by Pentecostals as their warrant for this doctrine are open to an alternative and preferable exegesis.

After lengthy investigation of the relevant passages F. D. Bruner[2] asserts (and, in our view, correctly) that in the New Testament conversion, baptism, the laying on of hands and the gift of the Holy Spirit are essentially and unconditionally connected, though they may vary in the form and order of their manifestation: there is not, as the Pentecostals suggest, an additional gift of the Spirit, a 'second blessing', which is conditional upon a more holy life and a more zealous striving. J. D. G. Dunn drew similar conclusions from the evidence: 'We shall see that, while the Pentecostal's belief in the dynamic and experiential nature of Spirit Baptism is well founded, his separation of it from conversion-initiation is wholly unjustified.'[3] Cardinal Suenens puts the matter very directly: 'For us, as well as for the majority of Christian Churches, there is not a duality of baptisms, one in water and one in the Spirit. We believe there is but one baptism. Baptism in the Holy Spirit is not a sort of super-baptism, or a supplement to sacramental baptism which would then become the pivot of the Christian life.'[4] Seeking to re-express in a less ambiguous way the experience that is called 'baptism in the Spirit', the Cardinal speaks of 'a deeper aware- ness of the presence and the power of the Holy Spirit', 'a very special grace ... a renewal of [the] spiritual life accompanied by a feeling of peace and joy of a kind hitherto unknown', 'a release of the latest potentials of the Spirit ... a new and more developed awareness of our true Christian identity which only faith can reveal to us; and which brings alive this faith, giving it a new reality and an awakened eagerness to spread the Gospel' (p. 81).

The last of these attempted re-expressions recalls Simon Tug- well's view:[5]

> In the New Testament, in the early church, all that Pente- costals understand by 'baptism in the Spirit' is referred quite strictly and simply to what it means to be a christian at all. The experience of the Spirit is not subsequent to that of con- version and faith; the experience of Pentecost is identical with the baptismal confession that 'Jesus is Lord' (and how often the New Testament warns us against Pentecostal mani- festations divorced from this confession!)

With this affirmation made, Tugwell finds himself compelled to concede:

> Unfortunately, we have to recognise that, generally, our own experience of baptism, of being christians, falls far short of this wholeness, this integrity. The Pentecostal doctrine is in- tended to be one way of coping with this situation, by allow- ing an independent reality to conversion, and to the experi- ence of the Spirit in his fulness.... It throws a very direct challenge to those who are content to have been validly bap- tised, without aspiring to supernatural awareness or to a ministry and witness in the power of the Spirit, indeed with- out expecting to be 'changed' ..., those, in fact, who only know 'from hearsay' that they have been baptised at all.

But there is a salutary warning offered: 'There should be no question of seeking something *extra*, something other than the basic reality of the salvation wrought in Christ, and our incorporation into Christ in baptism. There are no "perks", there must be no looking for "experiences", only a desire to see the work of Christ made real in us and through us.' Although it is unlikely that strict Pentecostals will give assent to this kind of interpretation or re-interpretation of 'baptism in the Spirit', in our opinion it stands closer to New Testament teaching on the experience and vitalising power of the Spirit in the Christian.

We must now proceed from the 'gift' to the 'gifts', the spiritual gifts available to the 'Spirit-filled' believer or, in our terms, 'the authentic Christian', the newly created man in Christ. We are glad to pass over 'speaking with tongues' – a subject on which there is an enormous literature – only pausing to reiterate what we affirmed in an earlier chapter, that the phenomenon described in Acts 2 is not the same as the gift which Paul deals with in 1 Corinthians: whether that gift – exposed to serious misunderstanding and misuse, requiring to be subjected to testing and discrimination, needing to be put and kept in its proper place – was 'speaking in heavenly languages', or 'utterances in ecstatic or mystical speech' as well as 'a way in which the Spirit prays in us, inciting us to praise of God's wonderful achievements, expressing the intoxicating novelty of belonging to the new creation brought into being by the resurrection of Jesus Christ from the dead, and at the same time pointing to the mysteriousness of this belonging, which we cannot apprehend while we are still in "the body of this death" ' ,[6] is not a question we have to answer here. It is the gift of prophecy with which we must deal, as that gift has been revived in the whole Pentecostal movement. If personal participation in Pentecostal worship and direct witnessing of prophesying are necessary for anyone who wishes to comment on the phenomenon, then the present writer has no claim to do so, for, apart from listening to a recording of prophetic utterances given at a conference of Roman Catholic charismatics in Belgium, he has not heard prophetic speech. Nevertheless, our approach will be as fair and balanced as this acknowledged limitation and the literature consulted will permit.

The spiritual gift of prophecy is exercised in most Pentecostal assemblies: someone who is filled with the Spirit will speak, in the vernacular, sentences or phrases reminiscent of a biblical passage or an amalgam of biblical passages: the utterances are usually of an exhortatory kind and most often with an eschatological and sometimes visionary context and content. (This is true to my recollections of the 'prophecies' heard on the recording just referred to: they were admonitory, couched entirely in biblical phraseology, eschatologically oriented, and accompanied by declarations like 'Behold!' ... and 'I see ...'.) Prophecy is similar to glossolalia in occurring most frequently in an ecstatic or para-ecstatic condition and in understanding itself as a medium of the Spirit: indeed, it is even claimed that prophecy differs from speaking in tongues only in that it is spoken in understandable speech. Prophecy is usually defined, even by more careful exponents of Pentecostalism, as something more than simply Spirit-inspired utterance, as, in fact, the voice of the Holy Spirit himself: in prophecy we have, in the words of Donald Gee,[7] 'the *speaking* Spirit'. Since prophecy is considered to be spontaneous and direct spiritual communication, strict Pentecostals feel that it ought not to be confused with preaching or prepared remarks and addresses where the substance is obtained by more conventional or indirect means than immediate inspiration. The Spirit delivers *his* message directly and spontaneously to the assembly through the prophet. In his book *The Era of the Spirit*[8] J. Rodman Williams writes:

> In prophecy God speaks. It is as simple, and profound, and startling as that! What happens in the fellowship is that the Word may suddenly be spoken by anyone present, and so, variously, a 'Thus saith the Lord' breaks forth in the fellowship ... in prophecy God uses what he finds, and through frail human instruments the Spirit speaks the Word of the Lord.

Prophecy therefore adds to the inner illumination of the believer by the Spirit the element of public proclamation (thus evoking an element of public discernment) and it is this that Pentecostals have extended beyond a narrow circle of inspired leaders to all 'Spirit-baptised' believers: the gift of prophecy may be expected by every 'Spirit-filled' Christian.

The exercise of the gift of 'the interpretation of tongues' in Pentecostal meetings is generally regarded as a form of prophecy, not as a translation or a paraphrase of a message in another language, unknown or foreign, but rather as an interpretation or reproduction in conventional speech or comment provided by someone who is inspired to understand the import of the mysterious, glossolalic utterance. The interpreter, it would seem, like the prophet, addresses the assembly in an earnest, ecstatic, exhortatory and usually eschatological manner of speech, as an instrument of the Spirit and for the edification of the congregation.

Thus far in our description of the gift of prophecy today we have been reflecting the views of classical Pentecostals. We must now see what writers from within the Neo-Pentecostal or 'charismatic' movement have to say about the phenomenon. After affirming that 'in Jesus the Prophet we are a prophetic people', Simon Tugwell[9] alludes to the fact that scholars are reminding us that petitionary prayer, and especially intercession, is a prophetic function to be exercised only by those endowed with the divine Spirit, Genesis 20.7 ('he is a prophet and he will pray for you ...') being the scriptural warrant for the view. However, he goes on to assert that 'all prophecy is, first and foremost, the proclamation of what God has done in Christ, it is praise of his mighty deeds' (p. 61).

> Praise, then, is a prophetic function, in these last days; it is also ... a sign that we have indeed begun to enter into the freedom of the sons of God, that we have reached the point of the 'coming of faith', that *metanoia* [=that 'repentance' which leads a man into new life] has become a reality for us (p. 62).

The recently published book *New Heaven? New Earth?: An Encounter with Pentecostalism*[10] – probably the most serious attempt yet made to write a 'charismatic theology' – contains four essays by British Roman Catholic theologians, two of which contribute to the theme of our inquiry. Under the sub-title 'Receiving God's Word' – one of the distinctive features of Pentecostalism – Peter Hocken briefly discusses the gift of prophecy.

This spiritual gift, he says, 'illustrates the gift-character of the Word of God, not just as given once and for all, but as constantly uttered and renewed; by its regular exercise Pentecostalism shows that Christians are not simply hearers but also speakers of the Word', uttering, under the influence of the Holy Spirit, a word of God addressed to a particular contemporary situation. Although he notes that W. J. Hollenweger[11] is critical of the typical Pentecostal restriction of spontaneous prophecy to exhortation for edification, Hocken feels that the Pentecostal practice of prophecy confronts other Christians and Churches with what they officially declare the ministry of preaching to be, namely, an activity which partakes of the character of the Word of God and not simply a human adumbration of that Word. (That this high evaluation of preaching is 'official' and widespread in Protestant circles is, in our opinion, rather questionable.) Hocken goes on:

> Prophecy often shocks visitors to Pentecostal Churches because ordinary human beings claim to receive a Word from God – so whilst in theory the Pentecostal belief that prophecy is for all generations adds little to received theologies of the Word and of its ministry, in practice their prophecy challenges other Christians to believe that they can receive a Word from God to speak in the name and strength of Jesus Christ.
>
> Relating prophecy to preaching as common yet distinct instances of man empowered to speak God's Word shows how spiritual gifts need to be situated in ordinary Christian life, avoiding the danger of treating charismata as freak phenomena unconnected with day-to-day Christian living and worship (p. 25).

For Tugwell 'prophecy' manifests itself as praise and proclamation; for Hocken it is closely related to the activity of preaching, despite the fact that the latter is normally, unlike (classical) Pentecostal prophesying, an utterance of some length. Of particular interest are Hocken's observations on the possible comparison between, on the one hand, the relationship between biblical inspiration and Pentecostal prophecy and, on the other hand, the relationship between Scripture and tradition as understood in contemporary post-Vatican II Catholic theology. He sees as common to both the following features:

> the attribution of a clear priority and a 'once and for all' character to the biblical Word: the interpretation and application of the 'once and for all' biblical Word in an ongoing Christian ministry that shares in the authority of the Word, who is Jesus Christ: the impossibility of a total separation between the contrasting elements, the original and the ongoing, there being a sense in which both Christian prophecy and Christian tradition precede and find embodiment in the written Word.
>
> All these activities are both human and divine, the Spirit of God working in, among and through men; both Christian prophecy and Christian tradition are open to some degree of abuse, with the possibility of their expressing human cussedness and immobility, personal pride and arrogance, as well as the saving Word and Gospel of the Lord.
>
> So whilst classical Pentecostals have little time for the notion of tradition, their practice and beliefs concerning prophecy imply a high degree of continuity between the apostolic Church and subsequent generations, with a view of Christian cooperation in the one completed work of Jesus Christ that is closer to the Catholic than to the Protestant tradition (pp. 25–26).

If, in this context, Hocken means by 'the Protestant tradition' the classic Calvinist view that the so-called 'miraculous' spiritual gifts (glossolalia and prophecy) belonged only to the apostolic, or pre-canonical age, then his claim may be justified. The theory that the extraordinary manifestations of the Spirit in the apostolic age served the purpose of inaugurating the Christian dispensation and were then withdrawn because they were no longer needed is foreign to Paul's thought. Of course, the charismata are all, in a sense, temporary in Paul's view because 'the perfect', i.e. the parousia, is imminently expected: but he does not envisage them as passing away or ceasing before the 'face to face' knowledge of the parousia.[12] In defence of the gift-withdrawal theory characteristic of main-stream Protestantism it has to be said that, since the Reformers reacted sharply and correctly against the crude religious 'magic' of the medieval Church, it is understandable that their heirs became and have, to a large extent, remained suspicious of anything mysterious or miraculous, including the revival of the apostolic gifts. But Pentecostalism – and for this we must be grateful – simply forces us all to come face to face with the contemporary exercise of *all* the spiritual gifts. He would be a singularly brave (or prejudiced) man who would claim that there is not room in the Church today for the careful and discerning exercise of the charismata God appointed for the edifying of the Church – not because the New Testament provides a blueprint or normative pattern of Church life and organisation – but because the Church in the twentieth century needs the benefits of spiritual gifts.

> For at a time when Christians of all traditions realise deeply the imperfections of the church, Christ has given gifts 'for the perfecting of the saints' (Eph. 4: 12, AV). At a time when the continued existence of the Christian ministry is at stake, with panic, uncertainty and surrender on every hand, there are gifts 'for the work of ministry' (Eph. 4:12). At a time when Christians are ashamed at their divisions but embarrassed by misdirected efforts to heal them, gifts are available 'until we all attain to the unity of the faith' (Eph. 4.13). At a time when heresy and half-truth and doctrines of men bewilder Christians, God has given his gifts, 'so that we may no longer be children, tossed to and fro and carried about with every wind of doctrine, by the cunning of men, by their craftiness in deceitful wiles. Rather, speaking the truth in love, we are to grow up in every way into him who is the head, into Christ' (Eph. 4:14, 15).[13]

The second essay in *New Heaven? New Earth?* which is pertinent to our discussion is by George Every and is entitled 'Prophecy in the Christian Era'. With great erudition the author traces the history of prophetism and of theological evaluations of it through the centuries, but, for our purposes, what is most significant is Every's understanding of what 'prophecy' was and is. At the beginning of his essay he asserts that 'Among Christians the typical exercise of prophecy is the spiritual interpretation of Scripture, of the Old Testament in the New, and of the whole Bible thereafter', although this spiritual or allegorical interpretation has never been limited to scriptures in any religion. Other writings are read in the same way, and signs of the times interpreted spiritually. 'Every Christian who meditates on the work of Christ, and reads the signs of his presence in the Bible, in the history of the world and of the Church, and in the course of his own life, has some share, through the power of the Spirit, in the prophetic office of all Christians' (p. 163). This description of prophecy is reminiscent of the understanding of 'prophetic word' that we mentioned at the beginning of this chapter. With reference to Pentecostal groups, in particular, Every claims that in them 'a wide variety of prophetic or spiritual interpretation is used, not only in the choice and exposition of texts from all the Scriptures, but in the interpretation of signs of the times in events of the day, in the situation of the group, and in particular intimations or hunches that may be given to members of it'. Despite the oddness of the last clause in that quotation, Every has shrewd words to say about the evaluation of Pentecostal prophecies:

> No doubt in discerning what is truly of the Spirit in such prophecies the Bible is one of our standards, but one that can be misused. There is nothing surprising in the frequent use of the language of King James' version in modern prophecies, and no reason to regard them as fabricated imitations for this reason, but the emphatic 'Thus says the Lord' may betray uncertainty on the defensive rather than genuine faith, and direct citations from Scripture may often belong to the penumbra of the message rather than to the essential core of the meaning. In the discernment of spirits a wider range of comparison is needed than can be provided by the text of the New Testament and modern Pentecostal and Neo-Pentecostal literature (p. 164).

In discerning spirits, Every contends, the whole history of

allegorical interpretation of Scripture is relevant and, with it, the history of the other forms of prophecy that evolved in the Church in the age of the Fathers and the Dark Ages (e.g. monastic vigils, visions, the distinction made by Aquinas between natural prophecy – which is akin to imaginative or extra-sensory perception – and Spirit-inspired, revelatory prophecy). 'Discernment of spirits is more than a matter of discerning truth from error and delusion. It is also a matter of distinguishing between the group's common mind [= natural prophecy] and the illumination of the Spirit when he tells us more than we think and more than the prophetic speaker and those who listen to him can immediately understand' (p. 198). One cannot help but wonder how a classical Pentecostal would react to that!

Every agrees that the interpretation of tongues is a form of prophecy. Paul's exhortation 'to excel in building up the church' (1 Cor. 14.12) and his commendation of prophecy over tongues helps us in a situation when bursts of enthusiastic praise, of singing hymns and singing in tongues, need to be interrupted by a controlled utterance, bringing the group back to the actual situation. This may take the form of a reading, from Scripture or from some spiritual writer, with or without comment, or of a prophetic saying (which may be descriptive of a vision or symbolic image), or a prophetic action that implies judgment on the situation. 'All these forms of prophecy', the writer claims, 'have a history in Christian tradition' (p. 192).

In our view, Every's essay 'Prophecy in the Christian Era' – despite its display of recondite learning – is marred by the fact that (i) it begins from a narrow and unusual definition of prophecy as the spiritual or allegorical interpretation of Scripture; and (ii) it casts the net so wide (in history and tradition) that almost any means of bringing insight and judgment to bear on a (group) situation is classed as the exercise of the prophetic gift. We have here a kind of 'domestication', almost a 'demythologising' of the charisma, and this is a tendency we detect in some other Neo-Pentecostal interpretations of prophecy in the Church today. Is reading from some spiritual writer, even if it brings insight and judgment to bear on the

community, really the exercise of prophecy? Is 'spiritual interpretation' of biblical passages and other texts, whether in words
or in deeds or both, an adequate description of the 'gift of prophecy' in the light of the information which the New Testament
documents provide, directly and indirectly, about the phenomenon? In an earlier chapter of this book we have suggested
that spiritual interpretation or charismatic exegesis of Scriptural (Old Testament) passages – similar to the Qumran *pesher*-
ising technique – may have formed part of the New Testament
prophet's function, but is probably more characteristic of the
'teacher' (*didaskalos*) in the Christian community. Those Pentecostal and Neo-Pentecostal writers who describe the 'gift of prophecy' in terms of edificatory exhortation (*paraklēsis*) seem
closer to what in our view Paul, Acts and the book of Revelation
consider to be the chief function of prophets.

Before we attempt to draw together the strands of our discussion in this chapter, we must deal with two arguments which
are critical of the entire Pentecostal movement and, in particular, of its expectation of the spiritual gifts, including prophecy,
within the life of Christian communities. The first – which we
have already mentioned – is that the gifts, being given for the
inauguration of the Church, have ceased or been withdrawn
as no longer necessary: this view has no clear Scriptural warrant; requires the dismissal as counterfeit of some of the experiences of sincere Christians today who can offer evidence in their
own lives and ministries of the rediscovery of spiritual gifts; and
creates an artificial division (as admittedly its opposite view
often does) between gifts dramatic and gifts less dramatic which
God has given for the functioning and growth of the Church.

As an expression of the second criticism – which is directed
at Pentecostalism as a whole – we quote from Don Cupitt's
review[14] of the book *New Heaven? New Earth?*:

The book ... does not remove my misgivings about the
dangers of what I cannot help seeing as a retreat into fantasy.
Let me elaborate, very briefly. There is a true and a false
ecstasy in Christianity. The true ecstasy, inspired by God,
is that intellectual self-transcendence by which we are able

to *repent*, and that intellectual world-transcendence by which we are able to have *faith* in God. Repentance and faith are supernatural (because they have an element of transcendence in them) and they are realised in us by the divine Spirit; and they are intellectual acts, in which the divine reason enables us to transcend in freedom our ordinary one-level thinking. The false ecstasy is a kind of nature-religion, and it perceives the divine in the freakish or extraordinary in nature: in abnormally intense emotion, in subjective intensity of conviction, in fantasy, in the occult and so on. It confuses the true transcendent with the abnormal and, instead of exalting reason, repudiates it.

Lest it be thought that this kind of view emanates only from so-called 'liberal' theologians, we draw attention to remarks made in the fairly conservative Calvinistic periodical *The Reformed Journal* by Roy M. Anker. He is not directly criticising Pentecostalism, but rather the distortion (among evangelicals) of the biblical understanding of faith. Nevertheless, he has some aspects of Pentecostalism in mind:

> There is an ever-growing tendency today ... to make faith a kind of game in which God is always the loser, in which we tease God and ourselves with sensational wagers over his existence. We make magic with God: we seek miraculous healings, tongue-speakings, and extra-providential acts as a vindication of our credulity. God is put to the test to get definite empirical confirmation that he exists, which is really to confess a lack of faith, make him our servant, at our beck and call for our often trivial demands.... In today's fractured world, and in Christ's, the presence of God needs most to be manifest not in sensational gimmickry, gratifying mostly oneself, but in the thirst for and embodiment of 'the Harvest of the Spirit ... love, joy, peace, patience, kindness, goodness, fidelity, gentleness and self-control' (Gal. 5:22).[15]

The 'repudiation of reason', 'making magic with God', striving for the gifts of the Spirit instead of thirsting for the "fruits of the Spirit"': these are indeed very serious charges against

Pentecostalism and its most significant feature, the revival of spiritual gifts. Are they justified? The exercise of even the most dramatic of the spiritual gifts need not be at the expense of the growth in the charismatic of the 'fruits of the Spirit'. Of course, sometimes – perhaps too often – the possession of spiritual gifts leads to jealousies, rivalries, invidious comparisons with and criticism of fellow Christians, insensitivity, divisiveness and so on. But this state of affairs is not the inevitable result of the possession and exercise of charismata. Every Pentecostal would agree that the greatest charism of all is 'love' (*agapē*): and many will testify that Pentecostal groups are the most accepting, loving and liberating companies of Christians they have encountered. With reference to the suggestion that God is being 'tested' to provide evidential proof of himself in miraculous gifts, we would reply that if this is the spirit or intention of Pentecostals (or any other Chrstians) it is rightly condemned: but, in our view, Pentecostals exercise gifts that are *given*, that are *available* to those who have surrendered themselves wholly to God in Christ: they are not seeking 'experiences' to confirm God's presence, through the Spirit, in the individual, the Church and the world.

Cupitt's claim about 'false ecstasy' and the 'repudiation of reason' may be answered, *with reference to prophecy*, by drawing attention to the fact that if the Pentecostals' exercise of the gift is governed by the Pauline understanding of and injunctions about it, then it is not a repudiation of reason nor an anti-intellectual phenomenon. For Paul, prophecy communicates at the level of the mind (1 Cor. 14.19, 31); it does not absolve the individual believer or the Christian community from reasoning about their faith (1 Cor. 14.29 ff., 'the discerning of spiritual utterances'): on the contrary, where prophecy is active the community is compelled to think *more deeply* about its faith and its life. At the same time, of course, prophecy does not permit faith to be solely a matter of rational thought (and with that Cupitt would agree): for, in an existential way, prophecy opens up the community to itself and the believer to himself: it makes the believer conscious of wider dimensions of reality ('transcendence' surely?) and sets him in the context of ultimate

reality. This is how 'edification' takes place.[16] Genuine prophecy is not evidence of some kind of 'nature-religion which
perceives the divine in the freakish and extraordinary in
nature': rather it ought to help us 'to transcend in freedom our
ordinary one-level thinking' by recalling us to the fact that the
living Spirit of God is not only 'high above us' but also 'deep
within us', bearing – it is to be hoped – his own fruits and giving
his own gifts for the growth and vitality of the Church. Spirit-
inspiration is not opposed to rationality, but it is often a necessary supplement to it.

In conclusion we shall now try to relate the major insights we
have gained on the exercise of prophecy today to what has been
said, in the preceding chapters, on prophecy in the New Testament.

(1) The expectation, common to all Pentecostals, that the
gift of prophecy will be exercised by any believer who has been
grasped by the living Spirit of God is consonant with the witness
of Acts, Paul and the Revelation to an understanding of the
Church as composed of men and women who are *all* potentially
prophets. According to the New Testament, some Christians,
by reason of their profound or lasting endowment with the gift,
are called 'prophets': Pentecostalism, so far as we are aware,
does not distinguish between the office of prophet (given only
to a few) and the gift which can be desired by all 'Spirit-filled'
believers. (The classical Pentecostal understanding of 'baptism
in the Holy Spirit' as a 'second blessing' does not appear to
have any warrant in the New Testament teaching on conversion, baptism and the reception of the Spirit.)

(2) The expectation and presence of the gift of prophecy,
and all other charismata, within the life of Christian communities (house-groups, prayer-meetings, as well as larger assemblies)
is in substantial agreement with New Testament teaching: for
it is clear from Paul's writings and implicit – if not explicit –
in Acts and the book of Revelation that prophecy is exercised
in the context of congregational worship, for the benefit of the
community and not for the individual's self-glorification.

(3) If, with Simon Tugwell, we see certain types of prayer,

and especially praise, as prophetic in character, then we are in touch with one strand of Pauline teaching: 1 Corinthians 14.13 ff. suggests that we should not rigidly distinguish between prophecy and prayer in the setting of worship, and comparison of the lists in 1 Corinthians 14.26 and 14.6 reveals that in the former 'a hymn' takes the place of 'prophecy' in the latter. Prayer and praise therefore appear to be associated with prophecy: and in the captivity epistles Paul speaks of 'psalms, hymns and spiritual songs' (Col. 3.16; Eph. 5.18 f.), the last mentioned presumably being songs inspired by the Spirit. To this extent prophecy expresses not only the word of God to men but also the response of men to God and his word, a response initiated and sustained by the Spirit.

(4) Despite some criticism for so doing, Pentecostalism usually restricts prophecy to edificatory exhortation. If our suggestion that a very important part of the New Testament prophet's ministry was to offer *paraklēsis*, i.e. exhortation, encouragement, warning and so forth, in the form of 'pastoral preaching', then we have a large measure of common ground between the type and intention of 'prophetic speech' within Pentecostal assemblies and the New Testament churches. In the former, however, the giving of the prophetic exhortation is not restricted to a particular group, nor would Pentecostals regard prepared discourses (such as a sermon) as prophetic, because they lack the immediacy of the Spirit's inspiration.

(5) If prophecy in Pentecostal circles sometimes has a visionary context and content, it must be remembered that the book of Revelation – composed by a prophet and called, in its entirety, *prophēteia* – has a large amount of visionary material within it: symbols and imagery (occasionally even rather grotesque) are also found in it, and these forms of 'communication' are often present in Pentecostal prophecies.

(6) It does not seem that the New Testament regards the interpretation of tongues as a form of prophecy: these are two separate gifts in the series listed by Paul, and obviously the apostle did not want them to be confused in the Corinthian situation. The gift of 'discerning spirits' is associated by Paul with prophecy in that it provides a test of prophetic utterance

and a control against its abuse: it functions in relation to prophecy as the 'interpretation of tongues' does to glossolalia. It
may be that Pentecostals do not always distinguish 'prophecy'
and 'speaking in tongues' and therefore confuse the gifts by
which each is interpreted.

(7) Some of the activities that came to be regarded as prophetic in the later history of the Church (and which were
mentioned by Every in the essay discussed above) cannot be
paralleled in the New Testament teaching on prophecy, and
they would not, in our view, be consonant with that teaching.
That they are legitimate developments of New Testament
teaching will be affirmed by those who are disposed to hold
'tradition' in high regard. Monastic vigils that are regarded as
'prophetic' and the distinction between 'natural' and 'inspired'
prophecy do not seem to conform to anything we can find in
the New Testament teaching concerning the gift.

(8) The view, expressed by Every, that prophecy is properly
defined in terms of spiritual or allegorical interpretation of
Scripture, which is then used to discern the signs of the times
in the events of the day and to clarify the situation of the charismatic group, does not, in our view, do justice to the New Testament witness. Charismatic exegesis of the Old Testament may
have formed part of the prophet's ministry, but it was – or so
we have argued – more characteristic of the Christian 'teacher'.
But do Pentecostals recognise 'teaching' as a spiritual gift? Presumably not, unless it be included in their understanding of
the gifts of 'the utterance of wisdom' and 'the utterance of knowledge', both non-dramatic charismata.

(9) If it is true that in classical Pentecostal assemblies prophecy occurs most often in an ecstatic or para-ecstatic condition, we have to bear in mind the fact that some commentators
on 1 Corinthians 14 maintain that for Paul prophecy was
uttered in ordinary, though probably excited, perhaps ecstatic,
speech, hence the need for the further gift of discernment. But
if Paul's approval of prophecy was based on its intelligibility
(over against the unintelligibility of glossolalia), then the condition of ecstasy in which it was uttered must have been subdued;
it could not have been an abandoned frenzy. At most it could

have been a state in which speech was automatic, i.e. not controlled by the conscious mind. However, our view is – and many scholars would assent – that for Paul prophecy or inspired speech was not uttered in any kind of ecstatic condition at all.

(10) Like Paul, Pentecostals strongly encourage the exercise of the gift of prophecy in the assembly; but unlike Paul, they seem to pay less attention to the gift which forms a pair with prophecy, i.e. 'the ability to distinguish between spirits' (1 Cor. 12.10). This is not a gift of interpreting spiritual revelations, but the evaluation of prophetic utterances by the community, an evaluation aimed at determining whether the word is a genuine word of the Spirit, or a word to be ignored and rejected. Why is this gift not emphasised by Pentecostals? Perhaps because it is found very difficult to decide what is genuinely of the Spirit today. Perhaps because it is not considered necessary in view of the fact that so much Pentecostal prophecy is entirely biblical in content, and therefore undoubtedly Spirit-inspired. This leads to the final comment we wish to make on the matter of prophecy today.

The exhortatory (and visionary) content of prophetic utterance in Pentecostal assemblies and groups is almost always reminiscent of scriptural passages or of an amalgam of scriptural passages. The emphatic 'Thus says the Lord ...' (itself recalling Old Testament prophetic speech) may, as Every suggests, 'betray uncertainty on the defensive' and seeking authority: we would suggest, however, that it gives to the utterance what really amounts to 'second-hand' inspiration. If the prophetically gifted person in Pentecostalism exhorts mainly by means of the repetition of biblical sentences, phrases, visions and images, is this really evidence of immediate and direct inspiration by the Spirit, or of the possession of a miraculous gift? Has the Spirit nothing to say that is new and still 'in conformity with the faith'? There are many who could interject into a prayer-group a word from the Bible but would in no sense regard themselves as exercising the prophetic gift. Is it the inspiration, or compulsion, or impetus to say the biblical word that is prophetic, rather than the content of what is actually said? The absolute authority of the word of God given in

Scripture (often in the King James' version), which is a fundamental tenet of classical or strict Pentecostal belief, may be the reason why prophecy is almost exclusively biblical in content, and therefore, in the absence of further contextualisation, explanation and application, not obviously or immediately helpful in guiding and directing the community in its life, witness and service. In our opinion, there is little difference between the Pentecostal's 'Thus saith the Lord ...' and an evangelist's 'The Bible says ...', followed by a selection of texts quoted out of context and without interpretation. The authority of inspiration belongs to Scripture: does it belong to the repetition of Scripture? Is a man exercising the gift of prophecy when he is impelled to utter a biblical passage *or* when he utters an immediately (i.e. first-hand) inspired word of judgment, exhortation, consolation or warning? This is a question which Pentecostals must face and answer. Perhaps – and we can put it no stronger than that – it is those who have grasped the meaning of Scripture, perceived its powerful relevance to the life of the individual, the Church and society, and declare that message fearlessly who are the true successors not only of the Old Testament prophets but also of the prophets in the New Testament: they – and they do not need to be preachers or ecclesiastical leaders – build up the Church for its prophetic mission in the world.

NOTES

CHAPTER ONE (pp. 1–47)

1. This section draws extensively on the excellent paper presented to the first meeting of the SBL Seminar on Christian Prophecy by M. E. Boring, ' "What are we looking for?" Toward a Definition of the Term "Christian Prophet" ', *Society of Biblical Literature Seminar Papers, 1973*, Vol. 2 (Scholars Press, Missoula, Montana), pp. 142–54

2. Cf. the remarks on etymology by James Barr, *The Semantics of Biblical Language* (Oxford University Press, 1961), pp. 107 and 109

3. T. M. Crone's book *Early Christian Prophecy: A Study of its Origin and Function* (St Mary's University Press, Baltimore, 1973) is really an analysis of the word or word-group. When he fails to find the term 'prophet' in the Qumran texts, in Josephus's description of his self-understanding, and in the rabbis' descriptions of their functions, he assumes that the phenomenon of prophecy (however defined) was absent. Since his study of prophecy in the New Testament is mainly a discussion of texts in which the word 'prophet' appears, important source material (relating to Paul himself, as well as in John's Gospel) may be omitted from consideration.

4. The history of this debate from Sohm and Harnack to the present can be found in Ulrich Brockhaus, *Charisma und Amt: Die paulinische Charismalehre auf dem Hintergrund der früchristlichen Gemeindefunktionen* (Wuppertal, 1972), pp. 1–89

5. It is a weakness in Wayne Grudem's valuable work *The Gift of Prophecy in the New Testament Church, with special reference to I Corinthians* (unpublished Ph.D. thesis, Cambridge University, 1976) that he makes his understanding of the authoritative character of the Old Testament prophet's message as 'words of God' the definitive criterion for the recognition of prophets in the New Testament. Were there no other influences upon the understanding and expression of the genuine prophetic phenomenon in New Testament times?

6. Boring, op. cit., p. 147

7. Boring, op. cit., p. 149

8. Cf. G. Friedrich, *TDNT*, Vol. VI, p. 853

9. *SBL Seminar Papers, 1974*, Vol. 2, p. 44

10. Ibid., p. 58

11. J. Lindblom, *Prophecy in Ancient Israel* (Blackwell, Oxford, 1962), p. 6

12. J. Hempel, 'Prophet and Poet', *JTS* (old series), Vol. xl (1939), pp. 113 ff., claimed that the great Greek poets exhibited the prophetic spirit, delivering the word of their god under a sense of inner compulsion: the writer

of Titus 1.12 who calls Epimenides a 'prophet' may reflect this idea, even if he is only reproducing a current conventional term.

13. C. H. Dodd, *The Bible and the Greeks* (Hodder and Stoughton, London, 1935), p. 178

14. E. Fascher, *PROPHĒTĒS: Eine sprach- und religionsgeschichtliche Untersuchung* (Giessen, 1927), p. 207

15. H. Krämer, *TDNT*, Vol. VI, pp. 793–5; another good summary of pagan Greek usage of *prophētēs* may be found in Crone, op. cit., pp. 12–39

16. R. Reitzenstein, *Die Hellenistischen Mysterienreligionen* (Leipzig, 1910), pp. 160 ff., 209 ff.: but see H. A. A. Kennedy, *St Paul and the Mystery Religions* (Hodder & Stoughton, London, 1913) and more, recently, G. Wagner, *Pauline Baptism and the Pagan Mysteries* (ET: Oliver and Boyd, Edinburgh, 1967)

17. A. J. Heschel, *The Prophets*, Vol. II (Harper, New York, 1962), p. 252

18. In *Israel's Prophetic Heritage* (*Festschrift* for J. Muilenburg, ed. B. W. Anderson and W. Harrelson: S.C.M. Press, London, 1962), pp. 98–107: quotation from p. 107

19. O. H. Steck, *Israel und das gewaltsame Geeschick der Propheten* (Neukirchen, 1967), especially pp. 60 ff.

20. B. Vawter, *The Conscience of Israel* (Sheed and Ward, London, 1961), p. 28

21. G. von Rad, *Theology of the Old Testament*, Vol. II (Oliver and Boyd, Edinburgh, 1965), p. 96

22. E.g. H. M. Teeple, *The Mosaic Eschatological Prophet* (SBL Monograph Series, Vol. 10: Philadelphia, 1957), pp. 2 f. and 111

23. J. Klausner, *The Messianic Idea in Israel* (New York, 1955), p. 260

24 *TDNT*, Vol. VI, pp. 815–16

25. For a review of the opinions on the dating of this work from the Testaments see A.-M. Denis, *Introduction aux pseudépigraphes grecs d'Ancien Testament* (Brill, Leiden, 1970), p. 58

26. R. H. Charles, *The Apocrypha and Pseudepigrapha of the Old Testament* (Oxford, 1913), ad. loc.; also his *The Greek Versions of the Testaments of the Twelve Patriarchs* (Oxford, 1908), p. 45

27. O. Eissfeldt, *The Old Testament: An Introduction* (ET: Blackwell, Oxford), p. 635

28. J. Blenkinsopp, 'Prophecy and Priesthood in Josephus', *JJS*, Vol. xxv (1974), pp. 239–62 (especially 241 f.): several of the points made in this section will reveal indebtedness to this important article.

29. Cf. G. Delling, 'Die biblische Prophetie bei Josephus', *Josephus-Studien* (*Festschrift* for O. Michel: Göttingen, 1974), pp. 109–21

30. Cf. J. Reiling, 'Pseudoprophētēs in the Septuagint, Philo and Josephus', *NovT.*, Vol. xiii (1971), pp. 147–56

31. Cf. E. Bammel, '*Archiereus Prophēteuōn*', Vol. lxxix (1954), pp. 351–6; C. H. Dodd, 'The Prophecy of Caiaphas: John xi. 47–53', *Neotestamentica et Patristica* (*Festschrift* for O. Cullmann: Brill, Leiden, 1962), pp. 134–43;

W. Grimm, 'Die Preisgabe eines Menschen zur Rettung des Volkes: Priester-liche Tradition bei Johannes und Josephus', *Josephus-Studien*, pp. 133–46

32. Cf. R. Meyer, *TDNT*, Vol. VI, p. 822, and H. A. Wolfson, *Philo* (Harvard University Press, Cambridge, Mass.), Vol. 2, p. 11

33. Cf. S. Sandmel, *Philo's Place in Judaism* (Ktav, New York, 1971), p. 183 note 366; J. Bréhier, *Philo d'Alexandrie* (Vrin, Paris, 1950), p. 185

34. For a general study of prophecy in rabbinic literature see J. Bowman, 'Prophets and Prophecy in Talmud and Midrash', *EQ*, Vol. xxii (1950), pp. 107–14, 205–20 and 255–75

35. R. Leivestad, 'Das Dogma von der prophetenlosen Zeit', *NTS*, Vol. xix (1972–3), pp. 288–99, especially pp. 289 f.

36. M. A. Chevallier, *Esprit de dieu: paroles d'hommes* (Neuchâtel, 1966), p. 85

37. Cf. H. M. Teeple, op. cit., p. 1

38. See R. Le Déaut, *La nuit pascale* (Institut Biblique Pontifical, Rome, 1963), pp. 65, 266 ff.

39. Cf. J. Jeremias, *TDNT*, Vol. II, pp. 933 f., and *S-B*, Vol IV, pp. 779–89

40. 'It surely is significant that even the "prophetic spirits" of Rabbinic Judaism did not declare "Thus saith the Lord", but appealed to a past revela-tion, "It is written" ', W. D. Davies, *Paul and Rabbinic Judaism* (S.P.C.K., London, [3]1970), p. 212: also C. K. Barrett, *The Holy Spirit and the Gospel Tradi-tion* (S.P.C.K., London, 1958), p. 123, who says that the rabbis 'have super-natural knowledge, but they do not utter inspired speech'. Cf. also J. Abelson, *The Immanence of God in Rabbinical Literature* (Macmillan, London, 1912), p. 260

41. Davies, op. cit., p. 212

42. Cf. G. Vermes, 'The Qumran Interpretation of Scripture in its Histori-cal Setting', *ALUOS*, Vol. vi (1966–8), pp. 84–97, especially pp. 88 f.; and F. F. Bruce, 'Jesus and the Gospels in the light of the Scrolls', *The Scrolls and Christianity* (ed. M. Black: S.P.C.K. London, 1969), pp. 72–4

43. M. Black, *The Scrolls and Christian Doctrine* (Ethel M. Wood Lecture: Athlone Press, London, 1966), pp. 6–8

44. Cf. F. F. Bruce, *Biblical Exegesis in the Qumran Texts* (Tyndale Press, London, 1959), pp. 9–10

45. Cf. Gert Jeremias, *Der Lehrer der Gerechtigkeit* (Göttingen, 1963), p. 141

46. See F. F. Bruce, 'The Book of Daniel and the Qumran Community', *Neotestamentica et Semitica (Festschrift* for M. Black: T and T. Clark, Edinburgh, 1969), pp. 221–35, especially pp. 226–9

47. See R. E. Brown, 'The Teacher of Righteousness and the Messiah(s)', *The Scrolls and Christianity*, pp. 37–44 and especially note 11 on p. 111

48. G. Jeremias, op. cit., p. 198

49. H. Conzelmann, *The Theology of Luke* (ET: Faber and Faber, London, 1960), pp. 23–5

50. W. Wink, *John the Baptist in the Gospel Tradition* (SNTS Monograph Series, Vol. 7: Cambridge University Press, 1968), pp. 51–5

51. For arguments to the contrary, see W. Wink, op. cit., pp. 58–62: cf. also P. Benoit, 'L'enfance de Jean-Baptiste', *Nov T*, Vol. iii (1957), pp. 169–94; and A. George, 'Le parallèle entre Jean-Baptiste et Jésus en Luc 1–2', *Mélanges Bibliques (Festschrift* for B. Rigaux: Gembloux, 1970), pp. 147–72

CHAPTER TWO (pp. 48–69)

1. Cf. G. Vermes, *Jesus the Jew* (Fontana Books, London, 1973), pp. 27–8

2. *Contra* O. Cullmann, *The Christology of the New Testament* (S.C.M. Press, London, ²1963), pp. 34–5.

3. Cf. F. Schnider, *Jesus der Prophet* (Freibourg/Göttingen, 1973), pp. 102–7

4. So most recently F. Schnider, op. cit., pp. 124 ff.; and J. Wancke, *Die Emmauserzählung* (Leipzig, 1973), pp. 60–4

5. Cf. J. Jeremias, *New Testament Theology*, Vol. 1: *The Proclamation of Jesus* (ET: S.C.M. Press, London, 1971), pp. 77–8, and literature there cited.

6. But see in respect of Elijah, J. L. Martyn, 'We have found Elijah', *Jews, Greeks and Christians (Festschrift* for W. D. Davies: Brill, Leiden, 1976), pp. 181–219

7. Cf. F. Gils, *Jésus prophète d'après les Évangiles synoptiques* (Louvain, 1957), pp. 25–30

8. Cf. F. Schnider, op. cit., pp. 108–15; and W. Wink, *John the Baptist in the Gospel Tradition*, p. 43: *contra* F. Hahn, *The Titles of Jesus in Christology* (ET: Lutterworth Press, London, 1969), p. 379; and G. Friedrich, *TD N T*, Vol. VI, p. 846

9. W. D. Davies, *The Setting of the Sermon on the Mount* (Cambridge University Press, 1964), p. 92

10. Cf. É. Cothenet, *Le Prophétisme dans le Nouveau Testament (S D B*, Paris, 1971), cols. 1253–4

11. F. Hahn, op. cit., p. 380; and O. Cullmann, op. cit., p. 36

12. M. E. Boismard, 'Jesus, le Prophète par excellence, d'après Jean 10, 24–39', *Neues Testament und Kirche (Festschrift* for R. Schnackenburg, Herder, Freiburg, 1974), pp. 160–71

13. So N. Habel, 'The Form and Significance of the Call Narrative', *ZAW*, Vol. lxxvii (1965), pp. 297–323, especially p. 306; and P. E. Broughton, 'The Call of Jeremiah: the relation of Dt. 18.9–22 to the Call of Jeremiah', *Australian Biblical Review*, Vol. vi (1958), pp. 37–46

14. See J. Carmignac, 'Pourquoi Jérémie est-il mentionné en Matt. 16.14?', *Tradition und Glaube (Festschrift* for K. G. Kuhn: Göttingen, 1971), pp. 283–98

15. G. Friedrich, *TD N T*, Vol. VI, p. 841

16. Cf. E. Schweizer, 'Formgeschichtliches zu den Seligpreisungen Jesu', *NTS*, Vol. xix (1972–3), pp. 121–6.

17. Jeremias, op. cit., p. 95

18. G. Bornkham, *Jesus of Nazareth* (ET: Hodder and Stoughton, London,

1960), p. 60; R. Meyer, *Der Prophet aus Galiläa* (Darmstadt, [2]1970), pp. 11f.; G. Friedrich, *TDNT*, Vol. VI, p. 844; and J. D. G. Dunn, *Jesus and the Spirit* (S.C.M. Press, London, 1975), p. 83

19. Dunn, op. cit, p. 84
20. Jeremias, op. cit., p. 282
21. Cf. J. Jeremias, 'Die Drei-Tage-Worte der Evangelien', *Tradition und Glaube*, pp. 221–9; and M. Black, 'The "Son of Man" Passion Sayings in the Gospel Tradition', *ZNW*, Vol. lx (1969), pp. 1–8
22. A long review of recent research is available in D. Wenham, 'Recent Study of Mark 13', *TSF Bulletin*, no. 71 (1975), pp. 6–15 and no. 72 (1975), pp. 1–9; and a review of past work forms part of K. Grayston's fresh and perspicacious essay, 'The Study of Mark XIII', *BJRL*, Vol. lvi (1974), pp. 371–87
23. L. Hartman, *Prophecy Interpreted: The Formation of Some Jewish Apocalyptic Texts and of the Eschatological Discourse, Mark 13 and Parallels* (Gleerup, Lund, 1966)
24. Cf. Jeremias, *New Testament Theology*, Vol. I, pp. 56 ff.
25. H. Schlier, *TDNT*, Vol. I, p. 341
26. Jeremias, op. cit., pp. 35–6
27. V. Hasler, *Amen: Redaktionsgeschichtliche Untersuchung zur Einführungsformel der Herrenworte 'Warlich, ich sage euch'* (Zurich/Stuttgart, 1969).
28. K. Berger, *Die Amen-Worte Jesu: Eine Untersuchung zum Problem der Legitimation in apokalyptischen Rede* (de Gruyter, Berlin, 1970) and 'Zur Geschichte der Einleitungsformel "Amen, ich sage euch"', *ZNW*, vol. lxiii (1972), pp. 45–75
29. J. Strugnell, '"Amen, I say unto you" in the Sayings of Jesus and in Early Christian Literature', *HTR*, Vol. lxvii (1974), pp. 177–82
30. Cf. W. D. Davies, op. cit., p. 56
31. R. Bultmann, *The History of the Synoptic Tradition* (ET: Blackwell, Oxford, [2]1968), p. 153
32. Cf. R. H. Fuller, *The Foundations of New Testament Christology* (Fontana Books, London, 1969: original 1965), pp. 127–8
33. G. Vermes, *Jesus the Jew* (Fontana Books, London, 1973)
34. Cf. O. Cullmann, op. cit., pp. 43–50
35. It can be plausibly argued that Jesus fused the Servant theme and the Son of Man title to create a third and more profound concept, viz. the suffering Son of Man/Messiah. Is this a pattern which Christian prophets adopted subsequent to Jesus' ministry as they exegeted already existing biblical themes and their development in such a way that the latent meanings became actual as applied to the person and ministry of Jesus?

CHAPTER THREE (pp. 70–93)
1. The widely accepted dating of the Revelation to the Domitianic period (*c.* AD 95) has been formidably and, in our view, convincingly challenged

by J. A. T. Robinson, *Redating the New Testament* (S.C.M. Press, London, 1976), pp. 221–53: he dates it to late AD 68 or 69

2. The view that the church(es) in Asia Minor owe their prophetic character and organisation to the fact that they were founded by Jewish-Christian refugees from Palestine who left their country before or shortly after the catastrophe in AD 70 (so A. Satake, *Die Gemeindeordnung in der Johannesapokalypse* (Neukirchen-Vluyn, 1966), pp. 162–95 : cf. G. Bornkamm, *TD N T*, Vol. VI, pp. 669 f.) would, if correct, lend support to an earlier date for the composition of the book of the Revelation (but see Note 1 above), for towards the end of the first century the letters of Ignatius reveal the dominance of a rigid episcopate. Furthermore, Satake's hypothesis would imply that the prominence of the prophet(s) in the church of Asia Minor, being a feature imported from the early Palestinian community, makes that church a kind of Jewish-Christian conventicle, and not typical of the Church in general in John's own time (*c.* AD 95). But if the book is dated earlier, may we not be back in a period when the spiritual and prophetic element still had a leading voice both theologically and constitutionally?

3. Cf. H. H. Rowley, *The Relevance of Apocalyptic* (Lutterworth, London, ²1955); and D. S. Russell, *The Method and Message of Jewish Apocalyptic* (S.C.M. Press, London, 1964), pp. 92 ff.

4. Vielhauer, 'Apocalyptic', *New Testament Apocrypha*, Vol. 2 (ET: ed. R. McL. Wilson, Lutterworth, London, 1965), pp. 595–7

5. G. von Rad, *Theology of the Old Testament*, Vol. 2 (ET: Oliver & Boyd, Edinburgh, 1965), p. 303. For a fresh presentation of the case for apocalyptic being an unbroken development of prophecy, see P. D. Hanson, *The Dawn of Apocalyptic* (Fortress Press, Philadelphia, 1975)

6. Cf. G. E. Ladd, 'The Revelation and Jewish Apocalyptic', *EQ.* Vol. xxix (1957), pp. 94–100

7. J. Kallas, 'The Apocalypse – an Apocalyptic Book?', *JBL*, Vol. lxxxvi (1967), pp. 69–81

8. Cf. B. W. Jones, 'More about the Apocalypse as Apocalyptic', *JBL*, Vol. lxxxvii (1968), pp. 325–7

9. It is sometimes suggested that the committing of the revelation to 'a book which is written and read' is an apolcalyptic feature, in contrast to the prophet's direct address to a situation. But the written character of the Revelation may be due to the fact that John is absent from the churches he addresses; in any case, several Old Testament prophets were, like the author of Revelation, divinely commissioned to write their message.

10. J. Comblin, *Le Christ dans l'Apocalypse* (Paris, 1965), pp. 5 f., 85

11. W. C. van Unnik, 'A Formula describing Prophecy', *NTS*, Vol. ix (1962–3), pp. 86–94

12. But see the critique of this view by P. von der Osten-Saken, *Die Apokalyptik in ihrem Verhältnis zu Prophetie und Weisheit* (Munich, 1969)

13. G. von Rad, op. cit., pp. 303 ff.

14. Cf. W. G. Rollins, 'The New Testament and Apocalyptic', *NTS*,

Vol. xvii (1970–1), pp. 454–76 (especially p. 473) which examines critically E. Käsemann's thesis that 'apocalyptic is the mother of Christian theology'.

15. Cf. W. G. Kümmel, *Introduction to the New Testament* (ET:S.C.M. Press, London, ²1975), pp. 461 f.; also M. Rissi, 'The Kerygma of the Revelation to John', *Interpretation*, Vol. xxii (1968), pp. 3–17, especially p. 5

16. A. Oepke, *TDNT*, Vol. III, p. 588; and L. Goppelt, *Apostolic and Post-Apostolic Times* (ET: Black, London, 1969), p. 111: 'The Book of Revelation did not, like the Jewish apocalypses, describe the course of world history with particular reference to contemporary events in order to be able to describe the Emperor and his officials as merely ephemeral phenomena. Instead, like early Christian prophecy, it traced the essential character of the final events, in particular the picture of the world-ruler of the end times, in order that the Church, in spite of all the deceiving appearances and threats to its comfort, might not worship the Emperor rather than God, asking him for both daily bread and salvation.'

17. L. Goppelt, 'Heilsoffenbarung und Geschichte nach der Offenbarung des Johannes', *TLZ*, Vol. lxxvii (1952), pp. 513–22

18. A. Feuillet, *L'Apocalypse: État de la question* (Paris, 1963), p. 8

19. Most of the prophetic formulae are discussed by F. Hahn, 'Die Send-schreiben der Johannesapokalypse: Ein Beitrag zur Bestimmung prophe-tischer Redeformen', *Tradition und Glaube* (*Festschrift* for K. G. Kuhn: Göttingen, 1971), pp. 362–90; and by M. E. Boring, 'The Apocalypse as Christian Prophecy', *Society of Biblical Literature Seminar Papers, 1974*, Vol. 2 (Scholar's Press, Missoula, Montana), pp. 43–62 (and to Boring's paper parts of this chapter are deeply indebted). The letters of chapters 2 and 3 of Revelation are embedded in what is prophetic proclamation from beginning to end (1.3; 22.7, 10, 18 f.)

20. Cf. Isa. 32.3; Jer. 28.15; Amos 7.16; Dan. 10.11, etc., and the repeated injunction of the 'prophet' Moses, Deut. 4.1, 6.3, 4 ('Hear, O Israel, …'); 5.1, 9.1, 32.1

21. P. S. Minear, *I saw a New Earth* (Corpus Books: Washington, DC, 1968), p. 43

22. T. Holtz, *Die Christologie der Apokalypse des Johannes* (Berlin, 1962), p. 209: cf. the role of the Spirit in Rom. 8.26 and of the Paraclete in the Fourth Gospel whose activity has to do, in part, with the proclamation and inter-pretation of the message of Jesus.

23. F. Hahn, op. cit., p. 373

24. Cf. R. E. Brown, *The Semitic Background of the Term 'Mystery' in the New Testament* (Fortress Press, Philadelphia, 1968), pp. 36–8

25. For a longer discussion of Rev. 10.7 and 11.18, see D. Hill, 'Prophecy and Prophets in the Revelation of St John', *NTS*, Vol. xviii (1971–2), pp. 407–409: John, of course, uses *doulos* and *douloi* as a term for Christians in general (2.20, 7.3, 19.2 and 22.3)

26. Cf. W. F. Arndt and F. W. Gingrich, *A Greek–English Lexicon of the*

New Testament and other Early Christian Literature (Cambridge University Press, 1957), p. 479

27. See H. B. Swete, *The Apocalypse of St John* (Macmillan, London, 1909), p. 225

28. Cf. F. Hauck, *TDNT*, Vol. IV, p. 586 note 19.

29. D. Hill, loc. cit., p. 412. Cf. also P. S. Minear, op. cit., pp. 4 and 194. On the witness terminology in New Testament tradition-history see O. Michel, 'Zeuge und Zeugnis', *Neues Testament und Geschichte (Festschrift* for O. Cullmann: Zürich/Tübingen, 1972), pp. 15–31, and the recent monograph by A. A. Trites, *The New Testament Concept of Witness* (Cambridge University Press, 1977)

30. Although the Revelation often brings witnessing and death by violence into close association (e.g. 2.13, 11.3, 17.6), it never calls the death of persecuted Christians *martyria*, nor does it ever say that the faithful render their witness in or by their death: the fact that the witnesses are those who die violently does not justify the identification of *martyria* with martyrdom: the witnesses of Christ are not so named because they die, but they die because they are witnesses. Cf. N. Brox, *Zeuge und Märtyrer: Untersuchungen zur frühchristlichen Zeugnisterminologie* (München, 1961), pp. 92–105; and A. T. Nikolainen, '*Über die theologische Eigenart der Offenbarung des Johannes*', *TLZ*. Vol. xciii (1968), pp. 164–7

31. G. von Rad, op. cit., p. 37

32. See p. 15 above: also K. Koch, *The Growth of the Biblical Tradition* (Scribner's, New York, 1969), pp. 189 ff.

33. E. Käsemann, 'Sentences of Holy Law in the New Testament', *New Testament Questions of Today* (ET: S.C.M. Press, London, 1967), pp. 66–81

34. Käsemann, op. cit., p. 76

35. Ulrich B. Müller, *Prophetie und Predigt im Neuen Testament* (Gütersloh, 1975), pp. 104 ff.: he regards the 'Overcoming words' as paraenetical in character.

36. Ulrich B. Müller, op. cit., pp. 57–104: P. S. Minear, op. cit., pp. 41–61, offers a simpler analysis of the form of the seven letters.

37. C. Westermann, *Basic Forms of Prophetic Speech* (ET: Lutterworth, London, 1967)

38. The suggestion made by E. Lohse (*Die Offenbarung des Johannes*, Göttingen, 1960, p. 23) that the letters recall the pattern of Old Testament covenant formularies like Exod. 19.3–8; Jos. 24 is not convincing.

39. Cf. É. Cothenet, op. cit., col. 1325

40. R. H. Charles, *The Revelation of St John* (Clark, Edinburgh, 1920): Charles has rather too much scissors-and-paste in his approach to the book and its use of sources. The recent commentary on the book in the Anchor Bible series, *Revelation*, by J. Massyngberde Forde (Doubleday, New York, 1975) puts forward the unusual, but stimulating, hypothesis that most of the Revelation emanates from a John the Baptist school, which represented a primitive form of Christianity and inherited the Baptist's prophetic and

apocalyptic tendencies: it is interesting to note that Dr Ford assigns the writing of the book to a period prior to the Gospel of Mark and emphasises that it does not fit the apocalyptic genre.

41. Cf. F. Hahn, op. cit., pp. 357 ff.

42. See J. A. T. Robinson, op. cit., pp. 242–50

43. Cf. R. Bauckham, 'Synoptic Parousia Parables and the Apocalypse', *NTS*, Vol. xxiii (1976–7) pp. 162–76

44. P. S. Minear, op. cit., pp. 214–27, considers eight different literary forms which express John's hortatory intention: most of these we have alluded to in our analysis of the vocabulary and contents of the prophet's message.

45. According to Minear, the judgments and tribulations described in the fourth vision (11.19–15.4) are directed not at persecutors of the Church but at faithless Christians misled by false teachers (op. cit., pp. 113–27): but in the Foreword to the book (pp. ix–xiii) M. M. Bourke casts doubts on the correctness of this claim, and justifiably so, in our opinion.

46. M. E. Boring, op. cit., pp. 50–1

47. Cf. G. Friedrich, *TDNT*, Vol. VI, pp. 849, 853

48. Cf. D. Hill, op. cit., p. 415

49. G. Bornkamm, *TDNT*, Vol. VI, p. 669

50. A. Satake, op. cit.: his thesis is criticised on exegetical and historical grounds in a review by T. Holtz, *TLZ*, Vol. xciii (1968), pp. 262–4

51. On this, see Hill, op. cit., pp. 406–10, and A. Satake, op. cit., pp. 119–33

52. E. Schweizer, *TDNT*, Vol. VI, p. 449 note 816, and *Church Order in the New Testament* (ET: S.C.M. Press, London, 1961), pp. 134 f.

53. E. Schweizer, *TDNT*, Vol. VI, pp. 449 f.; P. S. Minear, op. cit., pp. 11 and 22; W. G. Kümmel, op. cit., p. 459

54. O. Cullmann, *Early Christian Worship* (ET: S.C.M. Press, London, 1953), p. 7. Attention is drawn to a number of liturgical formulae in the Revelation by É. Cothenet, op. cit., col. 1327–8

55. M. E. Boring, op. cit., p. 54

56. F. Hahn, op. cit., p. 381

57. Cf. É. Cothenet, op. cit., col. 1328

CHAPTER FOUR (p. 94–109)

1. Cf. B. M. Metzger, 'Ancient Astrological Geography and Acts 2:9–11', *Apostolic History and the Gospel (Festschrift* for F. F. Bruce: Paternoster Press, Exeter, 1970), pp. 123–33

2. J. D. G. Dunn, *Jesus and the Spirit* (London, 1974), p. 171

3. É. Cothenet, *Le Prophétisme dans le Nouveau Testament*, col. 1281

4. E.g. M. H. Scharlemann, *Stephen: A Singular Saint* (Rome, 1968); C. H. H. Scobie, 'The Origins and Development of Samaritan Christianity', *NTS*, Vol. xix (1972–3), pp. 390–414; and 'North and South: Tension and Reconciliation in Biblical History', *Biblical Studies (Festschrift* for W. Barclay: Collins, London, 1976), pp. 87–98

5. Cf. J. Daniélou and H. Marrou, *Nouvelle histoire de l'Église*, Vol. I (Paris, 1963), pp. 151–5

6. É. Cothenet, op. cit., col. 1283

7. E. E. Ellis, 'The Role of the Christian Prophet in Acts', *Apostolic History and the Gospel*, p. 58

8. E. C. Selwyn, *The Christian Prophets* (Macmillan, London, 1900), pp. 24 f.

9. Cf. G. Friedrich, *TDNT*, Vol. VI, p. 854; also ch. 5, pp.

10. J. W. Bowker, 'Speeches in Acts: A Study in Proem and Yelammedenu Form', *NTS*, Vol. xiv (1967–8), pp. 96–111

11. J. W. Doeve, *Jewish Hermeneutics in the Synoptic Gospels and Acts* (Assen, 1953), p. 175

12. E. Haenchen, *The Acts of the Apostles* (ET: Blackwell, Oxford, 1971), pp. 415 ff.; H. Conzelmann, *Die Apostelgeschichte* (Handbuch zum N.T.: Tübingen, 1963), p. 75; U. Wilckens, *Die Missionsreden der Apostelgeschichte* (Neukirchen, ²1963), pp. 50 ff.

13. E. Haenchen, op. cit., p. 416

14. E. Käsemann, 'Sentences of Holy Law in the New Testament', *New Testament Questions of Today*, p. 77: cf. also pp. 74 and 76

15. E. E. Ellis, op. cit., p. 61

16. Thus Haenchen, op. cit., p. 376

17. E.g. É. Cothenet, op. cit., col. 1283, and T. M. Crone, *Early Christian Prophecy*, p. 198

CHAPTER FIVE (pp. 110–40)

1. Questions about the genuineness of some of the letters ascribed to Paul are not of much significance here. With reference to the place and function of prophets in the church, only a few verses from the possibly deutero-Pauline Letter to the Ephesians and from the very probably deutero-Pauline Pastorals are relevant.

2. Cf. F. F. Bruce, 'Is the Paul of Acts the Real Paul?', *BJRL*, Vol. lviii (1976), pp. 282–305; also C. K. Barrett, 'Acts and the Pauline Corpus', *ExpT*, Vol. lxxviii (1976–7), pp. 2–5

3. See J. M. Myers and E. D. Freed, 'Is Paul also among the Prophets?', *Interpretation*, Vol. xx (1966), pp. 40–3: on the prophetic nature of Paul's call; see also J. Munck, *Paul and the Salvation of Mankind* (ET: S.C.M. Press, London, 1959), pp. 24–35; T. Holtz, 'Zum Selbstverständnis des Apostels Paulus', *TLZ*, Vol. xci (1966), cols. 321–30; and K. Stendahl, *Paul among Jews and Gentiles* (S.C.M. Press, London, 1977), pp. 6–10

4. Cf. M. Black, 'The Throne-Theophany Prophetic Commission and the "Son of Man"', *Jews, Greeks and Christians* (Brill, Leiden, 1976), pp. 57–73: to the passages Black discusses there might be added Rev. 1.9 ff.

5. Myers and Freed, op. cit., pp. 44–6

6. 'We may see the authority of the Lord operating with and through the human tradition (which is now enshrined in Scripture)', C. K. Barrett,

The First Epistle to the Corinthians (A. and C. Black, London, ²1976), pp. 265–6

7. T. W. Manson put it this way: 'He (Paul) did not confuse the Church with the hierarchy. He gloried in his independence of the *styloi* (pillars), and his complete dependence on Christ. The pillar apostles might recognise him – they had not made him. Nor would Paul confuse the Church with any outward form of organisation'; *On Paul and John* (S.C.M. Press, London, 1963), p. 78

8. See J. H. Schütz, *Paul and the Anatomy of Apostolic Authority* (Cambridge University Press, 1975)

9. G. W. H. Lampe, 'Grievous Wolves (Acts 20.39)', *Christ and Spirit in the New Testament* (Cambridge University Press, 1973), p. 258

10. On these matters, see K. H. Rengstorf, *TDNT*, Vol. I, pp. 398–447; C. K. Barrett, *The Signs of an Apostle* (Epworth Press, London, 1970); W. Schmithals, *The Office of Apostle in the Early Church* (ET: London, 1971); R. Schnackenburg, 'Apostles before and during Paul's Time', *Apostolic History and the Gospel* (Paternoster Press, Exeter, 1970), pp. 287–303; and J. A. Kirk, 'Apostleship since Rengstorf: Towards a Synthesis', *NTS*, Vol. xxi (1974–5), pp. 249–64

11. Cf. E. Käsemann, 'Ministry and Community in the New Testament', *Essays on New Testament Themes* (ET: S.C.M. Press, London, 1964), pp. 78, 81

12. Myers and Freed, op. cit., p. 53

13. This is the position Wayne Grudem takes up and defends in his (unpublished) thesis, *The Gift of Prophecy in the New Testament Church, with special reference to 1 Corinthians*, (Cambridge University, 1976)

14. H. Greeven, 'Propheten, Lehrer, Vorsteher bei Paulus', *ZNW*, Vol. xliv (1952), p. 3

15. R. P. Martin, *Worship in the New Testament* (Marshall, Morgan and Scott, London, ²1974), p. 136

16. So É. Cothenet, *Le Prophétisme dans le Nouveau Testament*, col. 1301; and G. Friedrich, *TDNT*, Vol. VI, p. 854

17. Cf. H. Greeven, op. cit., pp. 5–6

18. J. Lindblom, *Gesichte und Offenbarung* (Gleerup, Lund, 1968), p. 179

19. H. von Campenhausen, *Ecclesiastical Authority and Spiritual Power in the Church of the First Four Centuries* (ET: A. and C. Black, London, 1969), p. 61

20. H. Greeven's remarks on glossolalia are of interest: 'In glossolalia primitive Christianity did not hear the helpless stammering of the person in ecstasy for whom, under the vision of heavenly revelation, language broke down and, so to speak, shattered. It is not the ruins of human speech, but superhuman language that is perceivable on the lips of those who speak in tongues'; op. cit., p. 17 note 39

21. P. Vielhauer, *Oikodomē* (Karlsruhe, 1940), pp. 91 ff.

22. G. Dautzenberg, *Urchristliche Prophetie* (Stuttgart, 1975), pp. 246–53

23. We may observe that Ignatius of Antioch (*Phil.* 7) describes the

expected effects of spirit-inspired prophecy on *members of the church* (not un-believers) in similar terms, *ta krypta elenchei*. Ignatius utters with the voice of God (*theou phonē*) the warning, which the spirit announces through him, on divisive tendencies within the Church and the necessity for a return to unity. Con-viction, warning and advice are all mediated through prophetic speech.

24. E. B. Allo, *Première Épître aux Corinthiens* (Paris, 1934), p. 367

25. C. K. Barrett, op. cit., p. 326: cf. also J. P. M. Sweet, 'A Sign for Un-believers: Paul's Attitude to Glossolalia', *NTS*, Vol. xiii (1966–7), pp. 240–57

26. G. Bornkamm, *Early Christian Experience* (ET: S.C.M. Press, London, 1969), p. 177 note 4

27. E. Schweizer, *Church Order in the New Testament* (ET: S.C.M. Press, London, 1961), p. 226 (28c)

28. Cf. J. P. M. Sweet, op. cit., pp. 240–6

29. Cf. K. H. Rengstorf, *TDNT*, Vol. VII, p. 259

30. J. D. G. Dunn, *Jesus and the Spirit*, p. 231

31. In 'Christian Prophets as Teachers or Instructors in the Church', *Pro-phetic Vocation in the New Testament and Today* (Brill, Leiden, 1977), pp. 108–30

32. M. A. Chevallier, *Esprit de Dieu, paroles d'hommes* (Neuchâtel, 1966), p. 198

33. F. J. Leenhardt, *L'Épître aux Romains* (Neuchâtel, 1957), p. 174

34. Cf. C. K. Barrett, op. cit., pp. 321 f.; Greeven, op. cit., p. 10; and H. Schlier, *Die Zeit der Kirche* (Freibourg, ⁵1972), p. 259

35. Cf. K. Beyer, *TDNT*, Vol. III, pp. 638f.

36. H. Schlier, 'Le caractère propre de l'exhortation selon St Paul', *Essais sur le Nouveau Testament* (Paris, 1968), pp. 393–412: quotation from p. 394

37. E. E. Ellis, 'The Role of the Christian Prophet in Acts', p. 57

38. H. von Campenhausen, op. cit., p. 62; É. Cothenet, op. cit., col. 1298; C. E. B. Cranfield, '*Metron Pisteōs* in Romans xii.3', *NTS*, Vol. viii (1961–2), pp. 345–51; and E. Käsemann, *An die Römer* (Mohr, Tübingen, ²1974), p. 326. It is interesting that Käsemann regards the interpretation of the phrase in terms of the prophet's own faith as 'utterly meaningless' (*schlechterdings unsinnig*)!

39. G. Dautzenberg, 'Botschaft und Bedeutung der urchristlichen Pro-phetie nach dem ersten Korintherbrief (2.6–16; 12–14)', *Prophetic Vocation in the New Testament and Today* (Brill, Leiden, 1977), pp. 131–61

40. For a contrary view, see E. E. Ellis, 'Spiritual Gifts in the Pauline Com-munity', *NTS*, Vol. xx (1973–4), pp. 128–44

41. Cf. E. Schweizer, *TDNT*, Vol. VI, p. 423

42. B. Rigaux, *Les Épîtres aux Thessaloniciens* (Paris, 1956), pp. 538f.; H. von Campenhausen, *Aus der Frühzeit des Christentums* (Tübingen, 1963), p. 37; É. Cothenet, op. cit., col. 1289

43. G. Friedrich, *TDNT*, Vol. VI, p. 855

44. Cf. H. Greeven, op. cit., pp. 20 ff.

45. H. von Campenhausen, *Ecclesiastical Authority and Spiritual Power*, p. 61

46. Cf. C. K. Barrett, op. cit., p. 328; F. F. Bruce, *1 and 2 Corinthians* (Oliphants, London, 1971), p. 134; and É. Cothenet, col. 1296

47. So H. Greeven, op. cit., p. 6; M. A. Chevallier, op. cit., p. 190 f.; G. Friedrich, *TDNT*, Vol. VI, 851; and H. Conzelmann, *1 Corinthians* (Fortress Press, Philadelphia, 1975), p. 245

48. G. Dautzenberg, 'Zum religionsgeschichtlichen Hintergrund der *diakrisis pneumatōn* (1 Kor. 12.10)', *BZ*, Vol. xv (1971), pp. 93–104

49. U. B. Müller, *Prophetie und Predigt im Neuen Testament*, p. 27

50. E. E. Ellis, 'Christ and the Spirit in 1 Corinthians', *Christ and Spirit in the New Testament*, pp. 275 ff., and 'Spiritual Gifts in the Pauline Community', *NTS*, Vol. xx (1973–4), pp. 154 ff.

51. Cf. R. P. Martin, *Worship in the New Testament*, p. 136

52. Cf. Greeven, op. cit., p. 3 note 6; F. F. Bruce, op. cit., p. 124; and C. K. Barrett, op. cit., p. 299

53. Cf. W. Schmithals, *Gnosticism in Corinth* (ET: Abingdon Press, Nashville, 1971), p. 175

54. C. K. Barrett, op. cit., p. 301

55. G. Dautzenberg, *Urchristliche Prophetie*, pp. 159–255

56. A spirited and detailed defence of Pauline authorship is made by A. van Roon, *The Authenticity of Ephesians* (Brill, Leiden, 1974)

57. Cf. J. D. G. Dunn, op. cit., p. 347

58. Cf. É. Cothenet, op. cit., cols, 1306–9, and the authorities listed there who favour this view.

59. J. Murphy-O'Connor, *La Prédication selon S. Paul* (Paris, 1966), p. 34

60. Cf. É. Cothenet, op. cit., col. 1314

61. Cf. E. Schweizer, *Church Order in the New Testament*, p. 79 (6c); C. Spicq, *Les Épîtres Pastorales* (Paris, 1947), p. 136

CHAPTER SIX (pp. 141–59)

1. H. A. Guy, *New Testament Prophecy* (Epworth Press, London, 1947), p. 112

2. Cf. W. G. Kümmel, *Introduction to the New Testament* (ET: S.C.M. Press, London, ²1975), p. 397

3. For a discerning review of the matter see F. F. Bruce, ' "To the Hebrews" or "To the Essenes" ', *NTS*, Vol. ix (1962–3), pp. 217–32

4. Cf. S. Kistemaker, *The Psalm Citations in the Epistle to the Hebrews* (Amsterdam, 1961); but here the resemblances between the methods of exegesis tends to be exaggerated.

5. M. Barth, 'The Old Testament in Hebrews: An Essay in Biblical Hermeneutics', in *Current Issues in New Testament Interpretation* (*Festschrift* for O. Piper: New York, 1962), p. 58,

6. J. A. T. Robinson, *Redating the New Testament* (S.C.M. Press, London, 1976), pp. 217 ff.

7. W. Manson, *The Epistle to the Hebrews* (Hodder and Stoughton, London, 1951), p. 171

8. Robinson, op. cit., p. 219

9. G. Bornkamm, *TDNT*, Vol. VI, pp. 670–1

10. Oslo–Hamburg, 1959

11. B. Lindars, *Behind the Fourth Gospel* (S.P.C.K., London, 1971), pp. 43–60

12. B. Lindars, *The Gospel of John* (Oliphants, London, 1972), pp. 52–3

13. Cf. D. Moody Smith, 'Johannine Christianity: Some Reflections on its Character and Delineation', *NTS*, Vol. xxi (1974–5), pp. 222–48, especially p. 233 and the authorities cited in notes 1 and 2.

14. *NTS*, Vol. xiii (1966–7), pp. 133–32

15. Brown, op. cit., p. 126. The intimate relation of the Paraclete and his functions to Jesus has been discusssed by M. E. Boring in a paper published in *NTS* entitled 'The Influence of Christian Prophecy on the Johannine Portrayal of the Paraclete and Jesus', *NTS*, Vol. xxv (1978–9), pp. 113–23

16. Boring, op. cit.

17. S. H. Sasse, 'Der Paraklet im Johannesvangelium', *ZNW*, Vol. xxiv (1925), pp. 260–77

18. Cf. D. Moody Smith, op. cit., p. 233 and note 4

19. Fortress Press, Philadelphia, 1976. Cf. also his paper 'Christian Prophecy and the Q Tradition', *SBL Seminar Papers, 1976*, Vol. 2 (Scholars Press, Missoula, Montana), pp. 119–26

20. R. A. Edwards, 'Christian Prophecy and the Q Tradition', p. 126

21. Ibid., p. 122

22. *NTS*, Vol. xvi (1969–70), pp. 213–30: cf. also his commentary *The Good News according to Matthew* (ET; S.P.C.K., London, 1976), pp. 178 ff.

23. E. Käsemann, 'The Beginnings of Christian Theology', *New Testament Questions of Today* (ET: S.C.M. Press, London, 1969), p. 91

24. See D. Hill, '*Dikaioi* as a Quasi-technical Term', *NTS*, Vol. xi (1964–5), pp. 296–302

25. É. Cothenet, *Le Prophétisme dans le Nouveau Testament*, col. 1271

26. P. Minear, 'False Prophecy and Hypocrisy in the Gospel of Matthew', *Neues Testament und Kirche (Festschrift* for R. Schnackenburg: Freibourg, 1974), pp. 76–93

27. Cf. D. Hill, 'False Prophets and Charismatics: Structure and Interpretation in Matthew 7, 15–23', *Biblica*, Vol. lvii (1976), pp. 327–48

28. Cf. H. A. Fischel, 'Prophet and Martyr', *JQR*, Vol. xxxvii (1946–7), p. 279

29. J. A. Sanders, 'From Isaiah 61 to Luke 4', in *Christianity, Judaism and Other Graeco-Roman Cults (Festschrift* for Morton Smith, Vol. 1: Brill, Leiden, 1975), pp. 75–106

30. Seabury Press, New York, 1976

CHAPTER SEVEN (pp. 160–85)

1. *The History of the Synoptic Tradition* (ET: Blackwell, Oxford, ²1968), pp. 127 f.

2. Especially in his essay 'Sentences of Holy Law in the New Testament', *New Testament Questions of Today* (ET: S.C.M. Press, London, 1969), pp. 66–81

3. *Rediscovering the Teaching of Jesus* (S.C.M. Press, London, 1967), pp. 15, 22, 27, 186

4. J. Jeremias, *New Testament Theology I: The Proclamation of Jesus* (ET: S.C.M. Press, London, 1971), p. 2

5. M. Dibelius, *From Tradition to Gospel* (ET: Cambridge and London, 1971), p. 24

6. F. Neugebauer, 'Geistsprüche und Jesuslogien', *ZNW*, Vol. liii (1962), pp. 218–28

7. B. Gerhardsson, *Memory and Manuscript* (Lund-Copenhagen, ²1964) and *Tradition and Transmission in Early Christianity* (Lund-Copenhagen, 1964)

8. H. Schürmann, *Traditionsgeschichtliche Untersuchungen zu den synoptischen Evangelien* (Dusseldorf, 1968), pp. 39–65

9. M. E. Boring, 'How may we identify Oracles of Christian Prophets in the Synoptic Tradition? Mark 3:28–29 as a Test Case', Vol. xci (1972), p. 502

10. P. Vielhauer, *New Testament Apocrypha* II (ET: Lutterworth Press, London, 1965), p. 606

11. J. H. Bernard, *The Odes of Solomon* (Cambridge University Press, 1912), *ad loc.* The quotation from W. Bauer comes from *Neutestamentliche Apokryphen* Vol. II (Tübingen, 1964), pp. 623 f. (Bauer's translation of and comments on the Odes are not included in the English version of the book.)

12. H. von Soden, *Das Interesse des apostolischen Zeitalters an der evangelischen Geschichte* (Freiburg, 1892), pp. 153 f.

13. Bultmann, op. cit., p. 163

14. 'The Beginnings of Christian Theology', *New Testament Questions of Today*, pp. 82–107; 'On the Subject of Primitive Christian Apocalyptic', ibid., pp. 108–37

15. 'Sentences of Holy Law in the New Testament', *New Testament Questions of Today*, pp. 66–81

16. K. Berger, 'Zu den sogenannten Sätzen heiligen Rechts', *NTS*, Vol. xvi (1969–70), pp. 10–40, and 'Die sogenannten "Sätze heiligen Rechts" im NT: Ihre Funktion und ihr Sitz im Leben', *ThZ*, Vol. xxviii (1972), pp. 305–30

17. *Rediscovering the Teaching of Jesus*, p. 22

18. 'An Apology for Primitive Christian Eschatology', *Essays on New Testament Themes* (ET: S.C.M. Press, London, 1964), pp. 169–85; the quotation is from pp. 187 f.

19. *Essays on New Testament Themes*, pp. 48–62

20. *New Testament Questions of Today*, p. 68

21. G. F. Hawthorne, 'Christian Prophets and the Sayings of Jesus: Evidence of and Criteria for', *SBL Seminar Papers, 1975*, Vol. 2 (Scholars Press, Missoula, Montana), pp. 105–29. Page references to quotations from this essay are given in the text.

22. Cf. E. E. Ellis, *The Gospel of Luke* (Oliphants, London, 1966), p. 172

23. V. Hasler, *Amen: Redaktionsgeschichtliche Untersuchung zur Einfürungsformel der Herrenworte 'Warlich, Ich sage euch'* (Zürich, 1969)

24. *JBL*, Vol. xci (1972), pp. 501–21

25. 'Christian Prophecy and Matthew 10.23: A Test Exegesis', *SBL Seminar Papers, 1976*, Vol. 2 (Scholars Press, Missoula, Montana), pp. 127–33. Page references to quotations from this essay are given in the text.

26. Hawthorne, op. cit., p. 117

27. Ellis, op. cit., p. 173

28. Shortly after this book was completed J. D. G. Dunn published a balanced and careful study which relates to the content of this chapter under the title 'Prophetic "I"–Sayings and the Jesus Tradition: The Importance of Testing Prophetic Utterances within Early Christianity', *NTS*, vol. xxiv (1977–8), pp. 175–98. After reviewing considerations for and against Bultmann's hypothesis (see pp. 160 ff. above) – the latter being, in our view, both more relevant and more damaging than the former are favourable – Dunn cogently argues that all the available evidence (1 Corinthians, 1 John, Didache, Shepherd of Hermas) strongly suggests that all prophetic utterances in the early Christian communities would have been tested as to their origin and significance for the congregation addressed, and that it is wholly improbable that an utterance which ran counter to the community's kerygma would have passed that test. On this criterion he excludes Mark 3.28–29 (Boring's test-case, see above, pp. 182 ff), but allows that some post-Easter prophetic words entered the Jesus-tradition: among such he is inclined to include Matthew 10.5; 11.28–30; 18.20, Luke 11.49–51 and possibly (with Hawthorne) Luke 22.19b. The article is a healthy corrective to the extravagant claims of Bultmann and Käsemann concerning the frequency with which 'I'-sayings gained entry into the Synoptic tradition as sayings of Jesus.

CHAPTER EIGHT (pp. 186–92)

1. Cf. H. Chadwick, *The Early Church* (Penguin Books, Harmondsworth, 1967), pp. 46 f.

2. B. H. Streeter, *The Primitive Church* (Macmillan, London, 1929), pp. 149–50: author's italics retained.

3. J. Reiling, *Hermas and Christian Prophecy: A Study of the Eleventh Mandate* (Brill, Leiden, 1973)

4. See *New Testament Apocrypha*, Vol. II (Lutterworth Press, London, 1965), pp. 686–7.

5. G. Friedrich, *TDNT*, Vol. VI, p. 861

6. E. Käsemann, 'An Apologia for Primitive Christian Eschatology', *Essays on New Testament Themes* (ET: S.C.M. Press, London, 1964), p. 188

7. *Ecclesiastical Authority and Spiritual Power* (ET: A. and C. Black, London, 1969), pp. 178–212

8. F. von Campenhausen, op. cit., p. 178

CHAPTER NINE (pp. 193–213)

1. P. Tillich, *The Shaking of the Foundations* (S.C.M. Press, London, 1949), pp. 7–9

2. F. D. Bruner, *A Theology of the Holy Spirit* (Hodder and Stoughton, London, 1971), pp. 153–284

3. J. D. G. Dunn, *Baptism in the Holy Spirit* (S.C.M. Press, London, 1970), p. 4

4. Léon J. Suenens, *A New Pentecost?* (Collins, Glasgow: Fountain Books, 1977), p. 80

5. S. Tugwell, *Did You Receive the Spirit?* (Darton, Longman and Todd, London, 1972); quotations from pp. 47–9

6. S. Tugwell, 'The Gift of Tongues in the New Testament', *ExpT*, Vol. lxxxiv (1972–3), pp. 137–40; quotation from p. 139

7. D. Gee, 'Speaking with Tongues and Prophesying', *Pentecost*, No. 34 (Dec. 1955), p. 11. Until his death in 1966 Gee was widely regarded as one of the most important Pentecostal writers.

8. Plainfield, Illinois, 1971, p. 27

9. S. Tugwell, *Did You Receive the Spirit?*, pp. 60–2

10. Darton, Longman and Todd, London, 1976. Page references are given in the text.

11. W. J. Hollenweger, *The Pentecostals* (S.C.M. Press, London, 1972), p. 345

12. Cf. D. Bridge and D. Phypers, *Spiritual Gifts and the Church* (Inter-Varsity Press, London, 1973), pp. 26–31

13. Bridge and Phypers, op. cit., pp. 30–1

14. *Theology*, Vol. lxxx (March 1977), pp. 143–4

15. *The Reformed Journal*, Vol. xxvii (Feb. 1977), pp. 14–16

16. Cf. J. D. G. Dunn, *Jesus and the Spirit* (S.C.M. Press, London, 1975), p. 233; and G. Bornkamm, 'Faith and Reason in Paul', in *Early Christian Experience* (ET: S.C.M. Press, London, 1969), pp. 39 ff.

SELECT BIBLIOGRAPHY

Barrett, C. K., *A Commentary on the First Epistle to the Corinthians* (A. and C. Black, London, ²1976)
—— *The Holy Spirit and the Gospel Tradition* (S.P.C.K., London, 1947, ²1966)
Beare, F. W., 'Sayings of the Risen Jesus in the Synoptic Tradition', *Christian History and Interpretation (Festschrift* for John Knox, eds. W. R. Farmer, C. F. D. Moule and R. R. Niebhur: Cambridge University Press, 1967), pp. 161–81
—— 'Speaking with Tongues: A Critical Survey of the New Testament Evidence', *JBL* Vol. lxxxiii (1964), pp. 229–46.
Berger, K., 'Zu den sogennanten Sätzen heiligen Rechts', *NTS*, Vol. xvii (1970–1), pp. 10–40
—— 'Die sogennanten "Sätze heiligen Rechts" im Neuen Testament', *ThZ.* Vol. xxviii (1972), pp. 205–30. These two articles subject to rigorous examination E. Käsemann's view as to the origin of the so-called 'Sentences of Holy Law' (see below) and offer an alternative solution: the 'Sentences' have their origin in sapiential and catechetical exhortation
Bittlinger, A., *Gifts and Ministries* (Hodder and Stoughton, London, 1974). Written from within the charismatic movement, this little book examines, with care and fairness, the New Testament concept of spiritual ministries and the spiritual gifts that equip Christians for service in them
Black, M. (ed.), *The Scrolls and Christianity* (S.P.C.K., London, 1969)
Blenkinsopp, J., 'Prophecy and Priesthood in Josephus', *JJS*, Vol. xxv (1974), pp. 239–62. One of the very few contributions to Josephus's understanding of and participation in the prophetic tradition
Boismard, M. E., 'Jesus, le Prophète par excellence, d'apres Jean 10, 24–39', *Neues Testament und Kirche (Festschrift* for R. Schnackenburg, ed. J. Gnilka: Herder, Freiburg, 1974), pp. 160–71. A fresh approach to the interpretation of a difficult passage
Boring, M. Eugene, 'How may we identify Oracles of Christian Prophets in the Synoptic Tradition? Mark 3.28–29 as a Test Case', *JBL*, Vol. xci (1972), pp. 501–21
—— 'The Apocalypse as Christian Prophecy', *SBL Seminar Papers 1974*, Vol. 2, ed. G. W. MacRae (Scholars Press, Missoula, Montana), pp. 43–62
—— 'Christian Prophecy and Matthew 10.23: A Test Exegesis', *SBL Seminar Papers 1976*, Vol. 2, ed. G. W. MacRae (Scholars Press, Missoula, Montana), pp. 127–33

—— ' "What are we looking for?" Toward a Definition of the Term "Christian Prophet" ', *SBL Seminar Papers 1973*, Vol. 2, ed. G. W. MacRae (Scholars Press, Missoula, Montana), pp. 142–54

Bornkamm, G., 'On the Understanding of Worship', *Early Christian Experience* (ET. S.C.M. Press, London, 1969), pp. 161–79

Bridge, D. and Phypers, D., *Spiritual Gifts and the Church* (Inter-Varsity Press, London, 1973). An assessment of the charismatic movement in the light of New Testament evidence by two conservative evangelical Christian writers

Brown, R. E., 'The Paraclete in the Fourth Gospel', *NTS*, Vol. xiii (1966–7), pp. 113–32

Bruce, F. F., *Biblical Exegesis in the Qumran Texts* (Tyndale Press, London, 1959)

—— *1 and 2 Corinthians* (New Century Bible: Oliphants, London, 1971)

—— 'The Spirit in the Apocalypse', *Christ and Spirit in the New Testament (Festschrift* for C. F. D. Moule, eds. B. Lindars and S. S. Smalley: Cambridge University Press, 1973), pp. 333–44

Bruner, F. D., *A Theology of the Holy Spirit: The Pentecostal Experience and the New Testament Witness* (Hodder and Stoughton, London, 1970). A thorough and critical examination of the Pentecostalists: valuable both as a reference book and as a source book

Campenhausen, H. von, *Ecclesiastical Authority and Spiritual Power in the Church of the first Three Centuries* (ET. A. and C. Black, London, 1969). Particularly valuable for its fourth chapter 'Spirit and Authority in the Pauline Congregation' and its eighth chapter 'Prophets and Teachers in the Second Century'

Chevallier, M.-A., *Esprit de Dieu, paroles d'hommes: Le rôle de l'esprit dans les ministères de la parole selon l'apôtre Paul* (Delachaux et Niestlé, Neuchâtel, 1966)

Clements, R. E., *Prophecy and Tradition* (Blackwell, Oxford, 1975). A fairly straightforward discussion of the relationship of Old Testament prophets to tradition.

Conzelmann, H., *1 Corinthians* (ET. Hermeneia Series: Fortress Press, Philadelphia, 1975)

Cothenet, É., *Le Prophétisme dans le Nouveau Testament* (published separately and in *Supplément au Dictionnaire de la Bible* (Paris, 1971), columns 1222–337). Probably the most comprehensive and balanced discussion of the phenomenon of Christian Prophecy within the New Testament.

Crone, T. M., *Early Christian Prophecy: A Study of its Origin and Function* (St Mary's University Press, Baltimore, 1973). Difficult to obtain, and, unlike Cothenet, goes beyond the New Testament evidence into the Patristic Age etc.: spoiled by the fact the author confines himself to occurrences of the *prophētēs/prophēteia/prophēteuō* terms, on the assumption that only on the basis of the actual appearance of the word(s) can we discuss the phenomenon of Christian 'prophecy'.

Cullman, O., *The Christology of the New Testament* (ET. S.C.M. Press, London, 1959). Quite useful on Jesus as 'prophet' and 'eschatological prophet'.

Dautzenberg, G., 'Zum religionsgeschichtlichen Hintergrund der *diakrisis pneumatōn* (1 Kor. 12.10)', *BZ*, Vol. xv (1971), pp. 93–104. Argues that the Greek phrase refers to the interpretation of inspired revelations, not to the discernment or distinguishing of spirits.

——, *Urchristliche Prophetie* (Kohlhammer, Stuttgart, 1975). This very important study surveys the literature and sources relevant to early Christian prophecy and reviews the major questions posed by recent research: it deals extensively with 1 Cor. 12–14, treating of discernment of spirits as the interpretation of revelations, of prophecy as understanding of mysteries and knowledge, of seeing in a mirror and in an enigma, and of the place and function of prophecy within Christian worship

Davies, P. E., 'Jesus and the Role of the Prophet', *JBL*, Vol. lxiv (1945), pp. 241–54

Dodd, C. H., 'Jesus as Teacher and Prophet', *Mysterium Christi*, eds. G. K. A. Bell and A. Deissmann (Longmans, London, 1930), pp. 53–66

Dunn, J. D. G., *Jesus and the Spirit* (S.C.M. Press, London, 1975). As its sub-title makes clear this book is 'a study of the religious and charismatic experience of Jesus and the first Christians as reflected in the New Testament'. It is a work of judicious and well documented scholarship which repays careful study and deserves the warm reception it has been accorded

Edwards, R. A., *A Theology of Q: Eschatology, Prophecy and Wisdom* (Fortress Press, Philadelphia, 1976)

—— 'Christian Prophecy and the Q Tradition', *SBL Seminar Papers 1976*, Vol. 2. Ed. G. W. MacRae (Scholars Press, Missoula, Montana), pp. 119–26

Ellis, E. E., *The Gospel of Luke* (New Century Bible: Oliphants, London, 1966; rev. ed. 1974)

—— 'The Role of the Christian Prophet in Acts', *Apostolic History and the Gospel* (*Festschrift* for F. F. Bruce, eds. W. W. Gasque and R. P. Martin: Paternoster Press, Exeter, 1970), pp. 55–67

—— ' "Spiritual" Gifts in the Pauline Community', *NTS*, Vol. xx (1973–4), pp. 128–44

Fascher, E., *PROPHĒTĒS: Eine sprach- und religionsgeschichtliche Untersuchung* (Töpelmann, Giessen, 1927). A basic work which gathers together all the references to *prophētēs* in secular and religious Greek literature

Friederich, G., '*Prophētēs:* D: Prophets and Prophecies in the New Testament. E: Prophets in the Early Church', *TDNT* Vol. VI, pp. 828–61. Although almost twenty years old, this contribution is still the most widely used and easily available treatment of the subject; but in those twenty years many works have appeared which make Friedrich's article rather dated: however, it is still a useful study with which to begin

Fuller, R. H., *The Foundations of New Testament Christology* (Lutterworth Press, London, 1965; Collins, Fontana Library, 1969)

Grayston, K., 'The Study of Mark XIII', *BJRL*, Vol. lvi (1974), pp. 371–87. A review of research on the chapter, with its own fresh suggestions

Greeven, H., 'Propheten, Lehrer, Vorsteher bei Paulus', *ZNW*, Vol. xliv (1952–3), pp. 1–43. A most important study of the function of prophets and other 'office-bearers' in the major Pauline epistles

Grudem, Wayne, *The Gift of Prophecy in the New Testament Church, with special reference to 1 Corinthians* (unpublished Ph.D. thesis: Cambridge University 1976). This work aims to provide the reader with a clear definition of prophecy in the New Testament church. In each of the four chapters ('The Authority of Prophecy', 'The Psychological State of the Prophet', 'The Function, Content and Form of Prophecy' and 'The Qualifications for Being a Prophet') the relevant sections of 1 Cor. 12–14 are examined in detail, and then related passages from the New Testament are discussed more briefly by way of comparison. The author tends to make the authoritative messenger-status of the Old Testament prophet the decisive criterion for the genuineness of a New Testament prophet

Guy, H. A., *New Testament Prophecy: Its Origin and Significance* (Epworth Press, London, 1947). The last book on the subject published in Britain. Its treatment of the relevant New Testament material was superficial even when it was written. It is now out of date and of very little value

Haenchen, E., *The Acts of the Apostles* (ET. Blackwell, Oxford, 1971)

Hahn, F. 'Die Sendschreiben der Johannesapokalypse: Ein Beitrag zur Bestimmung prophetischer Redeformen', *Tradition und Glaube* (*Festschrift* for K. G. Kuhn, eds. G. Jeremias, H.-W. Kuhn and H. Stegemann: Vandenhoeck and Ruprecht, Göttingen, 1971), pp. 362–90. An analysis of the prophetic-speech formulae in the circular letters of Revelation 2–3

—— *The Titles of Jesus in Christology* (ET. Lutterworth Press, London, 1969)

Hawthorne, G. F., 'Christian Prophecy and the Sayings of Jesus: Evidence of and Criteria for', *SBL Seminar Papers 1975*, Vol. 2, ed. G. W. MacRae (Scholars Press, Missoula, Montana), pp. 105–29. This paper attempts to present a fresh case for allowing to Christian prophets a creative role in respect of a small number of *logia* preserved as authentic sayings of Jesus

Hill, D., 'On the Evidence for the Creative Role of Christian Prophets', *NTS*, Vol. xx (1973–4), pp. 262–74. This article examines critically the arguments usually put forward in support of the view that Christian prophets were responsible for many *logia* which found their way into the tradition of Jesus' sayings

—— 'Prophecy and Prophets in the Revelation of St John', *NTS*, Vol. xviii (1971–2), pp. 401–18

Hocken, P., Tugwell, S., Every, G., and Mills, J. O., *New Heaven? New Earth?* (Darton, Longman and Todd, London, 1976). In addition to offering a theological analysis of Pentecostalism's central features, the writers aim to show how the encounter with Pentecostalism by Christians in the historic churches (in this case the Roman Catholic Church) can and should stimulate fresh theological reflection and even a new way of doing theology

Hollenweger, W., *The Pentecostals* (S.C.M. Press, London 1972). The most authoritative study available in English on Pentecostalism

Jeremias, J., *New Testament Theology I: The Proclamation of Jesus* (ET. S.C.M. Press, London, 1971)

Käsemann, E., *An die Römer* (Mohr, Tübingen, ²1974)

—— 'Sentences of Holy Law in the New Testament', *New Testament Questions of Today* (ET. S.C.M. Press, London, 1969), pp. 66–81

Kraft, H., 'Die altkirchliche Prophetie und die Entstehumg des Montanismus', *ThZ, Vol.* xi (1955), pp. 249–71. A distinguished essay by a notable church historian on the decline of prophecy and the rise of Montanism.

Leivestad, R., 'Das Dogma von der prophetenlosen Zeit', *NTS*, Vol. xix (1972–3), pp. 288–99. A short essay which asks interesting questions concerning the idea of the era in which prophets and the prophetic Spirit were not operative

Lindars, B., *The Gospel of John* (New Century Bible: Oliphants, London, 1972)

Lindblom, J., *Prophecy in Ancient Israel* (Blackwell, Oxford, 1962). One of the finest historical treatments of the subject in any language

Martin, R. P., *Worship in the New Testament* (Marshall, Morgan and Scott, London, 1974)

Meyer, R., *Der Prophet aus Galiläa* (Wissenschaftliche Buchgesellschaft, Darmstadt, ²1970). A thorough investigation of the prophetic character of Jesus' ministry according to the Synoptic evangelists

Minear, P. S., 'False Prophecy and Hypocrisy in the Gospel of Matthew', *Neues Testament und Kirche* (*Festschrift* for R. Schnackenburg, ed. J. Gnilka: Herder, Freiburg, 1974), pp. 76–93

—— *I Saw a New Earth* (Corpus Books, Washington, DC, 1968). A very lively commentary on the Revelation of St John

—— *To Heal and To Reveal: The Prophetic Vocation according to Luke* (Seabury Press, New York, 1976)

Müller, Ulrich B., *Prophetie und Predigt im Neuen Testament* (Mohn, Gütersloh, 1975). An incisive form-critical examination of materials from Revelation and the Pauline letters which suggests that Christian prophets were engaged in the consolation and exhortation of Christian communities, in the proclamation of divine judgment and in the preaching of salvation

Munck, J., *Paul and the Salvation of Mankind* (ET. S.C.M. Press, London, 1959). Particularly useful for its discussion of the prophetic character of Paul's call

Myers, J. M. and Freed, E. D., 'Is Paul also among the Prophets?', *Interpretation*, Vol. xx (1966), pp. 40–53

Neugebauer, F., 'Geistsprüche und Jesuslogien', *ZNW*, Vol. liii (1962), pp. 218–28. This short article offers a useful critique of the view that the early Church did not distinguish between utterances spoken by men under the influence of the Spirit and the tradition of Jesus' sayings

Nikolainen, A. T., 'Über die theologische Eigenart der Offenbarung des Johannes', *TLZ*, Vol. xciii (1968), pp. 161–70

Panagopoulos, J. (ed.), *Prophetic Vocation in the New Testament and Today* (Brill, Leiden, 1977). Papers read (in English, French and German) at the Consultation held (under the same title) at the Ecumenical Institute, Bossey, Switzerland, in September 1975

Reiling, J., *Hermas and Christian Prophecy: A Study of the Eleventh Mandate* (Brill, Leiden, 1973). In this book the discussion of Hermas's teaching on prophecy is preceded by a neat survey of the discussions on Christian prophecy from the time of Harnack

Robinson, J. A. T., *Redating the New Testament* (S.C.M. Press, London, 1976). A learned and provocative book which suggests that no book in the New Testament requires to be dated after AD 70

Ross, D. F., 'The Prophet as Yahweh's Messenger', *Israel's Prophetic Heritage* (*Festschrift* for J. Muilenberg, eds. B. W. Anderson and W. Harrelson: S.C.M. Press, London, 1962), pp. 98–107

Satake, A., *Die Gemeindeordnung in der Johannesapokalypse* (Neukirchener Verlag, Neukirchen-Vluyn, 1966)

Schlier, H., 'Le caractère propre de l'exhortation selon St Paul', *Essais sur le Nouveau Testament* (French trans.: Paris, 1968)

Schnider, Franz, *Jesus der Prophet* (Vandenhoeck and Ruprecht, Göttingen, 1973). The most recent and most extensive study of the prophetic character of Jesus' mission and ministry

Schweizer, E., *Church Order in the New Testament* S.C.M. Press ET., London, 1961)

—— *The Good News according to Matthew* (ET. S.P.C.K., London 1976) A first-class theological commentary on Matthew's Gospel

——'Observance of the Law and Charismatic Activity in Matthew', *NTS* Vol. xvi (1969–70), pp. 213–30

Steck, O. H., *Israel und das gewaltsame Geschick der Propheten* (Neukirchener Verlag, Neukirchen-Vluyn, 1967). This book emphasises the almost inevitable suffering involved in the prophetic vocation

Streeter, B. H., *The Primitive Church* (Macmillan, London, 1929)

Suenens, L. J., *A New Pentecost?* (ET. Fountain Books, Collins, Glasgow, 1977). This refreshingly optimistic book about the Church offers wise guidance on the significance of the charismatic movements today

Sweet, J. P. M., 'A Sign for Unbelievers: Paul's Attitude to Glossolalia', *NTS*, Vol. xiii (1966–7), pp. 240–57

Teeple, H. M., *The Mosaic Eschatological Prophet* (SBL Monograph Series, No. 10: Philadelphia, 1957)

Tugwell, S., *Did you receive the Spirit?* (Darton, Longman and Todd, London, 1972). This little book is a well-informed and balanced discussion of the doctrine and the gifts of the Holy Spirit as related to prayer and worship

Unnik, W. C. van, 'A Formula describing Prophecy', *NTS*, Vol. ix (1962–3), pp. 86–94. An analysis of the Rev. 1.19 and comparable texts

Vermes, G., *Jesus the Jew* (Fontana Books: Collins, Glasgow, 1976). This book – 'a historian's reading of the Gospels' – is particularly useful for its discussion of the setting of Jesus' ministry and its section on 'Jesus the prophet'
——— *The Dead Sea Scrolls in English* (Pelican Books: Harmondsworth, Middlesex, 1968)
——— 'The Qumran Interpretation of Scripture and its historical Setting', *ALUOS*, Vol. vi (1966–8), pp. 84–97
Vielhauer, P., *Oikodomē* (Harrassowitz, Karlsruhe, 1940)
——— 'Prophecy', *New Testament Apocrypha*, Vol. II (ET. ed. R. McL. Wilson, Lutterworth Press, London, 1965), pp. 601–7
Young, F. W., 'Jesus the Prophet: A Re-examination', *JBL*, Vol. lxviii (1949), pp. 285–99

INDEX OF PASSAGES
DISCUSSED

I. OLD TESTAMENT

II NEW TESTAMENT

III OTHER SOURCES